MICRO FINANCE IN INDIA

PROCEEDINGS OF NATIONAL CONFERENCE

EDITORS

Dr.MSV PRASAD

&

Dr.G.V.SATYA SEKHAR

DEPT OF FINANCE, GITAM INSTITUTE OF MANAGEMENT

GITAM UNIVERSITY

VISAKHAPATNAM

INDIA

1

DEPARTMENT OF FINANCE
GITAM INSTITUTE OF MANAGEMENT
GITAM UNIVERSITY
INDIA

NATIONAL CONFERENCE ON
MICRO FINANCE IN INDIA: ISSUES, CHALLENGES & STRATEGIES

ACKKNOWLEDGEMENTS

Dr.MSV. Prasad,
Associate Professor & Convener
Dr. G.V.Satya Sekhar,
Asst. Professor & Co-convener

We are indebted to our Honourable president Sr. M.V.V.S. Murthi, for his encouragement in our endeavours.

We express our heartful thanks to Prof. G. Subrahmanyam, Vice-Chancellor, GITAM university for his kind consent for conduction of national conference on MICRO FINANCE IN NIDIA : ISSUES, CHALLEGES & STRATEGIES.

We express our sincere gratitude to Prof. D. Harinarayana, Pro Vice-Chancellor, GITAM University for accepting as chief guest for valedictory function.

We would like to thank Sri. G. Lakshmi pathi Reddy, Zonal Manger, Indian Bank for sponsoring this conference for the send time. We thank Mr. M. Sudhakar Reddy, Chief Manager for providing all kinds of help throughout the conference. We have received overwhelming response from all parts of the country.

We also express our gratitude to Prof. K. Siva Rama Krishna, Dean and Principal for his guidance and supervision to organize this conference

PREFACE

V.Venkateswara Rao, Indian Bank, Chief Manager (Retd): Rebuilding Micro Finance- Issues- Challenges,

Contents

PART-I

- **CASE STUDY -1:**
  Prof P. Sheela & RLN Murthy: Role of Microfinance through Self Help Groups and its Impact On The Living Standards Of Rural Poor - A Case Study In Selected Rural Areas Of Visakhapatnam, A.P, India- Mr. R.L.N.MURTHY, research scholar, GITAM University, Visakhapatnam and Professor P. SHEELA, professor, Dept of Finance, GITAM Institute of Management, GITAM University, Visakhapatnam.

- **CASE STUDY- 2:**
  Self-help Groups Bank Linkage Programme in India: A study with reference to Andhra Pradesh **by Dr.S.S.S.DURGA GANESH,** *Associate Professor in Commerce,   Mrs.   AVN   College,   Visakhapatnam   and* **V.M.VEENA,** *Research Scholar, DCMS, Andhra University, Visakhapatnam*

- **CASE STUDY-3:** A Study on Psychological Empowerment Of Shg Members In Krishna District, Dr.N.Subramanyam, Mrs.N.Sailaja, Mrs.G.Madhu Sri

- **CASE STUDY-4 :** Entrepreneurship Development of Rural Women through Self Help Groups – A Case Study in Krishna District, **by Dr. Rajesh. C.Jampala,** Professor & Head, Department of Business Administration, P.B Siddhartha College of Arts & Science, Vijayawada & **Mrs G. Madhu Sri,** Research Scholar, Department of Commerce and Business Administration , P.B. Siddhartha College of Arts and Science, Vijayawada – 520 010.

- **CASE STUDY-5:** Role of Microfinance Institutions in Entrepreneurship Development in Visakhapatnam District, Andhra Pradesh, India, Dr. N. R. Mohan Prakash, Assistant Professor, Department of Marketing, GITAM Institute of Management, GITAM University, Visakhapatnam

- **CASE STUDY-6:** Implementation of CSR in Micro Finance to upscale skills deficiencies for micro credit borrowers in order to mitigate the rate of defaulters: A Study of an Integrated Model, Dr. Anitha Kumari, Sankar Mukherjee, Bengaluru School of Management Studies, GITAM University, Bengaluru

PART-I :

CHAPTER-1: Microfinance in India: Contemporary Issues and Challenges

Author
Dr.G.Renuka
Associate Professor,
Dept of Management
Rishi UBR P. G. College for Women,
Kukatpally, Hyderabad

Abstract: Microfinance refers to small savings, credit and insurance services extended to socially and economically disadvantaged segments of society. It is emerging as a powerful tool for poverty alleviation in India. This working paper tries to outline the prevailing condition of the Microfinance in India in the light of its emergence till now. The prospect of Micro-Finance is dominated by SHGs (Self Help Groups) - Banks linkage Program. Its main aim is to provide a cost effective mechanism for providing financial services to the poor. Recently Union Rural Development Minister Jairam Ramesh wanted the help of SHGs for the establishment of DRDO designed bio-toilets in rural areas. This paper discovers the prevailing gap in functioning of MFIs such as practices in credit delivery, lack of product diversification, customer overlapping and duplications, consumption and individual loan demand with lack of mitigation measures, less thrust on enterprise loans, collection of savings/loans and highest interest rate existing in micro finance sector. All these are clear syndromes, which tell us that the situation is moving without any direction. Finally paper concludes with practicable suggestions to overcome the issues and challenges associated with microfinance in India.

Key words: Microfinance SHGs, MFIs, NABARD

Chapter-2

Indian Microfinance – Status in India and Andhra Pradesh

- **Dr. Y. Aparna Rao,**
  Faculty, Department of Management Studies,
  G V P College of Engineering (A),
  Visakhapatnam

"Micro financing has been a noble way of reaching out to people at the lowest levels of society and cater to their financing needs while saving them from loan sharks. The trouble, however, is that some bad apples are giving the whole industry a bad name."
- *Ashvin Parekh, Partner and National Leader of Global Financial Services at Ernst & Young.*

CHAPTER-3

REGULATORY FRAMEWORK FOR MICROFINANCE

Ms. Santhoshi Kumari Gondesi
Ph.D. Research Scholar
Dept. of Finance,
GIM, GITAM University
Visakhapatnam

Abstract
Purpose:
The main purpose of this is to provide Microfinance regulation and to draft a regulatory framework in India. In the current environment, it is becoming difficult to stay abreast of new initiatives to regulate microfinance institutions (MFIs).The drafting of legal texts is an important step when setting up an appropriate legal framework for microfinance. **Three elements** establish a legal regime for microfinance. On the *legal side*, some kind of assessment of existing legislation should be conducted first. On the *political side*, new or amended legislation is only possible when sufficient political support exists. And, perhaps most importantly, on the *institutional side*, regulation will only be effective when institutional capacity and will are sufficiently strong.

Keywords: micro-finance; poverty; Muhammad Yunus; regulatory-framework; legal; financial-services; NGO.

CHAPTER-4

REGULATORY FRAMEWORK OF MICRO FINANCE INSTITUTIONS IN INDIA

-B. Omnamasivaya
Research Scholar,
GITAM Unviersity,
Visakahpatnam

Abstract:
        Microfinance institutions always been considered as one of the frontline institutions for the propagation of financial services to the poor. But Indian microfinance institutions they are making profit out of the poor. In 2010, Andhra Pradesh SKS microfinance held at the first IPO for a micro finance institution in India and drawing attention to the potential profits of the sector .the micro finance institutions were charging high interest rates and they are making out of poor because of the lack of regulatory mechanism. The farmer suicides in Andhra Pradesh in 2010 garnered excessive attention through print and electronic media for months on end owing allegedly to exorbitant interest rates being charged by private MFIs. The incident culminated in Andhra Pradesh and CM passed the AP Microfinance Ordinance 2010 (Passed) in to law in December which effectively shut down all private sector micro finance operations in the state . in response to this In October 2010, the RBI's Central Board of Directors set up a Sub-Committee, chaired by Y.H. Malegam, to study the issues and concerns in the micro finance sector. based on committee recommendations and report. Finally the ministry of finance proposed a comprehensive new bill for the regulation of MFI's

Key words : micro finance, micro finance institutions, RBI, development and regulation bill

CHAPTER-5

GROWTH OF UNORGANIZED SECTOR IN INDIA- A STUDY ON MICRO FINANCE AND POVERTY REDUCTION IN INDIA

Mr. KARTEEK MADAPANA,
Assistant Professor,
Gandhi institute of Engineering & Technology,
Gunupur, Rayagada,

A*bstract*

India falls under low income class according to World Bank. It is second populated country in the world and around 70 % of its population lives in rural area. 60% of people depend on agriculture, as a result there is chronic underemployment and per

capita income is only $ 3262. This is not enough to provide food to more than one individual. The obvious result is abject poverty, low rate of education, low sex ratio, and exploitation. The major factor account for high incidence of rural poverty is the low asset base. According to Reserve Bank of India, about 51 % of people house possess only 10% of the total asset of India .This has resulted low production capacity both in agriculture (which contribute around 22-25% of GDP) and Manufacturing sector. Rural people have very low access to institutionalized credit (from commercial bank).

Key terms: - Micro Finance, Financial Services, Poverty, NGOs, India.

CHAPTER-6

OPEN SOURCE MIS FOR MICROFINANCE IN INDIA: TRENDS AND CHALLENGES

D. Vijaya Geeta[*]
Associate Professor,
Department of Operations,
GITAM University

ABSTRACT

In recent times, open source markets are gaining popularity in the world of computing. Attributing to features like free or inexpensive licensing terms and availability of cloud services, open source markets has reached varied fields, comprising simple to complex applications. Initiatives such as Microfinance Open Architecture Project (MOAP) supports the cause of enforcing standards for building open source MIS for microfinance institutions. In this context, the paper studies the current scenario of development of MIS for microfinance in India especially in the area of open sourcing. The paper discusses the challenges faced in Indian microfinance institutes and proposes possible solutions to face them.

Keywords: Microfinance; MIS; Open Source; Microfinance Open Architecture Project; MiFOS

CHAPTER-7
FINANCIAL SUPPORT FOR ECONOMIC DEVELOPMENT

Pandu Ranga Rao, B
Assistant Director ,
KL University,

In a labour abundant and capital short economy like India there is a severe budgetary constraint for funds and the pressing need for higher investment in the frontiers of social development. Hence the people have to come forward to engage themselves in predictive activities by starting their own industrial of business ventures rather than depending on some employer for employment and livelihood when more and more persons come forward to state their own enterprises small it may be and run the enterprise efficiently the productivity of the nation automatically improves as the process of economic development involves improvement in the Gross National product and depends on the utilization of physical natural resources by the human resource to realise the productive potential of the nation It requires increase in production and consumption.

Chapter-8:
MICROFINANCE: EMPOWERING RURAL MASSES IN INDIA

Srinivas Vissapragada
Assistant Professor & Research Scholar
K L University Business School
K L University
Vaddeswarm,Guntur District
Andhra Pradesh

Abstract

Microfinance is not a magic sky-hook that reaches down to pluck the poor out of poverty. It can, however, be a strategically vital platform that the poor can use to raise their own prospects. In India more than 70% of the population lives in rural areas and most of these villages are deprived of basic enmities and underdeveloped. Indian financial system strives hard to empower rural people economically. Implementation new schemes and strategies in the rural areas can eradicate poverty, create employment opportunities and generate economic growth. Microfinance can be a critical element of an effective poverty reduction strategy. Improved access and efficient provision of savings, credit, and insurance facilities enable the poor to augment their consumption, manage their financial risks better, build their assets gradually and develop their micro enterprises. One of the major hindrances in the growth of the microfinance sector is the financial illiteracy of the people. This makes it difficult in creating awareness of microfinance and even more difficult to serve them as microfinance clients. Most microfinance institutions conduct educational training and awareness programmes for the benefit of the rural people. For many years, microfinance was considered as a panacea for poverty. However, since 2010, the sector has been damaged by various localized crises (competition among MFIs). In order to revert to the original social assignment of microfinance, a special legislative frame work and innovative economic models are required for effective delivery of microfinance.

Keywords: microfinance, poverty, financial literacy, economic model, employment

CHAPTER-9

ROLE OF MICRO-FINANCE IN RURAL INDIA

Dr. L.SRINIVAS REDDY,
Global Education Centre
(School of Business Management)
Hyderabad. INDIA

Abstract

India falls under low income class according to World Bank. It is second populated country in the world and around 70 % of its population lives in rural area. 60% of people depend on agriculture, as a result there is chronic underemployment and per capita income is only $ 3262. This is not enough to provide food to more than one individual. The obvious result is abject poverty, Low rate of education, low sex ratio, and exploitation. The major factor account for high incidence of rural poverty is the low asset base. According to Reserve Bank of India, about 51 % of people house possess only 10% of the total asset of India .This has resulted low production capacity both in agriculture (which contribute around 22-25% of GDP) and Manufacturing sector. Rural people have very low access to institutionalized credit.

Key words: Micro finance Institutions, Rural population , poverty

CHAPTER-10

The Importance and Role of Micro Finance in Poverty Alleviation and Profitable Agriculture Activities in India.

K.Madhava Rao
Assistant Professor
Department of Management Studies
Baba Institute of Technology and Sciences (BITS)
P.M.Palem, Visakhapatnam – 48

Abstract:

India falls under low income class according to World Bank. It is second populated country in the world and around 70 % of its population lives in rural area. 60% of people depend on agriculture, as a result there is chronic underemployment and per capita income is only $ 3262. This is not enough to provide food to more than one individual. The obvious result is abject poverty, low rate of education, low sex ratio, and exploitation. The major factor account for high incidence of rural poverty is the low asset base. According to Reserve Bank of India, about 51 % of people house possess only 10% of the total asset of India .This has resulted low production capacity both in agriculture (which contribute around 22-25% of GDP) and Manufacturing sector. Rural people have very low access to institutionalized credit (from commercial bank).

Key words: Agriculture, Reserve Bank of India, production capacity, Rural people, Commercial bank.

Chapter-11
Role Of Bharatiya Mahila Bank (BMB) for Women Empowerment

Through Self Help Groups

*Dr.K.Manjusree Naidu

**Dr.M.Jyothsna

Absract:

The budget 2013-14 is remarkable and innovative for one gender of the population because the Finance Minister announced the setting up of India's first women's bank as a public sector bank with Rs 1,000 crore as initial capital.BMB is a pet project of the Congress-led United Progressive Alliance (UPA) government. Exclusive women bank is defined as: "The bank is going to be run mostly by women and it would provide funds for the entrepreneurial initiatives by women". The announcement of First Women bank in India has received a huge appreciation from the countries around the world. Bharatiya Mahila Bank was inaugurated on 19th November, 2013 .BMB will have at least 25 branches—one each in all state capitals, by the end of this fiscal year.

Experts in the field of banking have expressed their opinion on the need and importance of exclusive women bank in India. At the national and international level there are many women banks which are operating successfully by achieving the objectives for which it has been started. The UPA governments innovative step is to see that India's first Women Bank has to operate in an effective and efficient direction by taking into consideration the experiences of the already existing women banks in India and abroad. What people (men and women) require from banks are **quality services** that meet their needs; based on their gender, age, financial background, these requirements may differ.

Objective of the study: Study the working of the successful women banks in India and abroad and to highlight how BMB can contribute to women empowerment through self help groups. The data below states how bank can empower women in unorganized sector by providing micro finance to self help groups.

CHAPTER-12

Micro Finance - The New Found Value in Women Through Self-help Groups.

* Prof. P.Sheela

**Dr. Rajeshwari Panigarhi

Abstract

Access to microfinance through self- help group has been identified as an important means to overcome poverty and has contributed much towards empowerment of women in particular and the society at large. Microfinance institutions have proved that lending to women is much emphasized that women are more reliable and providing them with the credit facilities raises the likelihood of timely payment. Poverty reduction also emphasizes on the well being of their family both economically as well as psychologically. The objective of this research is i) To analyze the value women were able to generate economically, psychologically and socially from being a part in this programme. ii) To analyze the possibilities of freedom women had derived from out of this programme iii) To understand how women were able to effectively utilize the financial benefits iv) To understand the involvement of women in making the decision on taking loan v) To offer suggestions for their better performances in the future. This research was focused in the rural areas of Visakhapatnam districts, covering sixteen groups who are actively participating in the microfinance finance programme and two groups who had discontinued from the programme. Both primary and secondary data was used in this research. The method used for data collection was through semi- structured interviews with focus group discussion (FGDs), informal conversations and observations were noted while interacting with the respondents. The outcome of the study had shown that there was a gradual increase in the all the three dimensions such as their economic, social and psychological status. The members in this study have expressed their deep satisfaction over the interaction with the other members within the group and with the officials at the microfinance institution. They have strongly considered the space provided to them through this programme is safe and they could share and learn better from each other's experiences, which in turn contributed a lot in developing their self confidence. The monitoring system of both the microfinance institutions as well as the leaders of the group focused on the client, repayment rates and loan disbursement was effective but very little focus was made on their social monitoring indicators, which would limit the process of empowerment in women. The members have strongly expressed had the microfinance institutions extend better training opportunities to both the team leaders as well as to all the member, would definitely help them in further enhancing their skills.

* Prof. P.Sheela., Professor, Dept of Fiance. GITAM Institute of Mnagement- GITAM University.
** Dr.Rajeshwari Panigrahi, Associate Professor, Dept of Marketing, GITAM Institute of Mnagement- GITAM University

Chapter-13
A Review of the Recent Developments in Micro Finance Literature

*Rajeshwari Panigrahi
**P.Sheela

Abstract

Purpose-Micro finance is India can trace its origins back to the early 1970s when the self employed Women's association SEWA of the state of Gujarat formed an urban cooperative bank, called Shri Ahila SEWA Sehkari Bank with the objective of providing banking services to poor women employed in the unorganised sector since then there has been continuous effort both from the government and non government sector taking initiatives to provide thrift finance to rural people. This subject has also gained lots of research interest thus, this study in intended to understand and explore the various dimension of search done in this area.

Design and Methodology -This study is a review of the studies taken place in the area of Microfinance to understand various dimensions of Micro-finance which have been researched and understand the trends of research undertaken in this area.

CHAPTER-14

Evaluation and Impact of Micro finance in Coastal Andhrapradesh

* Dr. Shaik Shamshuddin

** Dr. Haniefuddin S

*** Dr. Shaik Khadar Baba

ABSTRACT

This paper evaluates the aspects relating to microfinance in coastal Andhrapradesh, this study will be useful to accelerate economic growth, maintain political order, reduce poverty and adapt to climate change. The term microfinance is widely used to refer to institutions governing savings, credit, insurance and financial payments by relatively poor people, including those regulated by both official laws and comfortable norms. Analysis of microfinance is widely framed as a purely micro issue, centered on the motivation and behavior of specific users and providers. However, such analysis is almost invariably located whether explicitly or implicitly in a wider view of how the state, markets and society institute poverty.

These SHGs are mainly formed and managed by women and this has become an instrument, which has led to women's empowerment and social change. Most of the microfinance institutions in India attempt to go beyond savings and credit groups to provide microfinance services in the form of savings and insurance.

This paper first set out a general well-being regime framework that can be used for this analysis and sketch the role microfinance plays within it.

This paper provides a review of the literature on microfinance and a critical assessment of its effectiveness. It examines the experience of India, which has one of the largest microfinance sectors in the world, and particularly describing the microfinance status in coastal Andhra Pradesh.

Keywords: Microfinance, Microcredit, Self Help Group

CASE STUDY -1

ROLE OF MICROFINANCE THROUGH SELF HELP GROUPS AND ITS IMPACT ON THE LIVING STANDARDS OF RURAL POOR - A CASE STUDY IN SELECTED RURAL AREAS OF VISAKHAPATNAM, A.P, INDIA.

* Mr. R.L.N.MURTHY, research scholar, GITAM University, Visakhapatnam
**Professor P. SHEELA, professor, Dept of Finance, GITAM Institute of Management, GITAM University, Visakhapatnam.

Abstract

Microfinance has become increasingly popular as a tool for poverty reduction in developing and transition countries. The major challenge before developing countries is how to improve living standards of the poor. Microfinance has been chosen to shoot this problem. But, the question of how far microfinance is successful in improving living standards of the rural poor is still unanswered. It is in this context a research has been initiated to know the role of microfinance in improving living standards of the rural poor. Microfinance institutions are encouraging the self help groups to mobilize savings and turning the rural poor into income generating entrepreneurs.

This study aims at understanding the role of microfinance in improving living standards of the rural poor through self help groups. A questionnaire using likert type scale has been designed and executed to know whether the living standards have been improved through support of microfinance. The respondents have been selected on random basis covering selected rural areas of Visakhapatnam on all the beneficiary of the microfinance through SHGs. Responses to questions, such as increase in income, increase in savings, access to better health, access to better education, and improved financial position, have been sought to know whether their living standards have improved. Most of the respondents expressed their favorable response and did mention that microfinance through SHGs had helped them to a certain extent and also improved their living standards, the study also explored that few of the respondents were not fully aware the details of the program and is still relying on their group leaders instructions, which seems to be a bottle neck for their future endeavors.

CASE STUDY- 2
Self-help Groups Bank Linkage Programme in India: A study with reference to Andhra Pradesh

*Dr.S.S.S.DURGA GANESH
*Associate Professor in Commerce, Mrs. AVN College, Visakhapatnam

**V.M.VEENA
**Research Scholar, DCMS, Andhra University, Visakhapatnam

Abstract

The Self-Help Group Bank Linkage Programme (SHG-BLP) was an attempt to bring the 'unbanked' poor into the formal banking system and to inculcate among the poor the thrift and credit habits, a natural corollary is for the group members to adapt into seeking more and better livelihood opportunities with access to credit from formal financial institutions. The SHG-BLP has crossed many milestones - from linking a pilot of 500 SHGs of rural poor two decades ago to cross 8 million groups a year ago. Similarly from a total savings corpus of a few thousands of Indian rupees in the early years to a whopping Rs.27,000 crore today, from a few crore of bank credit to a credit outstanding of Rs.40,000 crore and disbursements touching Rs.20,000 crore during 2012-13. The SHG Bank Linkage is a great success story in Andhra Pradesh. In the current financial year, the government of Andhra Pradesh has facilitated Rs. 3966.82 crores of Bank Loans to 1.6lakhs SHGs up to end of October, 2013. The motive behind SHG-BLP is to combine the access to low-cost financial services with a process of self management and development. It is considered as most successful, promising and widely accepted model in India. The tremendous impact on the social status of the poor rural women becoming bread earners of their households through the instrument of SHGs has been highly commended by many researchers. The mushrooming of the Micro Finance Institutions (MFIs) smelling the 'business opportunities' with the poor, also led to an unhealthy trend of more and more credit being pumped without proper appraisal of the loanees and before assessing their capacity to repay. The grave crisis of confidence of MFIs and subsequent developments has had a highly negative impact on the micro credit initiative in the country had led to SHG-BLP. It is a pilot project started by NABARD is widely accepted model as one of the largest and successful one in the world. The present study is analytical and based upon secondary data which has been collected from different published reports, journals and existing available literature. The objective of this study is to evaluate the progress and impact of self help group bank linkage programme in Andhra Pradesh. The bank linkage programme for women self help groups is about Rs.20,000 crore and in five years time the government wants to increase this to Rs.1,00,000 crore.

CASE STUDY-3

A STUDY ON PSYCHOLOGICAL EMPOWERMENT OF SHG MEMBERS IN KRISHNA DISTRICT

*Dr.N.Subramanyam
**Mrs.N.Sailaja
***Mrs.G.Madhu Sri

Abstract

Microfinance has proved to be an effective tool for women empowerment. Microfinance includes micro credit, micro insurance and micro pension; etc. Micro credit is an extension of small loans to the poor to enable them to take up income generating activities. India now occupies a significant place and a niche in global microfinance through promotion of the self-help groups (SHGs) and the home grown SHG-Bank Linkage (SBL) model. The Indian model offers greater promise and potential to address poverty as it is focused on building social capital through providing access to financial services through linking with the mainstream. Though the access to credit has been seen as a motivational factor behind the formation of Self Help Groups (SHGs), SHGs have a potential that goes beyond mere economics of loan management. SHGs ensure people's participation in the development process as these are the grass root level democratic institutions of rural people. The vital function of the Self Help Group (SHG) programme is to provide access to credit in the context of poverty reduction and empowerment of women. With the aim to meet the millennium development goals and microfinance programme's role in supporting it, there has been an increasing expectation on their impact on women empowerment. However, the perception and expectations of the members of the SHGs vary from person to person. This paper focuses on the perceptions of the sample members, who are engaged in different income generating activities, in terms of psychological empowerment.

CASE STUDY-4

Entrepreneurship Development of Rural Women through Self Help Groups – A Case Study in Krishna District

Dr. Rajesh. C.Jampala
Professor & Head,
Department of Business Administration,
P.B Siddhartha College of Arts & Science,
Vijayawada,
Andhra Pradesh -520 008
Email: rajeshjampala@yahoo.com

Mrs G. Madhu Sri
Research Scholar,
Department of Commerce and Business Administration
P.B. Siddhartha College of Arts and Science,
Vijayawada – 520 010.
Email: gaganasahasra@gmail.com

Abstract

Empowerment of women has emerged as an important issue in recent times. Empowerment is an active, multidimensional process, which should enable women to realize their full identity and power in all spheres of life. Empowerment in the context of women's development is a way of defining, challenging and overcoming barriers in a women's life through which she increases her ability to shape her life and environment. Women must be empowered by enhancing their awareness, knowledge; skills and technology use efficiency, thereby, facilitating overall development of the society. The concept of Self Help Groups (SHGs) is proving to be a helpful instrument for the women empowerment. Entrepreneurship development and income generating activities are a feasible solution for empowering women. It generates income and also provides flexible working hours according to the needs of homemakers. The Self Help Groups (SHGs) have paved the way for economic independence of rural women. The members of SHGs in rural areas are involved in Micro –Entrepreneurships. Through that, they are becoming economically independent and are getting good recognition in the society. This paper deals with the success stories of the rural poor SHG members showing exemplary entrepreneurial qualities to come out of the vicious circle of poverty and indebtedness with the help of SHGs in Krishna District.

Keywords: Empowerment, Entrepreneurship development, Self Help Groups

CASE STUDY-5

Role of Microfinance Institutions in Entrepreneurship Development in Visakhapatnam District, Andhra Pradesh, India

Dr. N. R. Mohan Prakash
Assistant Professor,
Department of Marketing,
GITAM Institute of Management,
GITAM University, Visakhapatnma,

Abstract

Microfinance has been playing an important role in rural and semi-urban entrepreneurial development in Andhra Pradesh since its formation. Andhra Pradesh is a state of rich natural resource as well as healthy human resources potential to take up self employment. Microfinance and entrepreneurship help as a combine tool to contribute in development of an economy, particularly in Andhra Pradesh the combined contribution of these to are very much essential to cater the need of employability of people belongs to rural and semi-urban areas . Since formation of the state the people of Andhra Pradesh have been showing interest to earn money through self employment schemes by staring khadi and village industries in rural areas. The foremost objectives of this paper is to see the role of microfinance institutions in entrepreneurship development and also measure the level of satisfaction of microfinance institutions clients toward their respective banks considering primary source of data at state level. The sample of 300 microfinance bank clients residing in Andhra Pradesh has been interviewed. Data analysis and interpretation are the strength of this paper, descriptive analysis use in this paper and also non parametric test chi-square and Kruskal-Walli and Mann-Whitney test used. This study concludes that microfinance institutions play a significant role in entrepreneurship development in Andhra Pradesh and some of the clients who are taking loan from the public sector banks they use this amount to start a business than the other ones who use it for marriage, education house building purpose etc.

Keywords: Microfinance institution, Entrepreneurship, Mann-Whitney

CASE STUDY-6

Implementation of CSR in Micro Finance to upscale skills deficiencies for micro credit borrowers in order to mitigate the rate of defaulters:

A Study of an Integrated Model

Dr. Anitha Kumari, Sankar Mukherjee

Abstract: Eradication of abject poverty through the financial literacy was aimed to be accomplished under the armoury of Micro-Finance. Financial Literacy for the economically

Marginalised people in India have been the core of concern under the perspective of micro- economy. Micro-Finance has been coined a paramount important tool to combat the social evil particularly the mother of social evils called poverty. But owing to the anomalies of different structural loop holes there has been a concern of cloud appears over the process and financial health and hygiene of micro-finance in India. Micro credit in terms of repayment from the borrowers has over shadows the natural flow of Micro-Finance operation across the entire Micro-Finance companies. This hermeneutics study strive to open the logjam of this non-payment mechanism to foster the capital infusion that leads to capacity of lending and further strengthen the micro credit fabrics for holistic social empowerment. In modern times, when globalization, economic liberalization brings the world trade into a single converging point, multi disciplinary role became more dynamic and multi-dimensional to cater the need for each others. Human Resource is one the discipline which has its strategic significance to every sphere. Micro Finance needs this strategic support mechanism from the HR to understand the actual root of the problems of intensity of non-payment across the borrowers. Hence, this secondary based study, like to explore the strategic role that HR can play to mitigate the risk of lending of micro credit and it can replenish the mutual confidence between lenders and borrowers for accomplishing the holistic social inclusiveness.

PART-I :

Rebuilding Micro Finance- Issues- Challenges

Preface

V.Venkateswara Rao,
Indian Bank, Chief Manager (Retd)

Micro-finance to the poor through various organizations/Banks will help in improving the investment in small business, purchase of equipments etc. and thereby improving their income and standard of living. For delivering the micro-finance, financial inclusion is the first step in that direction. Micro Finance refers to provision of credit and other financial products of very small amounts to the poor in rural, semi-urban and urban areas. The Indian population is the second highest   in the world with 70% of them   living in rural areas. It is universally accepted that micro-finance is an effective tool to   accelerate the economic growth and alleviate poverty in the world. As of now there is lot of shortage of staff and kiosks opened in the villages for delivery of micro-finance are not opened regularly for the services of the public.

Financial Inclusion is for inclusive growth. RBI has directed that all Banks to bring all families in their service area villages into the banking fold by opening 'no frills' accounts(zero balance accounts) for each family. Surprisingly, there are good savings in these 'no frills accounts. The average balance is Rs.697/ in rural areas and Rs.934/- in the urban areas. As a first step Banks were advised to provide SB-cum-overdraft facility upto Rs.5,000/- per family. After repayment of the OD enhanced amount has to be given to these parties. It was observed the repayment in these accounts is poor and the NPAs at 97% and the Banks are reluctant to lend to these people.

CHALLENGES:

Though public and private sector banks are participating in micro-finance, their lending to the poor in the villages is minimal. Majority of the micro-finance lending is done by private organizations.   The finance is delivered and collected at their door step. They are charging higher interest rates from 5% to 10% per month and for recovery they are implementing coercive methods. Though there is improvement in the income of the poor, it is taken away by the private lenders in the form of interest. Still many families do not want to come to the banking fold in the villages due to lack of awareness about the services available with the Banks. Creation of awareness about the banking products is important for utilization of the micro-finance by the poor.

.The government used to announce the write off of the overdue agricultural loans for getting the electoral benefits of the ruling party. This has created an impression among the farmers that they need not pay the loans whenever there are general elections. Local political leaders in the villages always used to pressurize the Bank Managers for sanction of subsidy loans to their parties and the recovery in majority cases is poor which is causing NPAs to the Branch and Bank. The procedure for sanction of the loan is lengthy and the Banks requiring many papers. The poor in the villages are unable to obtain and produce these papers to the Bank and thereby the finance is avoided. They will be approaching the money-lenders for their financial needs.

STRATAGIES:

The concept of Self Help Groups a (SHGs) has helped the rural public to get the finance at cheaper rates of interest from both public and private sector banks and the state governments subsidizing the interest . SHG groups will be formed with 5 or 10 women members and SB accounts are opened with the Bank. Savings will be deposited with the Bank every month and after verifying the track record of savings the Banks will advance initially Rs.50,000/- (for 10 members). After getting the credit the savings will be continued and the repayment of loan will be made regularly. The women will utilize the money towards working capital for their businesses and for consumption needs such as expenses towards marriage, health, children education etc. This has helped the rural masses to get the credit through collective borrowing and prompt repayment. Records show that the repayment in SHG loans with Banks is very high at 98.5%. But the study indicates that very large number of poorest of the poor continues to remain beyond the reach of formal banking system. Steps to be taken both by the Government and Banks that one lady from each family should be a member of one SHG and for getting the finance. As per the directions of Ministry of finance and SLBCs all banks have to open kiosks in all their service area villages posting the Rural Development officers and also engaging retired/ experienced staff who are having good track record and having the required knowledge and make them available on the notified days regularly with all the services available. In other words, banking at the door step of the rural masses should be made available. Assessing the credit needs of the individual borrower, credit may be extended by making discreet enquiries about the integrity, honey and sincerity to avoid the loan becoming NPA.

CHAPTER-1

Microfinance in India: Contemporary Issues and Challenges

Author
Dr.G.Renuka
Associate Professor,
Dept of Management
Rishi UBR P. G. College for Women,
Kukatpally, Hyderabad

Abstract: Microfinance refers to small savings, credit and insurance services extended to socially and economically disadvantaged segments of society. It is emerging as a powerful tool for poverty alleviation in India. This working paper tries to outline the prevailing condition of the Microfinance in India in the light of its emergence till now. The prospect of Micro-Finance is dominated by SHGs (Self Help Groups) - Banks linkage Program. Its main aim is to provide a cost effective mechanism for providing financial services to the poor. Recently Union Rural Development Minister Jairam Ramesh wanted the help of SHGs for the establishment of DRDO designed bio-toilets in rural areas. This paper discovers the prevailing gap in functioning of MFIs such as practices in credit delivery, lack of product diversification, customer overlapping and duplications, consumption and individual loan demand with lack of mitigation measures, less thrust on enterprise loans, collection of savings/loans and highest interest rate existing in micro finance sector. All these are clear syndromes, which tell us that the situation is moving without any direction. Finally paper concludes with practicable suggestions to overcome the issues and challenges associated with microfinance in India.

Key words: Microfinance SHGs, MFIs, NABARD

INTRODUCTION

Micro Finance may be defined as "provision of thrift, credit and other financial services and products of very small amounts to the poor in rural, semi urban or urban areas, for enabling them to raise their income levels and improve living standards" [1]. At present, a large part of micro finance activity is confined to credit only. Women constitute a vast majority of users of micro-credit and savings services.

According to the United Nations, microfinance institutions can be broadly defined as provider of small-scale financial services such as savings, credit and other basic financial services to poor and low-income people. The term "microfinance institution" now refers to a wide range of organizations dedicated to providing these services and includes NGOs, credit unions, co-operatives, private commercial banks, NBFCs and parts of State-owned banks [2]. Microfinance is a dynamic field and there is clearly no best way to deliver services to the poor and hence many delivery models have been developed over a period of time.

Access s to financial services has been recognized as a human right. Strengthening credit-delivery services and increasing their outreach has always been an important component of Indian development strategy [3]. A large
number of the poor continued to remain outside the fold of the formal banking system, in spite of the expansion of the wide network of the organized banking system deep into rural areas. Market and the government both failed to provide credit access to the poor. In fact the failure of institutional initiatives of rural credit and to the weaknesses of the exploitative informal system of credit gave birth to Microfinance institutions. No doubt, microfinance has been successful in providing credit access to the poor. But in recent times the role of microfinance has become controversial, with various sections raising objections and criticisms in this regard. This article provides a brief overview of some of the important issues and challenges currently facing the microfinance institutions (MFIs) in India and finally concludes with practicable suggestions to overcome the issues and challenges associated with microfinance in India.

Objectives of the Study: In India so many micro lending institutions are working. Some are in very good condition in terms of lending, training to their clients for saving and small level entrepreneurship. Some are in bad condition and struggling for their existence. The present study is conducted to know the following things related to MFIs in India.

- The main objective of the study is to identify the main problems prevailing in microfinance in India.
- The other objective of this study is to find the solution of the problems faced by MFIs.

Review of Literature: There are lot of literature on opportunity and challenges of micro finance institution across the world, though only few studies have been carried out on the related topic, one such study done by Emerlson Moses [4], has studied that micro finance has emerged as a catalyst of rural development, especially in the overpopulated country like India. S.Sarumathil and Dr. K. Mohan [5] found that microfinance brought psychological and social empowerment than economic empowerment. Impact of micro finance is appreciable in bringing confidence, courage, skill development and empowerment. Devraja T.S. [6] has studied the India's achievement of the MDG of halving the population of poor by 2015 as well as achieving a broad based economic growth also hinges on a successful poverty alleviation strategy. In this backdrop, the impressive gains made by SHG-Bank linkage programme in coverage of rural population with financial services offers a ray of hope. In a similar study Mr. Nikhil considered that the microcredit movement has proved that it is possible to deliver financial services to poor people living in rural areas at a large scale, free from any reliance on subsidies. Manisha Raj in his research paper entitled "Microfinance Institutions in India and its Legal Aspects" states that Microfinance institutions have been proved a very important financial wing to incorporate the poor in the financial sector. Now on the other aspect like the challenges faced by the microfinance institutions Mr. Badrudduza found the positive results shown by MFIs in many countries but still there are a number of challenges before the microfinance industry, he shown in his paper. Rajesh and Ravi states in their paper, despite the role of microfinance is very good in poverty alleviation but the unethical and extortionist practices by MFIs led to arguably a draconian measure in its home turf Andhra Pradesh halting the industry in its tracks. In the line of challenges Dr. Sidhatha and their co authors found that the Microfinance delivery involves macro and micro challenges. The macro challenges faced by MFIs include the inaccessibility of the micro finance services to the rural poor, the capital inadequacy of the MFIs, the demand supply gap in provision of microcredit and micro savings and the lack of women orientation in marketing, evaluation and delivery of microfinance. The micro challenges include the inability to reduce the high

transaction cost involved in delivering microfinance, the non-availability of documentary evidence and collateral among majority of rural poor, difficulty in reducing the dependency of the rural poor on money lenders and lastly the problem of repayment tracking where lending is not based on documentary evidence. K. Muralidhara Rao found in his paper that Private MFIs in India, barring a few exceptions, are still fledgling efforts and are therefore unregulated. Jonathan Morduch and Stuart Rutherford in his study "Microfinance: analytical issues for India" states that the microfinance movement is thus striving to match the convenience and flexibility of the informal sector, while adding reliability and the promise of continuity and in some countries it is already doing this on a significant scale.

Statement of the Problem: We can say that the microfinance institutions are playing a vital role in the alleviation of poverty, uplifting living standard of very poor people. But what are the problems coming in the path of micro financing? The paper focuses on the issues and challenges prevailing in India regarding the micro financing. Are the microfinance institutions in very bad condition in India? An attempt is made through the paper to solve these problems.

Significance of the Study: The paper will help to know the condition of microfinance institutions in India. The research paper also tells why the microfinance institutions charges high interest to the borrowers. Here, in this research article, the attempt has been made to focus the problems of microfinance at social and cultural level, political level, educational level etc. The study presents some suggestions and recommendations to overcome from these problems.

The data for the present study is collected from the primary and secondary sources. Various magazines, news papers, research articles, referred journals and books have been studied and used for the collection of data.

Microfinance in India

An Overview: The field of Microfinance is much researchable. There is a lot of literature on Microfinance is available but there is hardly any universally accepted definition of microfinance. Researchers and microfinance visionaries have not a single opinion when it comes to microfinance. According to Sriram and Upadhyayula "It appears that what microfinance means is well understood, but it clearly articulated". However, microfinance is term that refers to the provision of a broad range of financial services such as deposits, loans, payment services, money transfers and insurance to poor and low-income households and their micro-enterprises. The need of microfinance comes from the disadvantaged sections of the society - who are unable to access to services of formal sector financial intermediaries - and are typically excluded from the formal banking system for lack of survival collateral, in short the poor and the very poor. The definitions of these groups vary from country to country. The clients of the microfinance institutes are normally employed in the informal sector, with closely interlinked household and business activities and earning low income [.In a much narrower sense though, microfinance is often referred to as microcredit for tiny informal businesses of micro entrepreneurs, the services being mainly delivered by socially oriented non-governmental organizations (NGOs).

Delivery Models of Microfinance: Microfinance is a dynamic field and there is clearly no best way to deliver services to the poor and hence many delivery models have been developed over a period of time. Each delivery model has its share of problem and success. In India, various delivery models have been adopted by microfinance institutions and they can be categorized in to following broad categories, discussed one by one.

Self Help Group Model: The Self Help Group (henceforth, SHG) model has evolved in the NGO sector and works on the belief that the poor can help themselves and the NGOs can provide networking and education to them. Almost 90% of the SHGs in India are female only due to the known fact that world's poorest households tend to rely more heavily on income generated by women of the house. In India, SHGs have been the most popular way to help the poor and make them bankable. An SHG is a small group of about 20 persons from a homogeneous class, who come together voluntarily to attain certain collective goals, social or economic. The group is democratically formed and elects its own leaders. The essential features of SHGs include members belonging to the same social strata and sharing a common ideology. Their aims should include economic welfare of all members. The concept of SHGs is predominantly used in the case of economically poor people, generally women, who come together to pool their small savings and then use it among themselves. The group members meet regularly (once in a week) and carry out their financial transactions .

The group mobilizes savings among its members only and provides need based loans to the members only (based on the funds created by savings). The rules and norms pertaining to finance or other matters are made by the group. The internal transactions are strengthened first and after that, the NGO supporting the group links them to banks for more financial assistance. There are many disadvantages of SHG models and they have been discussed in literature, a lot. Despite that fact, the advantages of the SHG have outnumbered the disadvantages and have made the SHGs as the most popular delivery model for microfinance in India. We can gauge the popularity from the following simple fact that even the government programs have SHG as the core of their strategies

Federated Self Help Group Model: Self Help Groups have been very successful in empowering women by providing direct and indirect benefits to them. However, SHGs are small in size (usually 10 – 15 members) and are limited in the types of financial services they can provide. Since Self Help Groups are a widely successful delivery model a need arises to scale them up without compromising with the success. The Federated Self Help Group model is one such way to scale up the previous model. Federation of SHGs bring together several SHGs. Compared to a single SHG, federation of SHGs have more than 1000 members. In Federated SHG model, there is a three tier structure the basic unit is the SHG, the middle tier is a cluster and the topmost unit is an apex body, which represents the entire SHG. At the cluster level, each SHG is represented by two of its members. The representatives of each SHG meet regularly. Information about the groups to the apex body and vice versa is given by the cluster unit. The apex body usually made up of 10 – 15 members and they form the link between the SHGs and the NGO supporting them. With the help of federations, an NGO with limited resources can have an impact on a large number of people. Few notable examples of Federated Self Help Group model are PRADAN, Chaitanya and SEWA.

Grameen Bank Model: The Grameen Bank model has been a case of exceptional success in Bangladesh. It turns out that many organizations in India have adopted the Grameen Bank model with little variations and good success. Some of the notable examples are SHARE Microfinance Limited, Activists for Social Alternatives (ASA) and CASHPOR Financial and Technical Services Limited. Some of the significant features of Grameen bank model are low transaction costs, no collateral (peer pressure is sufficient), repayment of loans in small and short interval and quick loan sanctions with little or no paper works and no formalities. Repayment of loans in small chunk is one of the major reasons of high loan recovery rate of a Grameen Bank. Furthermore, loans are provided for all purposes like housing loans, sanitation loans, supplementary loans etc. Also the interest rates are nominal making it easy for the poor people to repay their loans timely.

Co-Operative Model: A co-operative is an organization owned by the members who use its services. This model works on the principle that every community has enough human and financial resources to manage their own financial institutions. The members who own it are the members who use its services and can come from different sections of same community like agriculture, retail, wholesale etc. By proper networking small scale local institutions scale up and become sustainable while locals maintain ownership and control over their institution. The organization which has been vastly successful in co- operative form in India is Sahavikasa or Co-operativeDevelopment Foundation (CDF). CDF's approach relies on the well known Credit Union model involving a savings first strategy. Found in 1975 by a group of individuals, Sahavikasa has now emerged as the leading co-operative in India. Based on women's thrift group and men's thrift group, CDF has built up a network of financial cooperatives and had convinced the Andhra Pradesh government to form legislation for proper and flexible functioning of co-operatives in the state. The legislation is known as Mutually- Aided Societies Act (MACS). The act helps the CDF to register the thrift groups promoted by CDF under it. The activities of CDF involve assisting rural women and men in the areas of operation in forming and developing self sustainable co-operatives. CDF also provide education and training to the co-operators from its work area.

Key Issues in Microfinance in India

Low Outreach: In India, MFI outreach is very low. It is only 8% as compared to 65% in Bangladesh. Data show the great potential of MFIs in increasing their outreach and scale of operations. It has been observed that MF programmes focus a great deal of attention on women. It has been argued that women are better clients as they are more inclined to save than men, they borrow smaller amounts than men and their repayment performance is better than men. These characteristics of women clients constitute evidence in support of the inclination of MFIs to cater to the needs of women. Women may be better and more reliable clients, but in order to increase their outreach MFIs cannot ignore men as clients. **High Interest Rate:** MFIs are charging very high interest rates, which the poor find difficult to pay. It has been argued that MFIs are private entities and hence need to be financially sustainable. They do not receive any subsidized credit for their lending activities and that is why they need to recover their operational costs from borrowers. In the process, the basic reason for their existence-and their primary objective-is being lost. It is important that these NGOs should be willing to operate at narrow margins and to bear a low effective interest rate so that they can maintain a balance between their dual objectives of commercial viability and serving the poor.

Negligence of Urban Poor: It has been noted that MFIs pay more attention to rural areas and largely neglect the urban poor. Out of more than 800 MFIs across India, only six are currently focusing their attention on the urban poor. However, the population of the urban poor is quite large, amounting to more than 100 million. With increasing urbanization, this number is expected to rise rapidly in the coming years. In this situation, MFIs need to pay equal attention to the urban poor because they too need financial assistance for various activities.

Client Retention: Client retention is an issue that create a problem in growing the MFIs. There is about 28% client retention in the MFIs. This occurs because people are not properly informed and educated about services and products provided by the institutions more over the current client has higher default rate

Loan Default: Loan default is an issue that creates a problem in growth and expansion of the organization because around 73% loan default is identified in MFIs. Lack of understanding on the part of the clients, they also cannot correctly manage the loans given to them. As a result, they are not able to pay back the loan.

Low Education Level: The level of education of the clients is low. So it creates a problem in the growth and expansion of the organization because its percentage is around 70% in MFIs. Target population of MFIs is people of rural areas and they have no or less education level. As the percentage of people who have very less education.

Language Barrier: Language barrier makes communication with the clients (verbal and written) is an issue that creates a problem in growth and expansion of the organization because around 54% language barrier has been identified in MFIs. As the education level of clients is low so it is difficult to communicate with them. For this reason it is also difficult for the MFIs employees to make the clients to understand the policy and related details.

Late Payments: Late payments are an issue that creates a problem in growth and expansion of the organization because late payments are around 70% in MFIs. This usually occurs because clients are uneducated and they don't know how to manage their debt. They are unaware of the fact that late payment increases their loan payments..

Geographic Factors: Around 60% of MFIs agrees that the Geographic factors make it difficult to communicate with clients of far-flung areas which create a problem in growth and expansion of the organization. MFIs are basically aimed to facilitate the BPL population of the country but due to lack of infrastructure in those areas it becomes difficult to reach them.

Debt Management: Clients are uneducated about debt management 70% of the clients in MFIs are unaware of the fact that how to manage their debt. Because of the lack of education and understanding on the part of the clients, they also cannot correctly manage the loans given to them. So for this reason debt management creates a problem in growth and expansion of the organization.

Internal Environment

High Transaction Cost: High transaction cost is a big challenge for microfinance institution. The volume of transactions is very small, whereas the fixed cost of those transactions is very high. It cannot vary with the size of the loan. The higher a producer's fixed costs in the proportion of his total cost, the element of risk increases in the same proportion. Moreover, if the demand for the product falls or the marginal costs increases, it becomes very difficult to adjust the cost by cutting output. This cut will reduce revenue out of which he has to pay principal amount as well as interest on the loan. This needs to be rationalized.

Lack of access to Funding: Another factor contributing to the lack of growth in MFIs is that requisite financial support has not been provided to MFIs by concerned agencies. Around 68% of MFIs response was in favour of that government and SBP don't support them to meet the funds requirement as MFIs cannot alone remove the poverty from the country.

Loan Collection Method: Loan Collection Method is found an issue that creates a problem in growing the organization. Around 55% of MFIs agrees that due to weak law and legislation they are not able to make their loan collection system as effective as they want to do so.

Fraud: Fraud is an issue that creates a problem in growth and expansion of the organization because its percentage is around 67% in MFIs. Mismanagement of loans on the part of the clients creates the problem of fraud and financial embezzlement on the part of clients.

External Environment: Increased Competition: Increased competition is an issue that creates a problem in growth and expansion of the organization because its percentage is around 72%. As there has been growth in the banking sector with regard to the loan facilities therefore there is a greater competition among such institutions.

Uneven Population Density: Uneven population density is an issue which create problem in growth and expansion of the organization because loans and funds are required by rural population not urban areas.

Challenges Before the MFIs: No doubt, microfinance programme has shown impressive achievements, but a number of challenges are there: Did this programme reach the underprivileged? Whether everyone in need of microfinance intervention had been reached by any of the agencies? Even if everyone had been reached, did they get the required quantum of assistance to have sustainability? These questions are still very inconvenient to be answered because there are certain challenges associated with this programme. Some of the main challenges have been discussed in the following paragraphs.

Quality of SHGs: The third challenge is how to ensure the quality of MFIs in an environment of exponential growth. Due to the fast growth of the SHG-Bank Linkage Programme, the quality of MFIs has come under stress. This is reflected particularly in indicators such as the poor maintenance of books and accounts etc. The deterioration in the quality of MFIs is explained by a variety of factors including:

The intrusive involvement of government departments in promoting groups;

Inadequate long-term incentives to NGOs for nurturing them on a sustainable basis; and Diminishing skill sets on part of the MFIs members in managing their groups. In my assessment, significant financial investment and technical support is required for meeting this challenge.

Regional Disparity: It has been observed that the microfinance programme is mainly run by formal financial institutions with the help of SHGs. As a result, microfinance programme is progressing in those areas of the country where there is tremendous growth of formal financial institutions. Microfinance institutions were expected to reach those areas where the formal banking system failed to reach and the poor people have to depend on the money-lenders in order to meet their financial requirements. But actually, many big MFIs are activating in those states where the banking network is very strong. In the southern states, such as Andhra Pradesh, Tamil Nadu, Karnataka and Kerala, the spread of

SHG bank linkage programme as well as the MFI programme is very large. But the north and north-eastern region is almost neglected. In the southern India the spread of commercial bank branch network is the highest (27.94 per cent) and these states cover 48.15 per cent of the country's total SHG members and 54.77 per cent of the MFI members. So, approximately 50 per cent of the total microfinance programme beneficiaries belong to these four south Indian states. In contrast to this, in the north-eastern region of India, bank branch network is very limited and the coverage of microfinance programme is just 2.93 per cent. The table also shows the region-wise branch network and the microfinance members covered under SHG-Bank Linkage and MFI model in these different regions.

Deserving Poor are Still not Reached: The microfinance delivery models are not exclusively focused on those who are below the poverty line or very poor. Though the programme is spreading rapidly but with a slow progress in targeting the bottom poor households. About 50 per cent of SHG members and only 30 per cent of MFI members are estimated to be below the poverty line. According to Ghate (2008), approximately 75 million households in India are poor and about 22 per cent of these poor households are currently receiving microfinance services. In order to run the groups successively and to achieve higher repayment rates, they generally select the non-poor people as programme beneficiaries. The study finds that the core poor are often not accepted in group lending programmes by other group members because they are seen as a bad credit risk.

Inspite of the various institutional barriers, various psychological problems relating to the poor people restrict them to join the programme. The extreme poor often lack self-confidence so they hesitate to join a group where they have to deal with the other group members, bank officials and other promoting institutions. The core poor are generally too risk averse to borrow for investment in the future. They will therefore benefit only to a very limited extent from microfinance schemes.

Microfinance Outreach in Seven Poorest States of India:
Unfortunately, these seven states, Orissa, Bihar, Chhattisgarh, Jharkhand, Uttaranchal, Madhya Pradesh and Uttar Pradesh are lagging behind in microfinance programme. These states hold approximately 53.5 % of the total poor in India and the share of these seven states is just 23.60% of total microfinance outreach in India. The reasons for this skewed distribution of microfinance programme may be the intense support extended by the state governments, local culture and practice and concentration of MFIs.

Low Depth of Outreach: Another problem faced by the microfinance programme is the depth of services provided. Though the outreach of the programme is expanding, large number of people is provided with microfinance services but the amount of loans is very small. The average loans per member in both MFIs and SHGs are between Rs. 3,500] his amount is not sufficient to fulfil the financial needs of the poor people. The duration of the loans is also short. The small loan size and short duration do not enable most borrowers to invest it for productive purposes. They, generally, utilise these small loans to ease their liquidity problems.

Unregulated Microfinance Institutions: In India, micro finance is provided by a variety of institutions. These include banks (including commercial banks, RRBs andco-operative banks), primary agricultural credit societies and MFIs that include NBFCs, Section-25 companies, trusts and societies. But only the banks and NBFCs fall under the regulatory purview of the Reserve Bank of India. Other entities, e.g., MFIs are covered in varying degrees of regulation under their respective State legislations. There is no single regulator for this sector. As a result, MFIs are not required to follow some standard rules and are not subject to minimum capital requirements and prudential norms. This has weakened their management and governance, as they do not feel it mandatory to adopt some specific systems, procedures and standards. Therefore, there is a need for regulating the varied number of microfinance providers which are influencing the lives of millions of poor people. The regulation would, therefore, help in improving the growth of MFIs in an orderly approach.

Lack of Insurance Services: Poor people are vulnerable to financial shocks. A small change in their earning patterns due to natural calamities, health problems, death of earning member etc. Can push them to destitute. So, a provision of insurance under the microfinance programme is very essential to help the poor to cross the poverty line. But, in reality, the current microfinance programme in India is just focused on regular saving and micro-credit. SHG-BLP developed by NABARD is also providing

saving and credit services mainly and the provision of insurance is very less. However, some of the MFIs have started providing insurance services but the efforts are still at an experimental stage. A research report by Invest India Market Solutions Pvt. Ltd. (IIMS, 2007) indicates that the penetration of life insurance is only 12 per cent among the rural poor and 19 per cent among the urban low-income population [26] The penetration ratio for insurance in India was estimated at 4.80 in 2006, whereas for Asia it was 6.60 and for Europe at 8.30 [27]. So, in India the provision of insurance services is at the initial stage and this integral part of the microfinance programme is still neglected.

CONCLUSION

On the above findings we observe so many problems are associated with the MFIs. The Microfinance institutions are lagging behind in terms of loan and credit the real needy, regional imbalance, a proper regulation etc. Internal, external and client based challenges are prevailing from starting of the MFIs in India. Finally in my view MFIs in India have so many lacunas in their running, though the MFIs paid an important role in the poverty alleviation and enhancing the living standards of the poor. If the above shortcoming will be eliminate from the MFIs, it would have positive results on the economy, lead to greater efficiency and improvement of living standards of the thousands of poor.

Presently, there is no distinctive regulatory framework for the MFIs in India. Regulation of the MFIs is largely in the purview of the state governments. So there is a need of an exclusive regulation to regulate to MFIs in India. Ensure the quality of MFIs in an environment of exponential growth. Due to the fast growth of theSHG-Bank Linkage Programme, the quality of MFIs has come under stress. This is reflected particularly in indicators such as the poor maintenance of books and accounts etc. Proper training for the clients should be organized in an efficient way so that they could know each and every small things about their debt Ensure the uniform distribution of micro financing in both rural and urban areas of each states of Indi

REFERENCES

1.Microfinance and Its Delivery Models. StudyMode.com. Retrieved 08, 2007, from http://www. study mode.com/essays/Microfinance-Its-Delivery-Models-119718.html

2.Tenaw, S. and K.Z. Islam, 2009. Rural financial services and effects of microfinance on agricultural productivity and on poverty. University of Helsinki Department of Economics and Management (Discussion Papers series), 1: 28.

3.Nisha Bharti, 2007. Microfinance and Microfinance Institutions in India: Issues and Challenges, IRMA. 11: 2

4.Emerlson Moses, 2011. in his study "An Overview of Micro Finance in India", International Referred Research Journal, RNI-RAJBIL 2009/29954.VoL.III

5.Sarumathi, S. and K. Mohan, 2011. in their paper "Role of Micro Finance in Women's Empowerment", Journal of Management and Science, 1(1): 1-10.

6.Devaraja, T.S., 2011. "Microfinance in India - A Tool for Poverty Reduction".

7 Ghate, P., 20   08. Microfinance in India: A State of the Sector Report, 2007, Microfinance India Publications, New Delhi.

8 Srinivasan, N., 2009. Microfinance India State of the Sector Report 2008, Sage Publications, New Delhi.

9.A research report by Invest India Market Solutions Pvt. Ltd. (IIMS, 2007).

10Srinivasan, N., 2009. Microfinance India State of the Sector Report 2008, Sage Publications, New Delhi

11 *Sibghatullah Nasir* Middle-East Journal of Scientific Research 15 (2): 191-199, 2013 ISSN 1990-9233
© IDOSI Publications, 2013 , "Microfinance in India: Contemporary Issues and Challenges"

Chapter-2

Indian Microfinance – Status in India and Andhra Pradesh

- **Dr. Y. Aparna Rao,**
Faculty, Department of Management Studies,
G V P College of Engineering (A),
Visakhapatnam

"Micro financing has been a noble way of reaching out to people at the lowest levels of society and cater to their financing needs while saving them from loan sharks. The trouble, however, is that some bad apples are giving the whole industry a bad name."
- *Ashvin Parekh, Partner and National Leader of Global Financial Services at Ernst & Young.*

Introduction

Poverty alleviation programs in India gained prominence during the early 19th century. After independence, the government initiated several anti-poverty programmes. Micro Finance (MF) through the Self Help Group (SHG) concept emerged as a result of the failure of several Government run poverty alleviation programs. The MF concept promised poverty alleviation and sustainability to the rural poor, especially women.

Initially, micro finance was solely promoted by governmental agencies, nationalized banks, Micro Finance Institutions (MFIs) and NGOs, developmental financial institutions, such as the National Bank of Agricultural and Rural Development (NABARD) and the Small Industries Development Bank of India, (SIDBI). Subsequently, even private banks wanted to tap the potential of this sector and started micro lending. During the initial stages of micro finance operations in India, most MFIs operated as Non government organizations (NGOs) and focused on adapting the group-lending model from Bangladesh. Subsequently, NGO-MFIs began to transform into non bank finance companies (NBFCs) with a view to tap equity investment.

As such, the MFIs became highly leveraged and expanded their business initiatives by adopting a highly aggressive lending approach and by becoming highly leveraged. Thus, the risk associated with such a lending mechanism also increased tremendously. Lack of clarity in regulations and low transparency in operations of these NGO-MFIs together with the dual goals of social responsibility and profitability compounded the problem, reflecting as poor internal control systems, a lack of accountability, and suboptimal performances. Governance-related issues posed as the biggest challenge to the sustainability of India's microfinance institutions (MFIs).

Microfinance in India started in the early 1980s with small efforts at forming informal self-help groups (SHG) with the main objective of providing the rural poor with access to savings and credit services. Robinson (2001) defined microfinance as "small-scale financial services—primarily credit and savings—provided to people who farm, fish or herd". He also says that it "refers to all types of financial services provided to low-income households and enterprises."

Over the past decade, the microfinance sector in India has witnessed tremendous growth in size, prominence, stature, and visibility. The rapid growth brought with it, its share of problems too, some of them being over commercialization, questions on the premise on which the loans are made, the interest rates being charged by private players in the sector and the means by which the private players demand the repayment of loans from the borrowers.

Micro-finance, which initially started out as a means of extending financial services to the rural poor, who were ignored by the mainstream banks and exploited by loan sharks, in recent years has shifted from its original goal of working on the socio economic development of the poor, to large scale profit maximization. It has been felt off late, that the industry would require greater transparency, corporate governance and stringent legal regulations to keep it true to its original intent of helping the poor.

The Malegam Committee Report on regulating MFIs

In order to address the pressing issues in the micro finance sector, the Board of Directors of the Reserve Bank of India, at its meeting held on October 15, 2010 formed a Sub-Committee of the Board to study issues and concerns in the microfinance sector in so far as they related to the entities regulated by the Bank. The composition of the Sub-Committee; Shri Y.H. Malegam – Chairman, and other members are; Shri Kumar Mangalam Birla , Dr. K. C. Chakrabarty , Smt. Shashi Rajagopalan , Prof. U.R. Rao and Shri V. K. Sharma (Executive Director) – Member Secretary.

It is the first committee report for regulating Microfinance activities in India. The committee wanted to legitimize microfinance as an integral part of the Indian financial sector. The committee also recommended the creation of a new category of MFIs, called NBFC MFIs and continuation of priority sector funds for MFIs. However the committee has also highlighted key problem areas like ghost lending, multiple lending, over lending, while giving impetus on greater transparency with regard to interest rates through various measures. Stress was also given on the importance of off-site and on-site supervision of NBFC MFIs, and on corporate governance as the key to success of this sector. The main areas of concern of this report were; Unjustified high rates of interest, b) Lack of transparency in interest rates and other charges, c) Multiple lending, d) upfront collection of security deposits, e) over-borrowing, f) ghost borrowers, and g) coercive methods of recovery

The committee highlighted key problem areas like ghost lending, multiple lending, over lending, while giving impetus on greater transparency with regard to interest rates. Corporate governance as the key to success of this sector was stressed upon. The committee recommended the creation of a new category of MFIs, called NBFC MFIs and continuation of priority sector funds for MFIs. An NBFC-MFI may be defined as "A company (other than a company licensed under Section 25 of the Companies Act, 1956) which provides financial services pre-dominantly to low-income borrowers with loans of small amounts, for short-terms, on unsecured basis, mainly for income-generating activities, with repayment schedules which are more frequent than those normally stipulated by commercial banks and which further conforms to the regulations specified in that behalf". The Sub-Committee recommended that an NBFC classified as a NBFC-MFI should satisfy the following conditions:

a) Not less than 90% of its total assets (other than cash and bank balances and money market instruments) are in the nature of "qualifying assets."

b) For the purpose of (a) above, a "qualifying asset" shall mean a loan which satisfies the following criteria:-

i. the loan is given to a borrower who is a member of a household whose annual income does not exceed Rs. 50,000;

ii. the amount of the loan does not exceed Rs. 25,000 and the total outstanding indebtedness of the borrower including this loan also does not exceed Rs. 25,000;

iii. the tenure of the loan is not less than 12 months where the loan amount does not exceed Rs. 15,000 and 24 months in other cases with a right to the borrower of prepayment without penalty in all cases;

iv. the loan is without collateral;

v. the aggregate amount of loans given for income generation purposes is not less than 75% of the total loans given by the MFIs;

vi. the loan is repayable by weekly, fortnightly or monthly installments at the choice of the borrower.

c) The income it derived from other services is in accordance with the regulation specified in that behalf.

The Andhra Pradesh Micro Finance Institutions
(Regulation of Money Lending) Ordinance, 2010

Andhra Pradesh (AP) had been at the forefront of the micro finance sector in India. However, the year 2010 was witnessed a host of problems too in terms of coercive method of recovery resorted by the MFIs who were vital participants in the process. There were also cases where the borrowers are unable to repay the loan. In short, there were problems of lack governance, lack of proper regulations and legal dimension to micro lending. Although the establishment of MFIs was with a noble intention, implementation of the schemes became an issue as funding for the micro finance sector came at a very high cost. As such, the MFIs were forced to pass on the cost to their customers resulting in financial imbalances and further not providing the relief from money lenders, which was their foremost objective. It seemed as if the MFIs had only replaced money lenders with their high lending rates. It was felt that the Indian micro finance sector, which was so far a huge success in addressing poverty and related issues, was now eclipsed with growing number of suicides and this threatened the very existance of micro lending. This resulted in the State of Andhra Pradesh being the first State in the country to consider regulating the MFIs under a statute and thus came the aforementioned Ordinance. The Governor of Andhra Pradesh gave his assent to the Ordinance and enabled the enactment of the Ordinance with effect from 15th October 2010, which came into force from December 2010.

The legislation, strictly applicable in the state of Andhra Pradesh, aimed at regulating the sector by keeping a strict vigil on the activities of the MFIs in the state. It prohibited MFIs from lending to SHGs that were already covered by the formal banking system, without seeking prior approval of the banks. The MFIs were also required to change or rather, improve recovery practices from weekly basis to monthly basis. They were also asked to conduct their meetings with the borrowers in a prominent government facility like gram panchayat office. However, MFIs could advance loans to SHGs at interest subject to the provisions of the Ordinance.

Registration by MFIs

It has been made mandatory for all MFIs including the existing ones, to register with the district Registering Authority i.e the Project Director (PD) of District Rural Development Agency (DRDA) for rural areas and PD of Mission for Elimination of Urban Poverty in Municipal Areas (MEMPA) for urban areas. Additionally, they can also register with any other person appointed by the District Collector, to perform the function of the Registering Authority. Further, the MFIs can't grant or recover loans without obtaining registration from the Registering Authority. The registration is valid for a period of one year and can be renewed subsequently. The act also stated that the Registering Authority may, at any time, upon receipt of complaints by SHGs or the general public, cancel the registration of the MFI after issuing notice and affording reasonable opportunity to show cause against such notice.

Obligations of MFIs

MFIs have to specify the area of their operations, the rate of interest being charged or proposed to be charged, which cannot be subsequently increased and their system of conducting due diligence and recovery of the money lent while registering with the Registering Authority. An undertaking should be given by the MFI that it shall comply with the provisions of the Ordinance. In addition, the reporting norms, as prescribed by the ordinance need to be followed perfectly. The financial books and statement of accounts should be maintained properly.

Terms of lending

The ordinance says that MFIs cannot seek collateral from a borrower by way of pawn, pledge or any other security and any security obtained from a borrower before the commencement of the Ordinance will have to be released in borrower's favour. It also requires MFIs to display the interest rates charged in a prominent place at their offices in bold letters so that it is visible to general public. In case of SHGs with outstanding loans, the MFIs cant extend a further loan unless approved by the Registering Authority. Further, the MFIs cannot receive any payment without issue of a duly signed receipt. The amount of interest charged, should not be in excess of the principal amount and if any amount that is equal to twice the principal amount has been realized from the borrower, his loan will stand discharged and he shall be entitled to obtain refund of the excess amount. The ordinance also states that MFIs cannot deploy any agents or use any other coercive act for recovery of money from the borrower.

Conclusion

Both, the AP ordinance for regulation of MFIs as well as the Malegam Committee work towards achieving a harmony in terms of stabilizing and retaining the original flavour of the Micro finance Sector. Much still remains to be seen in terms of the benefits to the sector. But the sector has seriously transformed from being a simple tool for overty alleviation and economic and financial empowerment for the poor, especially women, to a tool for minting money.

References:

1. Andhra Pradesh Micro Finance Institutions (Regulation of Money Lending) Ordinance 2010
2. M S Sriram (2010), "The Anxiety of Growth in Microfinance", Unpublished Paper. Prof Sriram is Adjunct Professor, IIM - A
3. Ms Rajalaxmi Kamath and Prof Srinivasan (2009), "Microfinance in India: Small, Ostensibly Rigid and Safe", IIM B Working Paper
4. Srinivasan, N., "State of the Sector Report 2008", Sage Publications, London, UK, 2009.
5. Kamath, Rajalaxmi, Arnab Mukherji and Smita Ramanathan, "Ramanagaram Financial Diaries: Loan Repayments and Cash Patterns of the Urban Slums", IIMB Working Paper No. 268.
6. Performance and corporate governance in microfinance institutions Roy Mersland and Reidar Øystein Strøm Agder University, Norway May 2007.
7. MFI governance issues under lenders' lens, Rajesh Bhayani & Abhijit Lele, http://sify.com/finance.
8. Principles and Practices of Microfinance Governance, U.S. Agency for International Development, Global Bureau, Economic Growth Section.
9. http://www.gdrc.org/icm/govern/effective-govern.html.
10. Aloysius P. Fernandez (2010), Is Micro Finance leading to a Macro Mess, The AP Ordinance, Unpublished Paper.

CHAPTER-3

REGULATORY FRAMEWORK FOR MICROFINANCE

Ms. Santhoshi Kumari Gondesi
Ph.D. Research Scholar
Dept. of Finance,
GIM, GITAM University
Visakhapatnam

Abstract
Purpose:
The main purpose of this is to provide Microfinance regulation and to draft a regulatory framework in India. In the current environment, it is becoming difficult to stay abreast of new initiatives to regulate microfinance institutions (MFIs).The drafting of legal texts is an important step when setting up an appropriate legal framework for microfinance. **Three elements** establish a legal regime for microfinance. On the *legal side*, some kind of assessment of existing legislation should be conducted first. On the *political side*, new or amended legislation is only possible when sufficient political support exists. And, perhaps most importantly, on the *institutional side*, regulation will only be effective when institutional capacity and will are sufficiently strong.

Keywords: micro-finance; poverty; regulatory-framework; legal; financial-services; NGO.

Introduction:

Microfinance has become one of the primary means financial services to small traders and craftsmen working in informal sector of developing economies. Microfinance Institutions (MFIs) provide thrift, credit and other financial services and products of very small amount to the poor in rural, semi-urban and urban areas for enabling them to raise their income levels and improve their living standards.

Financial services are considered as an inclusive term that extends to savings, insurance, and fund transfers. Microfinance has been high on the public agenda after the UN Year of Microcredit in 2005 and since the Nobel Peace Prize went to Mohammed Yunus and Grameena Bank in 2006.[1] What should actually be attributed as the primary reason behind the success of the model of Grameena Bank is its existence as primarily a non-profit organization.

In India, the Reserve Bank of India ('RBI') has identified the growth of the microfinance sector as an important avenue through which the broader national goal

---

[1]Roy Mersland&ReidarØysteinStrøm, *Performance and Corporate Governance in Microfinance Institutions* 1 (Munich Personal RePEc Archive, Paper No. 3887, 2007).

of making a wide range of financial services accessible to increasing proportion of the population (usually referred to as financial inclusion goal). In addition, the RBI considers lending by banks to the microfinance sector as a part of their priority sector lending requirements. Both these aspects increase the importance of ensuring orderly development and sound governance and regulatory structures for the microfinance sector.[2]

The regulation of MFIs in India has, however, been a controversial subject. In 2010, SKS Microfinance Limited, the largest provider of microfinance services in India,[3] was in the spotlight because of its alleged violent recovery practices and a number of farmer suicides linked to inability to pay back its high-interest loans.

Finally, in 2011, the Ministry of Finance proposed a comprehensive new Bill for the regulation of MFIs. Amongst these changes, lie fundamental questions relating to the regulation of this sector.

Should MFIs be allowed to commercialize unfettered by issuing IPOs or should it be regulated to serve the poor? What kind of regulation is best suited to ensure that microfinance is able to achieve financial inclusion, and who should be this regulator?

VikramAkula, the founder of SKS Microfinance claims that "the path of the capital markets will lead to the greatest social impact".[4] Critics though, most notable among whom is Mohammad Yunus, argue that by offering an IPO buyers get the message that profit can be made out of poor people.[5] "This would push microfinance in the loan-sharking direction", says Yunus, who has, for the past one year been contradicting Akula's stance by saying that microfinance is, primarily, banking and therefore, MFIs need to work towards obtaining banking licenses, which will enable them to take deposits from the public and thereby become self-sustaining.[6]

---

[2] Reserve Bank of India MasterCircularon Micro Credit, RBI/2010-11/407; RPCD.FID. BC. No. 53/12.01.001/ 2010-11, February 14, 2011, available at http://www.rbi.org.in/scripts/ BS_CircularIndexDisplay.aspx?Id=6266 (Last visited on March 16, 2012).

[3] Crisil, India Top 50 Microfinance Institutions(2009), available at http://www.crisil.com/pdf/ ratings/CRISIL-ratings_india-top-50-mfis.pdf (Last visited on March 26, 2012).

[4] Interview of VikramAkula, founder and CEO of SKS Microfinance by India Knowledge@ Wharton, May 1, 2008, available at http://knowledge.wharton.upenn.edu/india/article.cfm?articleid=4284 (Last visited on April 21, 2011).

[5] Erika Kinetz, *SKS Launches India's First Microfinance IPO*, July 28, 2010, available at http:// abcnews.go.com/Business/wireStory?id=11270209 (Last visited on April 21, 2011).

[6] Mohammad Yunus, Founder and Managing Director, Grameen Bank at Clinton Global Initiative, Annual Meeting, 2010, *Special Session: Profiting from the Poor? A Discussion on Microfinance* IPOs available at http://www.clintonglobalinitiative.org/ourmeetings/2010/ meeting_annual_multimedia_player.asp?id=83&Section=OurMeetings&PageTitle=M ultime dia (Last visited on March 12, 2012).

Mohammad Yunus' critique about microfinance transforming into loan-sharking has come true in painful circumstances. Vikram Akula himself has accepted that 17 out of the 30 suicides in Andhra Pradesh were due to the interest rates imposed by SKS Microfinance.[7]

Microfinance Defined:

For the purposes of this study microfinance can be defined as any activity that includes the provision of financial services such as credit, savings, and insurance to low-income individuals which fall just above the nationally defined poverty line, and poor individuals which fall below that poverty line, with the goal of creating social value.

The creation of social value includes poverty alleviation and the broader impact of improving livelihood opportunities through the provision of capital for micro enterprise, and insurance and savings for risk mitigation and consumption smoothing.

A large variety of people and enterprises provide microfinance in India, using a range of Microfinance delivery methods. Since the founding of the Grameen Bank in Bangladesh, various actors have endeavored to provide access to financial services to the poor increative ways.Governments have piloted national programs, NGOs have undertaken theactivity of raising donor funds for on-lending, and some banks have partnered with public corganizations or made small inroads themselves in providing such services.

This has resulted in a rather broad definition of microfinance as any activity that targets poor and low-income individuals for the provision of financial services. The range of activities undertaken in microfinance include group lending, individual lending, the provision of savings and insurance, capacity building, and agricultural business development services.

Whatever the form of activity however, the overarching goal that unifies all actors in the provision of microfinance is the creation of social value. Microfinance is therefore defined as much by form as by intent of the lender or financial service provider.

Roots of Microfinance:

Microfinance in its modern form is a relatively new industry, not just in India, but worldwide. Globally, needy individuals have traditionally acked access to the financial services provided by banks, regardless of the sum of money involved. One of the primary reasons for this is- the significant transaction costs associated with servicing client accounts.

---

[7]Indian Express, *Post-suicides, SKS Microfinance willing to cut loan rates,* October 15, 2010, available at http://www.indianexpress.com/news/postsuicides-sks-microfinance-willing-to-c/698154/ (Last visited on March 18, 2012).

Another major reason is that the poor lack assets that can be used as collateral to secure loans, providing banks with little recourse against defaulting borrowers. As a result of being denied access to credit services from formal banking and lending institutions, impoverished individuals' access to credit was limited to either traditional development programs—which were criticized for failing to reach the world's neediest or to moneylenders known for their predatory lending practices.

In its initial phases, microfinance involved a standard procedure. Money would be lent to the needy; the principal amount would then be collected, with interest, and the proceeds from the collected payment would be contributed to a pool of capital that would be re-lent to other borrowers. It was intended that borrowers would use the loaned money to fund small entrepreneurial enterprises, which would hopefully provide them with an ongoing source of income.

A micro lender may, for example, loan a borrower enough money to cover the cost of a goat. Upon purchasing the goat, the borrower would be able to produce and sell the goat's milk. The profits from these sales would allow the borrower to maintain a constant income stream. Thus, rather than providing the borrower with temporary relief from financial distress, the microloan was intended to provide the borrower with an enduring source of financial support.

In the initial phases of microfinance, government agencies were the primary providers of "productive credit" to the needy. These lending programs, heavily subsidized by international donors, were criticized due to their large loan losses and the lending organizations' frequent need to recapitalize, or put new money into their business, in order to continue operations. This led to microfinance in its modern form, rooted primarily in the private sector, as a market-based solution that quickly became viewed as "an integral part of the financial system."

Traditionally, microfinance programs possessed *two features* that drove their success. **First,** impoverished people, particularly women, had excellent repayment rates that were often better than the formal financial sectors of most developing countries. **Second,** "the poor were willing and able to pay interest rates that allowed [micro lenders] to cover their costs." Thus, micro lenders were able to function sustainably while reaching a large number of clients. Throughout the 1990s and into the 2000s, microfinance was viewed as a tool of socioeconomic development, and was operated overwhelmingly as a non-profit enterprise, concentrated in developing countries throughout South Asia, Africa, and Latin America.

Efforts to establish and implement microfinance were lauded worldwide. One of the most exalted figures in microfinance is Muhammad Yunus, the founder of the Grameen Bank of Bangladesh and one of the industry's pioneers. The Grameen Bank arose out of a study conducted by Yunus, then a professor at the Chittagong University in Bangladesh, in which he interviewed impoverished residents of villages surrounding the University in order to better understand their experiences with poverty.

He concluded that the reason people were poor was that they "lacked access to credit at reasonable interest rates and under appropriate conditions." Yunus attempted, unsuccessfully, to convince traditional banks to lend small amounts of money to the needy.

The inability of traditional banks to provide adequate financing led him to conclude that "specialized financial institutions" were needed to provide these loans. Such institutions would need to be willing to provide loans to the impoverished individuals on terms and conditions that were appropriate for them. Yunus established the Grameen Bank using a model that was quite distinct from the traditional banking model. Strict qualification criteria were established to ensure a focus on the needy.

In order to provide incentives for repayment, the bank implemented an innovative lending scheme in which borrowers were required to form groups of five and "accept joint responsibility for repayment of loans." The ability to access future credit was conditioned upon repayment of each group members' loan.

Another unique feature of the Grameen Bank's model was that small loans were repaid in weekly installments over the period of one year. Furthermore, rather than require borrowers to travel to the bank for service, Grameen Bank workers traveled to the borrowers' homes to provide service.

This innovative framework distinguished the Grameen Bank from its peers in its ability to address the specific needs of the poor. Under this model, the Bank began in 1976 as a research project that served one local village and soon spread to neighboring villages. In 1983, the government of Bangladesh recognized the Grameen Bank as an independent bank.

The bank grew rapidly, expanding both in loan coverage and volume. In 2006, the organization and its founder were jointly awarded the Nobel Peace Prize, placing the microfinance industry inthe international spotlight. Today, the Bank boasts that it is "owned by the poor whom it serves," with borrowers owning 90% of its shares and the Bengali Government owning the remaining 10%.

While the Grameen Bank appears to have preserved its philanthropic roots by maintaining a structure that functions primarily to serve the needy, not every microfinance institution (MFI) can say the same. Over time, the industry's rapid growth has coincided with a shift from operations being funded primarily by the state or charitable donations to being largely dominated by the private sector. With this has come a shift from nonprofit to for-profit business models.

While this transformation has occurred worldwide, it is especially salient in India. The repercussions of this shift in India are discussed in more depth in the following subpart.

Literature review:

India possesses one of the largest microfinance industries in the world. Microfinance in India began in the 1980s.[8] By 2004, the industry's presence in the country consisted of 188 million accounts, representing 18% of the nation's total population.[9] In 2008, India experienced a 65% borrower growth rate, and by 2010, it possessed the largest and most concentrated microfinance industry in the world. The public persona of India's microfinance industry has changed dramatically over the past decade. Once lauded, the industry recently experienced a large backlash that has spurred widespread regulatory efforts.

This Part examines India's legal framework, which serves as the forum for these regulatory efforts as well as the basis for their controversy. This Partalso provides the necessary background for understanding the microfinance industry and the current demand for the industry's reform by examining the establishment of micro finance and its evolution.

Microfinance in India:

An understanding of India's poverty, economy, and growth helps in making informed statements about the commercialization of microfinance and its impact on micro finance outreach in India. This sets the stage for defining microfinance and analyzing the costs and benefits of a more commercial model of microfinance delivery. A more in-depth look at the country's financial sector and its regulation provides the context within which microfinance has evolved and outlines its constraints.

The Evolution and Regulation of Microfinance in India:

A complete understanding of the evolution and nature of a country's financial system, regulation, and government attitude toward the sector is integral to understanding he nature of microfinance in any particular country. Such knowledge allows one to understand what forces shape its growth and what factors constrain it.

Understanding the nature of microfinance regulation is especially important to assessing the costs and benefits of transforming from and NGO MFI to a Non-Banking Financial Corporation (NBFC), MFI because regulation outlines the nature of some of those benefits and costs while also providing the legal basis for the different types of legal form a MFI can take. The World Bank has called South Asia the "cradle of microfinance."

Statistics indicate that some 45% of all the people in the world who use microfinance services are living in South Asia. However, the overall percentage of the poor and

---

[8]M.S. Sriram& Rajesh S. Upadhyayula, *The Transformation of the Microfina*
[9]Robert Peck Christen, Richard Rosenberg, &VeenaJayadeva, *Financial Institutions with a "Double-Bottom Line": Implications for the Future of Microfinance*, OCCASIONALPAPER (Consultative Grp. to Assist the Poor, D.C.), July 2004, *available at*http://www.cgap.org/gm/document-1.9.2701/OP8.pdf.

vulnerable people with access to financial services remains small, amounting to less than 20 % of poor households in India.

The World Bank estimates that more than 87% of India's poor cannot access credit from a formal source and therefore they are not borrowing at all or have to depend on money-lenders who charge them interest rates ranging from 48% to120% per annum and sometimes much higher.[10] This demonstrates that there are potential clients for microfinance in India, depending on the level of demand for financial services, from those poor without access to it.

The provision of such services, if done correctly, could have a significant impact on the poor. This fact alone is very compelling and is reason enough to occupy oneself with the careful questioning of how microfinance can be provided to as many of the poor with a demand for it as possible. Integral to this questioning is the purpose of this study, understanding the costs and benefits of providing microfinance in the form of a financial company rather than an NGO.

With nearly 400 million people in India below or just below an austerely defined poverty line, approximately 75 million households are potential clients of MFIs. Of these,nearly 60 million are in rural India, the remaining 15 million being urban slum dwellers. We are then curious about the penetration of India's formal financial system thus far in order to understand the depth of outreach. Understanding the depth of the formal financial system is what drives the purpose of considering the benefits and costs to NGOs of becoming NBFCs.

MFI Model

Microfinance in India suffers from severe semantic difficulties. Microfinance is defined not by form but by the intent of the lender.[11] Therefore, a loan given by a market intermediary to a small borrower is not seen as microfinance. When an institution whose constituent intent is the distribution of such loans gives a similar loan, however, it is treated as microfinance.[12] The institution may be constituted as a society, NGO or a company (profit or not for profit).

The MFI model can be divided into examples which are state initiatives and private ones. National Bank for Agriculture and Rural Development ('NABARD') and Small Industries Development Bank of India ('SIDBI') are examples of state run MFIs. Besides, supporting small-scale financial institutions, commercial banks, RRBs, and co-operative banks provide separate retail services as well.[13]

---

[10]*Year of Micro-credit Conference: Microfinance can be the biggest instrument in the fight against poverty, says Bank Vice President*. The World Bank Group, Dec. 5 2005 (Accessed 02/16/2006); available

from http://www.worldbank.org.in.

[11]Sriram&Upadhyayula, *supra* note 23.

[12]*Id.*

[13]Today, there are about 60,000 retail credit outlets of the formal banking sector in the rural areas comprising 12,000 branches of district level cooperative banks, over 14,000 branches of the Regional Rural Banks (RRBs) and over 30,000 rural and semi-urban branches of commercial banks besides

The last decade has seen the emergence of private players dealing solely in the microfinance industry. These, institutions provide services that are similar to the state players' under the aegis of the prevailing legal and regulatory environment for private sector rural and microfinance operators. For the purpose of this paper, we intend to focus on the commercialization of this model and the regulation of the aforesaid private players.

Regulatory Framework

The financial regulatory framework in a given country can have a huge impact on even the viability of microfinance. The forms of legal organization an institution has available to them, registration requirements, interest rate caps, capitalization, etc. are all determined by the legal framework or lack thereof.

Regulatory structure in place in India

There have been many innovative initiatives undertaken by Indian MFIs over the past five to seven years. The efficacy of such initiatives has, however, been limited. Their operations have faced hurdles by the absence of a supportive regulatory environment. Here, we take a look at the regulatory structure for MFIs in three distinct phases, viz. prior to the Andhra Pradesh MFI crisis of 2010, the state response and the present regulations in light of the recommendations made by the Malegam Committee.

Recognizing the MFI Players, Prior to 2010

The foremost problems prior to the major crisis that hit MFIs in 2010 are the processes of registration involved. There is a multitude of ways to form and register a private MFI. In the absence of an umbrella regulatory mechanism regulation of MFIs has become an example of too many cooks spoiling the broth. The problem is that registering the MFI under each of the categoriess invokes different legislations to govern the MFIs. Despite a similar set of services being provided, there seems to be an inconsistency with the regulations governing the bodies.

---

almost 90,000 cooperatives credit societies at the village level. The numbers show a significant outreach. On an average, there is at least one retail credit outlet for about 5,000 rural people. *See* National Bank for Agriculture and Rural Development, *mF Institutions,* available at http://www.nabard.org/microfinance/mf_institution.asp (Last visited on March 14, 2011).

The table below provides the seven categories recognized by the RBI and the legal framework that governs their activities.

S.No.	Categories of Providers	Legal Framework governing their activities
1	Domestic Commercial Banks: Public Sector Banks; Private Sector Banks & Local Area Banks	RBI Act 1934 BR Act 1949 SBI Act SBI Subsidiaries Act Acquisition & Transfer of Undertakings Act 1970 & 1980
2	Regional Rural Banks	RRB Act 1976 RBI Act 1934 BR Act 1949
3	Co-operative Banks	Co-operative Societies Act BR Act 1949 (AACS) RBI Act 1934 (for sch. banks)
4	Co-operative Societies	State legislation like MACS
5	Registered NBFCs	RBI Act 1934 Companies Act 1956
6	Unregistered NBFCs	NBFCs carrying on the business of a financial institution prior to the coming into force of RBI Amendment Act 1997 whose application for CoR has not yet been rejected by the Bank Sec. 25 of Companies Act
7	Other providers like Societies, Trusts, etc.	Societies Registration Act, 1960 Indian Trusts Act Chapter IIIC of RBI Act, 1934 State Moneylenders Act

How to regulate micro finance institutions:

With the limitations of the mechanism being highlighted, it is imperative to look at the possible avenues where the legal lacunae may be filled. In addition to the Malegam Sub-Committee, the RBI setup a separate working group to look into the regulation of microfinance institutions on March 8, 2011.[14] The problem it seems is that there are too many regulators as there are varied ways to initiate a MFI in India. Fitch Rating, one of world's leading rating agencies, recognizes that the challenges

---

[14] The panel was headed by RBI Deputy Governor, Usha Thorat in light of the Malegam Sub- Committee Report. *See* Business Standard, *RBI working group under Thorat to study NBFC issues*, March 8, 2011, available at http://www.business-standard.com/india/news/rbi-working-group-under-thorat-to-study-nbfc-issues/427608/ (Last visited on March 18, 2011

faced by MFIs in India are similar to the global trend which includes regulatory concerns.[15]

"The experience of co-operative banks in India suggests that multiple regulators may not be as effective as a single strong regulator and may also make it difficult for MFIs to comply with different sets of guidelines."[16] Hiratsuka points out that that supervision in the sector by central banking authorities does not affect either sustainability or outreach.[17] The rider, however, being that such an observation does not apply to scenarios where institutions lay emphasis on sustainability and outreach along with returns on the investments made.[18]

The argument though put forth was that there should be governmental regulation for deposit acceptors. Any approach to regulation and supervision of MFIs needs to recognize their heterogeneity, and accommodate the flexibility and scope for development that MFIs need.[19]

The specific problems posed by the regulation of MFIs are an outgrowth of the fact that, almost by their very nature, these institutions are highly specialized.[20] The regulation of MFIs is broadly two-fold. At one end there are non-profit institutions which provide specific services and only lend out donor funds. It is believed that MFIs must be introduced to prudential norms in a gradual manner.[21]

Though, they may still be subject to other regulations, for example on record keeping.[22] The other limb of classification is profit making entities which seek returns. The IMF recommends that such MFIs should be treated as analogous to full-

---

[15]The Economic Times, *Microfinance companies needs stable regulation to survive: Fitch,* April 28, 2011, available at http://articles.economictimes.indiatimes.com/2011-04-28/ news/29482804_1_fitch-microfinance-companies-india-s-mfis (Last visited on March 13, 2012).

[16] *See id. See also* Interview of AnandaBhoumik, Senior Director (Financial Institutions), Fitch Ratings in the Economic Times, *Microfinance companies needs stable regulation to survive: Fitch,* (April 28, 2011), available at http://articles.economictimes.indiatimes.com/2011-04-28/ news/29482804_1_fitch-microfinance-companies-india-s-mfis, (March 26, 2012).

[17]Valentina Hartarska, *Governance and Performance of Microfinance Institutions in Central and Eastern Europe and the Newly Independent States* 13 (William Davidson Institute Working Paper Series, Paper No. 677, 2004).

[18]*Id.*

[19]Daniel C. Hardy, Paul Holden & Vassili Prokopenko, *Microfinance Institutions and Public Policy* 20 (IMF Working Paper No.WP/02/159, 2002).

[20]At least when they start their operations; they employ credit technologies which are specially designed for their target groups; they rely on close personal relationships with their clients as a substitute for conventional forms of collateral; and they have a specific governance and ownership structure which helps to ensure that they remain committed to their specific clientele, which is admittedly a difficult one to serve; *See* Schmidt, *supra* note 1, 114.

[21] B. Seth McNew, *Regulation and Supervision of Microfinance Institutions: A Proposal for a Balanced Approach,* 15 Law& Bus. Rev. Am. 287 (2009).

[22]*Supra* note 75.

fledged commercial banks.Thereby, they should be subject to the same prudential regulatory regime as applied to the commercial banks with which they compete.

In intermediate cases, any regulatory framework for MFIs would have to address the trade-off between depositor protection and other benefits of regulation on one hand, and stifling of financial innovation and competition as well as other costs of regulation on the other hand. In many situations, a reasonable compromise between these objectives might be approached by regulations that emphasize that MFIs should be bona fide and should establish adequate internal controls and record keeping (including on loan loss recognition). Regulations also need to be carefully gradated to allow for the development of MFIs from very small, local, and specialized institutions to full-service providers of financial services.

Suggested regulatory framework:

The legal, regulatory framework predates microfinance, and thus needs some reorientation to accommodate genuine constraints to expansion of MFIs. [23] The primary aim of regulation in this sector should be the creation of a 'level playing field'.[24]This should not be confused with having the same regulations for all financial institutions alike. The need of the hour is that regulations should cater to a clearly demarcated setup.

How to go about establishing a new framework?

At the level of financial institutions Chavez and Gonzalez-Vega distinguish between allocation, operational and dynamic efficiency. [25] The efficiency of the financial institutions is a measure of the efficiency of the regulatory framework. The gains in efficiency are a function of standardization. Standardization may be divided into two forms. Firstly, where regulation allows for reduction in operational costs and secondly, where the individual identity of each organization merges with the other ones.

There is a tradeoff between the objectives of efficiency and stability of the financial system. Measures to safeguard the soundness of the financial system always affect competition and therefore tend to incur efficiency losses. Efficient supervision means maximizing the probability of detecting infringements of regulations.

---

[23] Deutsche GesellschaftfürTechnischeZusammenarbeit (GTZ) GmbH, Stephan Staschen, *Regulation and Supervision of Microfinance Institutions: State of Knowledge*, August 1999, available at http://www.staschen.net/FINANZSYSTEME_Regulierung_State_of_Knowledge_1999e.pdf (Last visited on March 26, 2012).
[24]Rodrigo A. Chaves & Claudio Gonzalez-Vega, *Principles of Regulation and Supervision: Should They be Different for Microenterprise Finance Organizations?* (Ohio State University Rural Finance Program, Occasional Paper No. 1979, 1992)
[25]Allocation efficiency is aimed at channelizing the resources to their most productive use. The minimizing of the transaction costs leads to operational efficiency. Dynamic efficiency refers to the adaptability to changing circumstances. The circumstances referred to herein are the ability to stabilize and expand their outreach. *See* Chavez &Gonzalez-Vega, *id.*

As far as possible, the regulatory framework for financial institutions should stipulate a governance structure that is incentive compatible, i.e. that makes full use of the self-interest of the individuals (owner, manager, depositor, borrower, etc.), to arrive at the desired results. This can be particularly important with MFIs, because recourse to legal enforcement mechanisms would be impracticable and too costly due to the informality of the sector.

The ownership structure plays a large role here. The regulatory framework for financial institutions must be flexible enough to be able to react to regulatory avoidance, technological innovation, failures of certain regulatory measures, etc. This is particularly important in microfinance, since hardly any experience is available in other countries.

Regulation can be seen as an evolutionary process where individual institutional types or only some elements of their ownership and governance structure prevail and others are superseded. One of the great strengths of unregulated MFIs till now has been their ability to test innovative products. The functional perspective takes as given the economic functions performed by financial intermediaries and asks what the best institutional structure to perform those functions is.

In institutional regulation there are different regulatory frameworks that prescribe requirements for certain institutional types (e.g. a banking law alongside cooperatives legislation and a law for finance companies), but these rarely allow for an easy transition from one category to another. There would be enormous transaction costs that would be associated with each transition. Requiring MFIs to keep customary bank loan records for example would incur excessive costs, because they issue a large number of small short-term loans.

Similarly, the costs of supervision would be extremely high partly because of the sometimes huge number of MFIs in relation to their national economic significance and the related risk potential, so that banking supervisory bodies are often reluctant to regulate them and lack the requisite resources.[26] One of the major challenges, then, will be to find cost-saving but effective methods to regulate and supervise MFIs.

Capital Requirements:

While dealing with suggestions on a regulatory structure and suggestions as to what changes should be brought into regulations we consider foremost the parameters that we perceive contribute to the limitations of the extant regime. In consonance with the Basel Accords there are relative capital requirements obliging banks to have equity or other risk-bearing capital equivalent to a certain proportion of their assets, and, on the other, there are absolute capital requirements in the form of a minimum permissible amount of equity.

---

[26] Tor Jansson& Mark Wenner, *Financial Regulation and its Significance for Microfinance in Latin America and the Caribbean* (1997) *as cited in* Staschen, *supra note* 93, 14.

One of the main ingredients of banking regulation is the requirement that financial institutions must have sufficient capital. This requirement is mainly intended to protect depositors, but also helps to stabilize individual financial institutions and to safeguard the financial system against so-called systemic risks.

In India, depositor facilities with MFIs are relatively new. Capital requirements are predominantly seen as a measure to ensure stable institutions for lending capabilities. We propose that MFIs specifically, should be subject to higher relative capital requirements than are applied to "normal" banks, combined with strict, and strictly enforced, limitations on the range of activities in which they are permitted to engage.

In such a way this would ensure that there is a specific line of funds channeling through to the company and not just funds from the open market. In a way this would ensure that unethical practices such as cashing out by MFI managements are curtailed.

Creation of credit delivery mechanisms:

The second round of focus in light of a new legislation is the creation of credit delivery mechanisms. Financial liberalization in the 1990s spawned greater entry amongst NBFCs but also saw several instances of illegal behavior and scams costing millions of rupees to consumers. If entry-norms are diluted combined with a weak monitoring infrastructure there exists a risk of consumers getting ripped off.

The intrinsic trade-offs between appropriate supervision and regulation of these MFIs and their need to scale up to adequately serve the financial needs of the poor lies at the heart of the debate on regulatory reforms for microfinance. Additionally, creation of such 'micro' banks with different regulatory provisions, diluted entry norms and exemptions from regulations affecting banks will adversely impact existing institutional assets that comprise rural formal financial sector.

Many of these institutions are in precarious health, but others are not and cumulatively represent substantial investments of public resources over years. In a country as large and heterogeneous as ours, there is arguably a need to allow diverse delivery channels of credit for poor to flourish. Given the scale of our failure hitherto to solve the poor's credit problems, it is also advisable to keep an open and flexible stance. Yet history teaches us that when it comes to microfinance, it would make sense to keep expectations modest, monitor alertly and adapt as needed, and, on the legal and regulatory front, stay flexible but make haste slowly.[27]

Governance Issues:

Governance is scaffold of checks and balances designed to ensure that no party within an MFI impede the attainment of corporate objectives by diverting its resources for private gain. By governance, importance has to be given on the creation of sound internal governance. It is pointed out that with strong initiatives by the managing boards, MFIs achieve higher sustainability.

---

[27]Shrivastava, *supra* note 29, 3626, 3628.

A standard registration requirement which covers documents of establishment and governance structure should apply to MFIs such as NBFCs in the same manner that other business and social organizations are required to register. These basic documents include Articles and Memorandum of Association of the companies which clearly delineate the presence of the governing parties

What is necessary in India at the moment is the creation of guidelines for prudential regulation which accommodate MFIs and their needs from time to time. Boards of Directors, who represent the shareholders, members or donors, have the ultimate responsibility and accountability for internal oversight and governance over management in a MFI's operations. This requires that adequate risk management policies and procedures are in place.

High rates of interests:

In light of the *SKS Microfinance controversy* in Andhra Pradesh, the foremost concern was with the rate of interests imposed on the loans. The new RBI Master Circular on micro-credit states that " the interest rate applicable to loans given by banks to micro-credit organizations or by the micro-credit organizations to Self Help Groups/member beneficiaries would be left to their discretion".

It would be interesting to note that despite such guidelines, the RBI directions for NBFC-MFIs make no such stringent stipulations on interest rates. Such an inability to impose caps on interest rates is dumbfounding to say the least especially when there is a strong surge of commercialization of MFIs. In addition to the creation of caps there also needs to be some structure *qua* interest rates.

For example, interest rates charged by the MFIs are often not quoted in transparent annualized terms. Often, loans involve upfront fees and service charges, making calculation of effective interest rates complex and therefore non-transparent.

Conclusion:

India's microfinance industry today is at a crossroads: it can continue to lose money and be viewed in a negative light, or it can reinvent itself through its realignment with the RBI. Despite the criticism drawn by the industry in recent years, microfinance fulfills a social need. The industry offers a unique, frequently utilized service to the poor.[28] Lack in regulation, however, the microfinance industry has expanded without bounds, and has done so using tactics that have significantly harmed its borrowers.

This conduct has left the industry with a tarnished reputation. India's proposed Bill has the potential to further the positive aspects of microfinance that allow it to be a social utility while minimizing or eliminating the aspects that cause strife. The Bill provides certainty regarding the industry's capabilities and limitations, defining

---

[28]Polgreen& Bajaj, *supra* note 184.

permissible practices and establishing penalties for unconscionable conduct. It provides a government partner that will bring the legitimacy and security that investors require. Perhaps most importantly, the Bill limits excessive, purely profit-driven behavior, refocusing the industry's function on the altruistic foundation it was built on. Andhra Pradesh's draconian regulation offers no compromise; it threatens to regulate the microfinance industry to the point of futility, thus limiting the poor's access to capital.

Furthermore, it is possible that microfinance could be classified as either" banking" or "the Reserve Bank of India," both of which explicitly fall under the federal government's legislative purview. Alternatively, microfinance may be deemed a non-enumerated power, in which case it would also fall under the federal government's exclusive legislative authority. Even in the unlikely event the Supreme Court determines that microfinance does qualify as money lending, the federal government could still prevail by asserting that microfinance is a matter of "national interest" within their legislative authority.

.

References:

1. Aditya Alok& Nihal Joseph- regulating the growth of commercialization of micro-finance institutions in India.

2. Reinhard Schmidt, Banking Regulation contra Microfinance, 24 Savings and Development 111 (2000).

3. Briget Helms, Access for All Building Inclusive Financial Systems2 (2006)

4. See Mukul Asher & Savita Shankar, As Microfinance Grows, So Does The Need For Better Regulation, March 17, 2010, available at http://www.dnaindia.com/money/comment_as-microfinance-grows-so-does-the-need-for-better-regulation_1359900

5. Crisil, India Top 50 Microfinance Institutions(2009), available at http://www.crisil.com/pdf/ ratings/CRISIL-ratings_india-top-50-mfis.pdf

6. Erika Kinetz, SKS Launches India's First Microfinance IPO, July 28, 2010, available at http:// abcnews.go.com/Business/wireStory?id=11270209

7. Mohammad Yunus, Founder and Managing Director, Grameen Bank at Clinton Global Initiative, Annual Meeting, 2010, Special Session: Profiting from the Poor? A Discussion on Microfinance IPOs available at http://www.clintonglobalinitiative.org/ourmeetings/2010/ meeting_annual_multimedia_player.asp?id=83&Section=OurMeetings&PageTitle =Multimedia.

8. Mohammad Yunus, Founder and Managing Director, Grameen Bank at Clinton Global Initiative, Annual Meeting, 2010, Special Session: Profiting from the Poor? A Discussion on Microfinance IPOs available at

http://www.clintonglobalinitiative.org/ourmeetings/2010/
meeting_annual_multimedia_player.asp?id=83&Section=OurMeetings&PageTitle
=Multime dia (Last visited on March 12, 2012).

9. Indian Express, Post-suicides, SKS Microfinance willing to cut loan rates, October
   15, 2010, available at http://www.indianexpress.com/news/postsuicides-sks-
   microfinance-willing-to-c/698154/ (Last visited on March 18, 2012).

10. M.S. Sriram& Rajesh S. Upadhyayula, Transformation of the Micro financial
    institutions.

11. Robert Peck Christen, Richard Rosenberg, &VeenaJayadeva, Financial
    Institutions with a "Double-Bottom Line": Implications for the Future of
    Microfinance, OCCASIONAL PAPER (Consultative Grp. to Assist the Poor,
    D.C.), July 2004, available at http://www.cgap.org/gm/document-
    1.9.2701/OP8.pdf.

12. Year of Micro-credit Conference: Microfinance can be the biggest instrument in
    the fight against poverty, says Bank Vice President. The World Bank Group, Dec.
    5 2005 (Accessed 02/16/2006); availablefrom http://www.worldbank.org.in.

13. Sriram & Upadhyayula, supra note 23

14. Valentina Hartarska, Governance and Performance of Microfinance Institutions in
    Central and Eastern Europe and the Newly Independent States 13 (William
    Davidson Institute Working Paper Series, Paper No. 677, 2004).

15. Deutsche GesellschaftfürTechnischeZusammenarbeit (GTZ) GmbH, Stephan
    Staschen, Regulation and Supervision of Microfinance Institutions: State of
    Knowledge, August 1999, available at
    http://www.staschen.net/FINANZSYSTEME_Regulierung_State_of_
    Knowledge_1999e.pdf (Last visited on March 26, 2012).

16. Rodrigo A. Chaves & Claudio Gonzalez-Vega, Principles of Regulation and
    Supervision: Should They be Different for Microenterprise Finance
    Organizations? (Ohio State University Rural Finance Program, Occasional Paper
    No. 1979, 1992).

17. Polgreen& Bajaj, supra note 184.

CHAPTER-4

REGULATORY FRAMEWORK OF MICRO FINANCE INSTITUTIONS IN INDIA

-B. Omnamasivaya
Research Scholar,
GITAM Unviersity,
Visakahpatnam

Abstract:
        Microfinance institutions always been considered as one of the frontline institutions for the propagation of financial services to the poor. But Indian microfinance institutions they are making profit out of the poor. In 2010, Andhra Pradesh SKS microfinance held at the first IPO for a micro finance institution in India and drawing attention to the potential profits of the sector .the micro finance institutions were charging high interest rates and they are making out of poor because of the lack of regulatory mechanism. The farmer suicides in Andhra Pradesh in 2010 garnered excessive attention through print and electronic media for months on end owing allegedly to exorbitant interest rates being charged by private MFIs. The incident culminated in Andhra Pradesh and CM passed the AP Microfinance Ordinance 2010 (Passed) in to law in December which effectively shut down all private sector micro finance operations in the state . in response to this In October 2010, the RBI's Central Board of Directors set up a Sub-Committee, chaired by Y.H. Malegam, to study the issues and concerns in the micro finance sector. based on committee recommendations and report. Finally the ministry of finance proposed a comprehensive new bill for the regulation of MFI's

Key words : micro finance, micro finance institutions , RBI, development and regulation bill

Introduction:

        Micro Finance has become one of the primary means by which much required financial services are provided to small traders and craftsmen working in the informal sector of developing economies. MFIs provide thrift, credit and other financial services and products of very small amount to the poor in rural, semi-urban and urban areas for enabling them to raise their income levels and improve their living standards. Financial services are considered as an inclusive term which extends to savings, insurance, and fund transfers as well. Microfinance has been high on the public agenda after the UN Year of Microcredit in 2005 and since the Nobel Peace Prize went to Mohammed Yunus and Grameen Bank in 2006. What should actually be attributed as the primary reason behind the success of the model of Grameen Bank is its existence as primarily a non-profit organization.

        In India, the Reserve Bank of India ('RBI') has identified the growth of the microfinance sector as an important avenue through which the broader national goal of making a wide range of financial services accessible to increasing proportion of the population (usually referred to as financial inclusion goal) can be reached. In addition, the RBI considers lending by banks to the microfinance sector as a part of their priority sector lending requirements. Both these aspects increase the importance of ensuring orderly development and sound governance and regulatory structures for the microfinance sector.

The regulation of MFIs in India has, however, been a controversial subject. In 2010, SKS Microfinance Limited, the largest provider of micro-finance services in India, was in the spotlight because of its alleged violent recovery practices and a number of farmer suicides linked to inability to pay back its high-interest loans. Finally, in 2011, the Ministry of Finance proposed a comprehensive new Bill for the regulation of MFIs. Amongst these changes, lie fundamental questions relating to the regulation of this sector. Should MFIs be allowed to commercialize unfettered by issuing IPOs or should it be regulated to serve the poor? What kind of regulation is best suited to ensure that microfinance is able to achieve financial inclusion, and who should be this regulator ?

Vikram Akula, the founder of SKS Microfinance claims that "the path of the capital markets will lead to the greatest social impact". Critics though, most notable among whom is Mohammad Yunus, argue that by offering an IPO buyers get the message that profit can be made out of poor people. "This would push microfinance in the loan-sharking direction," says Yunus, who has, for the past one year been contradicting Akula's stance by saying that microfinance is, primarily, banking and therefore, MFIs need to work towards obtaining banking licenses, which will enable them to take deposits from the public and thereby become self-sustaining. Mohammad Yunus' critique about microfinance transforming into loan-sharking has come true in painful circum-stances. Vikram Akula himself has accepted that 17 out of the 30 suicides in Andhra Pradesh were due to the interest rates imposed by SKS Microfinance.

In light of these developments we contend that the commercialization of MFIs needs to be deterred. A corollary arising out of this would be to allow MFIs to exist only as not-for profit institutions as envisaged under § 25 of the Companies Act. Alternatively, if the argument put forward by the promoters of *SKS Microfinance* is tenable, independent regulator(s) must be introduced backed by sound guiding legislation. In order to control the micro finance institutions. there should be a strong regulatory frame work for monitoring the operations of micro finance institutions and micro finance business.

Need for the study:

Micro finance is the provision of financial services to low income individuals and households , as well as micro small and medium enterprises .many unbanked people are depending on microfinance institutions for credit but some micro finance institutions are charging the high interest rates , and harash recovery policy, Because of this many poor people are committed to suicide . micro finance institutions are really heppful for foster development of country if they are controlled hence there should be a separate regulatory framework to control the micro finance institutions activities and business.

Objectives of the study:
1.To know the regulatory framework for micro finance in India.

2.To understand the malgem report recommendations

3.To make aware of the micro finance institutions regulations and development bill 2012

Review of literature :

Aditya Alok & Nihaljoseph (2012) in their study, regulating the growing commercialization of micro finance institutions in India. The study revealed that MFI have always been considered as one of the frontline institutions for the propagation financial services to the poor. However, Indian MFI'S have not seen the kind of success as their counterparts in Latin America , Europe & Bangladesh . behind adoption of international models and subsequent commercialization by offering IPO has not seen desired results.

Anurag Priya Dashree & Asad K.Ghalib (2011) in their study they examined that the Andhra Pradesh micro finance crisis in India. they have been found that the absence of adequate regulatory mechanisms , resulted in over – lending to the poor and the singular focus of private sector MFIS on maximising profits in an inefficiency regulated environment, that give rise to the current circumstances.

Kenny Kline & Santadarshan Sadhu(2010) in their study they examined that the current micro finance regulatory structure , pending regulation , and MFI response to the RBI released in may 2011.

Denislewamoanga(2010) he examined that regulatory framework of microfinance in south Africa .in an attempt to find whether regulation enables(or) creates barriers to increasing access to financial services and reaching the unbanked population in south Africa . he found that while regulation is definitely not the sole responsible for the state of development of the south Africaan micro finance market. It constituted a facilitator to enhance the growth of the industry by setting standards, , increasing efficiency and promoting fair competition while strongly protecting consumers.

Regulatory framework of micro finance institutions:

The Malegam Report

In October 2010, the RBI's Central Board of Directors set up a Sub-Committee, chaired by Y.H. Malegam, to study the issues and concerns in the micro finance sector. In the terms of reference, the sub-committee was asked to review, examine and make recommendations regarding:

1.The definition of microfinance and MFIs

2.Prevalent practices with respect to interest rates, lending and recovery practices

3.Role of associations and bodies of MFIs could play

4.A grievance redressal system

Table 1. Key observations and recommendations of the Malegam Committee	
Issue	**Recommendations**
Regulatory scope	Separate category to be created for NBFCs operating in the microfinance sector.
	NBFC-MFIs can only lend to borrowers with a household income of less than Rs 50,000.
Interest rate	24% cap on individual loans; margin cap of 10% on large MFIs (loan portfolio exceeding Rs 100 crore) and 12% for rest.
	There should only be 3 components in pricing of the loan: (i) processing fee (not exceeding 1% of the gross
	loan amount), (ii) interest charge and (iii) insurance premium.
Loans	Maximum loan amount of Rs 25,000.
	Individual borrowers have to be a member of a JLG; borrower cannot be a member of more than one SHG/JLG.
	No more than two MFIs should lend to the same borrower.
Prudential norms	All NBFC-MFIs should have a minimum net worth of Rs 15 crore composed of Tier 1 capital.
	NBFC MFIs should maintain a capital adequacy ratio of 15%.
	MFIs should maintain an aggregate provision for loan losses (at least 1% of outstanding loan portfolio).
Conduct of MFIs	Responsibility of not using coercive methods of recovery lies with the MFIs.
	Each MFI should establish a grievance redressal procedure.
	Regulator should monitor that MFIs have a proper Code of Conduct and system of supervision of field staff.
	All recoveries should be made at a central place.
	Regulator should publish a client protection code to be be accepted and observed by MFIs.
Credit information bureau	One or more credit information bureaus should be established; all MFIs should join a bureau.

Legislative Brief The Micro Finance Institutions (Development and Regulations) Bill 2012

The Bill was introduced in the Lok Sabha by the Minister of Finance on May 22, 2012. The Bill was referred to the Standing Committee. on Finance (Chairperson: Shri Yashwant Sinha) on May 28, 2012. Still the BILL is in pending

Key issues and Analysis

The Bill provides safeguards against misuse of market dominance by MFIs to charge excessive rates. It allows RBI to set upper limits on lending rates and margins. However, there is no provision for consultation with the Competition

Commission of India.

The Bill allows MFIs to accept deposits. Unlike banks, there is no facility for insuring customer deposits against default by MFIs. The minimum capital requirement is also lower, though RBI may prescribe higher requirements.

The Development Fund for MFIs is to be managed by the RBI. The Bill also enables regulatory powers to be delegated to NABARD. Both these provisions could lead to conflict of interest.

The Bill provides for the creation of micro finance committees at central, state and district levels to oversee the sector. However, the formations of these committees are not mandatory.

PARTA: HIGHLIGHTS OF THE BILL

Micro finance is the extension of financial services, notably small loans, to low income groups. It can serve as a vehicle for financial inclusion. Regular banks tend not to lend to the poor because of the high cost per individual loan and lack of collateral. In India, micro finance overcomes these issues by lending to Self Help Groups[*] (SHGs), i.e., groups of pooled borrowings, and Joint Liability Groups (JLGs)[†], i.e., groups of pooled liability. Delivery largely takes place through two mechanisms: the National Bank for Agriculture and Rural Development (NABARD) sponsored SHG Bank Linkage programme, where banks lend directly to SHGs and through micro finance institutions (MFIs) lending to SHGs, JLGs, rural banks and individual clients. Taken together, the Banks-SHG programme and MFIs reached 76.7 million people in 2010-11, a 71% growth over 2006-07.

MFIs exist in various forms such as societies, trusts, co-operatives and non banking financial companies (NBFCs). In terms of market share, NBFCs dominate the industry, accounting for an estimated 90% of loan volume in 2010-11.NBFC-MFIs are regulated by the Reserve Bank of India (RBI) Act, 1934. There is no statute regulating the rest of the microfinance industry consisting of societies, trusts and co-operatives.

Figure 1: Current flow of credit and regulation in Indian micro finance

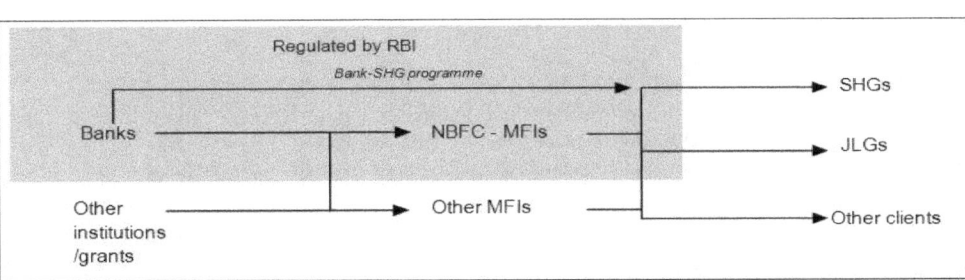

Key Features

The Bill establishes the RBI as the regulator for all entities providing micro finance services.

Definitions

- The Bill defines MFIs as organisations engaged in providing micro finance services. These organisations could include a society, company or a trust, whose object is to provide micro finance services. The Bill specifically excludes: banking companies, co-operative societies engaged in agriculture or industrial activity and any moneylender (including those registered under state laws).

- Micro finance services are defined as micro-credit facilities not exceeding Rs 5 lakh;   this can be exceeded (up to Rs 10 lakh) for purposes specified by the RBI. MFIs can also collect thrift (small deposits other than current accounts or demand deposits); provide pension and insurance services; and engage in remittance services.

- The RBI is empowered to issue directions about the classification of a micro finance institution based on the deployment of assets and proportion of clients

Registering Microfinance Institutions:

- The Bill requires any institution providing micro finance services to register with the RBI. The RBI should be certain that the institution will engage in providing micro finance services and have a net-owned fund (aggregate of paid up capital and reserves) of at least Rs 5 lakh.

- All organisations providing micro finance services will have to register within three months of the Act's commencement. Existing organisations registered with the RBI as an NBFC may continue to engage in micro finance activities subject to the rules and regulations issued by the RBI.

- Certificates of registration may be cancelled by the RBI if MFIs cease to provide micro finance services or fail to comply with any condition imposed by the RBI. MFIs can appeal to the central government against any rejection or cancellation of certificate.

Functioning of MFI's

- Registered MFIs will have to create a reserve fund containing an RBI-specified percentage of net profit or surplus. The fund can only be used for purposes specified by the RBI. NBFCs registered with the RBI are not obliged to create this reserve fund.

- The RBI can set a maximum limit on the interest rate an MFI can charge for micro credit facilities and the margin an MFI can make. In addition, the RBI can set a ceiling on the amount of loans given to clients and the number of individual clients an MFI has. The RBI can specify the tenure of micro credit facilities and other terms and conditions like periodicity of repayment schedules. MFIs will have to provide a breakdown of interest rates, processing fees or other charges on the loan document.

- For deposit acceptance, the RBI can provide directions relating to prudential norms like capital adequacy based on risk weights, accounting standards and deployment of funds.

- Any MFI restructuring, amalgamation or closure will have to be approved by the RBI.

Microfinance Development Fund

The RBI will create a Micro Finance Development Fund comprising of government grants, sums raised by donors and the public and any interest made out of investments. The Fund shall be used to provide loans, refinance, grant seed capital or any other micro credit facilities to any MFI. The fund can also be used to invest in existing MFIs.

Micro Finance Councils and Committees

District Micro Finance Committees may be formed by the RBI and would be responsible for overseeing micro finance activities at the district level, including monitoring over indebtedness and methods of recovery and submit quarterly reports to the RBI. State Micro Finance Councils may be created by the central government to coordinate activities of the District Committees. The Councils will oversee micro finance activities of the state including methods of recovery and indebtedness. Each State Micro Finance Council would be required to prepare a quarterly report for the central government. At the national level, the Micro Finance Development Council can be constituted by the central government and would have an advisory role regarding the formulation of policies and measures. The council shall also create a credit information bureau for MFIs to store data about clients and loans

Customer Protection

The Bill requires the RBI to create a grievance redressal mechanism for MFI clients. The scheme should provide for the nature of grievance and procedure for redressal of these grievances and complaints. The RBI shall specify performance standards for methods of operation, methods of recovery and governance. In addition, the RBI will be responsible for promoting customer education of MFIs for greater awareness

Offence and Penalties
If an offence is committed, both the person responsible and the MFI will be guilty. Contravening provisions of the Bill or default can result in a prison term not exceeding two years or a fine of up to Rs 5 lakh

Exemptions
The central government, in public interest, can exempt certain classes of MFIs from the provisions of the Bill.

PART B: KEY ISSUES AND ANALYSIS
Interest Rates
The interest rates charged by MFIs for loans are usually much higher than the rates charged by banks. This is because the cost structures of MFIs are higher than that of banks on two counts. Firstly, funding for MFIs is costlier; for example in 2009-10 the average cost of funds for MFIs was 9.3% (of the loan portfolio)[4] while for banks the equivalent figure was 5.1%. Secondly, MFI loans are smaller; individual loans typically range between Rs 10,000 and Rs 15,000.Consequently, the transaction cost as a percentage of the loan is higher for MFIs. In 2009-10, operating costs, which include administrative and personnel costs, was 12.3% of the amount lent for MFIs, while the equivalent figure for banks was 1.8%.

In order to prevent MFIs from charging excessive interest rates, the Bill enables RBI to set a limit on the interest rate and the margin (the difference between interest rates and cost of funds). In addition, RBI can specify the number of loans, size of loans and number of clients. Currently, the RBI has capped the margin at 10% for large NBFC MFIs (and 12% for the rest).

The provision allowing RBI to set a cap on interest rates is designed to address an issue that arises from limited competition. In micro finance, the price of the product is the lending rate charged by an MFI. Price ceilings are introduced to prevent a monopoly or dominant power in the market from setting too high a price; an issue that comes under the purview of the Competition Commission of India (CCI). However, the Bill does not include any provision for RBI to consult the CCI when setting interest rates.

Depositor Protection
The Bill permits MFIs to accept deposits. This would create an additional source of funding for MFIs, and also enable clients to have an option to save . however , depositor clients will bear the risk of default by an MFI , unlike borrower clients .currently ,banks and certain types of NBFCs can accept deposits and both are regulated by the RBI (see Table 1). The Bill empowers the RBI to issue directions to MFIs on prudential norms such as income recognition , accounting standards and capitals adequacy.

Table 1: Key current prudential norms

	Banks	Public deposit accepting NBFCs
Net owned fund	Rs 300 crore	Rs 2 crore
Capital adequacy ratio	Min. 9%	Min. 15%
Transfer to reserve fund	None	20% of profits
Period of deposit	No limit	1-5 years

Source: RBI; PRS

Deposit Insurance

The possibility of a financial institution defaulting and unable to repay deposits poses a significant risk to clients. Deposits in banks are protected, up to Rs 1 lakh, through the Deposit Insurance and Credit Guarantee Corporation. The Bill does not explicitly set out a similar provision for MFIs. Although the Bill requires MFIs to create a reserve fund which could potentially serve as protection for depositors, contributions to this fund are a percentage of profits or surplus. Consequently, any loss-making MFI would not have a fund, leaving depositors without a safety net.

Capital Requirement

While the Bill gives RBI the authority to set prudential norms, it specifically lays out the requirement for a minimum net-owned fund of Rs 5 lakh for MFIs. It is not clear whether RBI will specify a higher net-owned fund requirement for deposit taking MFIs. In comparison, banks require a net owned fund of Rs 300 crore while public deposit accepting NBFCs require Rs 2 crore

Borrower Protection

One of the major issues arising from the micro finance crisis in Andhra Pradesh was the method of debt-recovery; it was felt to be too aggressive and forceful. According to the Malegam Committee, methods of debt recovery arethe responsibility of MFIs and every MFI should establish a proper grievance redressal procedure. The Bill provides for RBI to specify guidelines for fair and reasonable methods of recovery, but does not specify what this would entail. RBI has the power to issue directions to MFIs about observing codes of conduct and setting up MFI-specific grievance redressal mechanisms. In addition, it will also issue a code of conduct for field staff, laying out minimum qualifications and training tools. and in particular, NBFC-MFIs. With regard to debt-recovery, the RBI has specified that recovery should be made at a designated central place and recovery at place of residence should only happen when the borrower fails to appear at the central location.

Development Fund

The BILL designates RBI to create a Micro Finance Development Fund The Fund will be managed by the RBI (under directions of the Central Board of Directors) and can be caused to provide loans or grants to MFIs and invest in equity or any other form of capital for MFIs .this allows an RBI managed Fund to be create shareholder of an MFI .or act as a creditor to an MFI .this could create a conflict of interest given the Role of RBI as a regulator .the committee on Banking sector Reforms (Narasimham committee II) had observed that it was inconsistent with the principles of effective supervision for the regulator to be the owner of a bank. Consequently, ownership of the State Bank of India was transferred to the central government with the enactment of the State Bank of India Amendment) Act, 2007. Given that a precedent has been set to prevent a conflict of interest, it is unclear why an RBI – managed fund is allowed to invest in and lend to MFI.

Delegation of Powers

The central government may, in consultation with RBI, delegate the powers of RBI to NABARD or any other agency. The only exceptions are the powers related to winding up of MFIs and imposition of penalties. As NABARD is also a lender to MFIs, there could be a conflict of interest if it is also given regulatory powers

Inclusion of Insurance and Pension Under Micro Finance
MFI's provide these services acting as agents. Currently, the insurance sector is regulated by the Insurance Regulatory and Development Authority while the pension sector is regulated by Pension Fund Regulatory Development Authority. There is no mention of either regulator in the Bill. The 2007 Bill did include insurance and pension services under the definition of micro finance services. However, unlike the current Bill, the 2007 Bill explicitly stated that insurance and pension services would be regulated by the respective regulatory authorities.

Micro Finance Development Councils and Committees
The Bill provides for the appropriate government to create the Micro Finance Development Council/Committee at the central, state and district levels to oversee the sector. The national council would promote the industry by advising the central government on policies, establishing a credit information bureau and the working of the grievance redressal mechanism. In addition, the central government is responsible for examining reports about recovery practices from states. The State Councils and District Committees also oversee micro finance activities in the states including methods of recovery and indebtedness. The Bill uses the word "may" and not "shall" for the constitution of these bodies. It is unclear why the establishment of the central and state councils and district committees is not mandatory.

Conclusion:

The farmer suicides in Andhra Pradesh in 2010 garnered excessive attention through print and electronic media for months on end owing allegedly to exorbitant interest rates being charged by private MFIs. Such dire situations are seen as a consequence of private MFIs turning to the market for capital. Criticisms to such a move include that since these institutions have gone public, there would be a demand for returns from the shareholders' money. In such a scenario the end user of the financial aid from the MFIs (largely rural farmers) would bear the brunt of such a demand. It seems *prima facie* that such criticism held certain merit a large number of farmers who committed suicide blamed, usurious interest rates and coercive means of loan recovery as the reasons for them taking such a step. The state of Andhra Pradesh owing to large scale media and political pressure cracked down with firstly, issuing an ordinance and later replicating it into legislation. This law criminalized coercive loan re-covery methods. In the immediate aftermath of the passing of the ordinance in October 2010, the state saw large scale arrests of MFI employees. The focus of the ordinance and later the Act has purely been on the lending and recovery mechanisms. The initial hypothesis put forth by us is that commercialization of MFIs needs to be deterred.

References :

1. Micro finance in India a new regulatory structure Kenny kline, santadarshansadhu

2. Regulating the growing commercialisation of MFI in india : Aditya alok & nishal joseph

3. Micro management constitutional and policy concerns arising from india's MFI development & regulation : ashely becker.

4. Existing legal and regulatory framework for the MFI in India: challenges and implications: sadhan

5. What should regulation do in the field of micro finance :renuke saneand susan Thomas

6. The Andhra Pradesh micro finance crisis in india :manifestation ,casual analysis , and regulatory response :anurag priyadarshee, k.ghalib

7. www.rbi.org

8. www.mfinindia.org

9. www.nabard.org

CHAPTER-5

GROWTH OF UNORGANIZED SECTOR IN INDIA- A STUDY ON MICRO FINANCE AND POVERTY REDUCTION IN INDIA

Mr. KARTEEK MADAPANA,
Assistant Professor,
Gandhi institute of Engineering & Technology,
Gunupur, Rayagada,

A*bstract*

India falls under low income class according to World Bank. It is second populated country in the world and around 70 % of its population lives in rural area. 60% of people depend on agriculture, as a result there is chronic underemployment and per capita income is only $ 3262. This is not enough to provide food to more than one individual. The obvious result is abject poverty, low rate of education, low sex ratio, and exploitation. The major factor account for high incidence of rural poverty is the low asset base. According to Reserve Bank of India, about 51 % of people house possess only 10% of the total asset of India .This has resulted low production capacity both in agriculture (which contribute around 22-25% of GDP) and Manufacturing sector. Rural people have very low access to institutionalized credit (from commercial bank).

Key terms: - Micro Finance, Financial Services, Poverty, NGOs, India.

INTRODUCTION

Microfinance is the provision of financial services to low-income clients, including consumers and the self-employed, who traditionally lack access to banking and related services. More broadly, it is a movement whose object is "a world in which as many poor and near-poor households as possible have permanent access to an appropriate range of high quality financial services, including not just credit but also savings, insurance, and fund transfers." Those who promote microfinance generally believe that such access will help poor people out of poverty.

Micro credit emphasizes the provision of credit services to low income clients, usually in the form of small loans for micro enterprise and income generating activities. Use of the term 'micro credit' is often associated with an inadequate amount of the value of savings for the poor. In most cases, the provision of savings services in 'micro credit' schemes simply involves the collection of compulsory deposit amounts that are designed only to collateralize those loans. Additional voluntary savings may collect but the clients have restricted access to their enforced savings. These savings become the main source of capital in the financial institutions.

Microfinance is considered as a tool for socio-economic development and can be clearly distinguished from charity. Families who are destitute or so poor they are unlikely to be able to generate the cash flow required to repay a loan, should be recipients of charity. Others are best served by financial institutions.

Role of Microfinance in Poverty Reduction:

Microfinance is about providing financial services to the poor who are not served by the Conventional formal financial institutions - it is about extending the frontiers of financial service provision. The provision of such financial services requires innovative delivery channels and methodologies. The needs for financial services that allow people to both take advantage of opportunities and better management of their resources. Microfinance can be one effective tool amongst many for poverty alleviation. However, it should be used with caution -despite recent claims, the equation between microfinance and poverty alleviation is not straight-forward, because poverty is a complex phenomenon and many constraints that the poor in general have to cope with. We need to understand when and in what form microfinance is appropriate for the poorest; the delivery channel, methodology and products offered are all inter-linked and in turn affect the prospect and promise of poverty alleviation. Access to formal banking services is difficult for the poor. The main problem the poor have to take when trying to acquire loans from formal financial institutions is the demand for collateral asked by these institutions. In addition, the process of acquiring a loan entails many bureaucratic procedures, which lead to extra transaction costs for the poor. Formal financial institutions are not motivated to lend money to them. In general, formal financial institutions show a preference for urban over rural sectors, large-scale over small scale transactions, and non-agricultural over agricultural loans.

Rural India and Microfinance

Micro financing has become important since the possibility of a sub-Rs 1,000 mobile handset has been ruled out in the near future. Rural India can generally afford handsets in the price range of Rs 1,500-2,000. To succeed in India, agribusiness must empower the farmer by making agriculture profitable, not by expropriating him foe this particular purpose the farmer should be funded for their basic and small needs.

Micro finance is expected to play a significant role in poverty alleviation and development. The need, therefore, is to share experiences and materials which will help not only in understanding successes and failures but also provide knowledge and guidelines to strengthen and expand micro finance programmes.

The development process through a typical micro-finance intervention can be understood with the help of the following Chart The ultimate aim is to attain social and economic empowerment. Successful intervention is therefore, dependent on how each of these stages has been carefully dealt with and also the capabilities of the implementing organizations in achieving the final goal, e.g., if credit delivery takes place without consolidation of SHGs, it may have problems of self-sustainability and recovery. A number of schemes under banks, central and state governments offer direct credit to potential individuals without forcing them to join SHGs. Compilation and classification of the communication materials in the directory is done based on this development process.

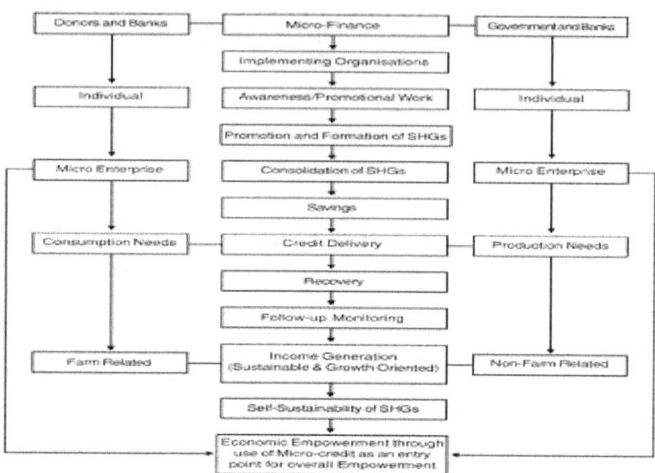

Few Schemes of a Government of India:

There are so many schemes for the upliftment of poor In India. One of them Micro-credit programmes is run primarily by NABARD in the field of agriculture and SIDBI in the field of Industry, Service and Business (ISB).

The success of Micro-credit programme lies in diversification of services. Micro Finance Scheme of SIDBI is under operation since January, 1999 with a corpus of Rs. 100 crore and a network of about190 capacity assessed rated MFIs/NGOs. Under the programme, total amount of Rs. 191 crore have been sanctioned up to 31st December, 2003, benefiting over 9 lakh beneficiaries.

Under the programme, NGOs/ MFIs are supposed to provide equity support in order to avail SIDBI finance. But they find it difficult to manage the needed equity support because of their poor financial condition. The problem has got aggravated due to declining interest rate on deposits. The office of the development commissioner (Small Scale Industries)

Under Ministry of SSI is launching a new scheme of Micro Finance Programme to overcome the constraints in the existing scheme of SIDBI, whose reach is currently very low. It is felt that Government's role can be critical in expanding reach of the scheme, ensuring long term sustainability of NGOs /MFIs and development of Intermediaries for identification of viable projects.

Salient Features of Micro-finance Programme of Government of India:

a) Arranging Fixed Deposits for MFIs/NGOs: Under this scheme government of India arrange money to MFI/NGO like SIDBI for micro credit to poor.

b) Training and Studies on Micro-Finance Programme: Government of India would help SIDBI in meeting the training needs of NGOs, SHGs, intermediaries and entrepreneurs and also in enhancing awareness about the programme. Institution building for 'intermediaries' for identification of viable projects: The Government of India would help in institution building through identification and development of 'intermediary organization', which would help the NGOs/SHGs in identification of product, preparation of project report, working out forward and back ward linkages and in fixing marketing/ technology tie-ups. The SISIs would help in the identification of such intermediaries in different areas.

c) Budgetary Provision for the Scheme During 10th plan: There was a budgetary provision in 10th five year plan and hoping more funds in next plan.

d) Administrative arrangement: A committee has been formed to control and monitor the administrative arrangement of MFI/NGOs.

Success Factors of Micro-Finance in Rural India

Over the last ten years, successful experiences in providing finance to small entrepreneur and producers demonstrate that poor people, when given access to responsive and timely financial services at market rates, repay their loans and use the proceeds to increase their income and assets. This is not surprising since the only realistic alternative for them is to borrow from informal market at an interest much higher than market rates. Community banks, NGOs and grass root savings and credit groups around the world have shown that these micro enterprise loans can be profitable for borrowers and for the lenders, making microfinance one of the most effective poverty reducing strategies.

For NGOs

- The field of development itself expands and shifts emphasis with the pull of ideas, and NGOs perhaps more readily adopt new ideas, especially if the resources required are small, entry and exit are easy, tasks are (perceived to be) simple and people's acceptance is high – all characteristics (real or presumed) of microfinance.
- Canvassing by various actors, including the National Bank for Agriculture and Rural Development (NABARD), Small Industries Development Bank of India (SIDBI), Friends of Women's World Banking (FWWB), Rashtriya Mahila Kosh (RMK), Council for Advancement of People's Action and Rural Technologies (CAPART), Rashtriya Gramin Vikas Nidhi (RGVN), various donor funded programmes especially by the International Fund for Agricultural Development (IFAD), United Nations Development Programme (UNDP), World Bank and Department for International Development, UK (DFID)], and lately commercial banks, has greatly added to the idea pull. Induced by the worldwide focus on microfinance, donor NGOs too have been funding microfinance projects. One might call it the supply push.
- All kinds of things from khadi spinning to Nadep compost to balwadis do not produce such concrete results and sustained interest among beneficiaries as microfinance. Most NGO-led microfinance is with poor women, for whom access to small loans to meet dire emergencies is a valued outcome. Thus, quick and high 'customer satisfaction' is the USP that has attracted NGOs to this trade.

B. For Financial Institutions and banks

Microfinance has been attractive to the lending agencies because of demonstrated sustainability and of low costs of operation. Institutions like SIDBI and NABARD are hard nosed bankers and would not work with the idea if they did not see a long term engagement – which only comes out of sustainability (that is economic attractiveness).On the supply side, it is also true that it has all the trappings of a business enterprise, its output is tangible and it is easily understood by the mainstream. This also seems to sound nice to the government, which in the post liberalisation era is trying to explain the logic of every rupee spent. That is the reason why microfinance has attracted mainstream institutions like no other developmental project. Perhaps the most important factor that got banks involved is what one might call the policy push. Given that most of our banks are in the public sector, public policy does have some influence on what they will or will not do. In this case, policy was followed by diligent, if meandering, promotional work by NABARD. The policy change about a decade ago by RBI to allow banks to lend to SHGs was initially followed by a seven-page memo by NABARD to all bank chairmen, and later by sensitisation and training programmes for bank staff across the country. Several hundred such programmes were conducted by NGOs alone, each involving 15 to 20 bank staff, all paid for by NABARD. The policy push was sweetened by the NABARD refinance scheme that offers much more favourable terms (100% refinance, wider spread) than for other rural lending by banks. NABARD also did some system setting work and banks lately have been given targets. The canvassing, training, refinance and close follow up by NABARD has resulted in widespread bank involvement.

Marketing of Microfinance Products
Contract Farming and Credit Bundling

• Banks and financial institutions have been partners in contract farming schemes, set up to enhance credit. Basically, this is a doable model. Under such an arrangement, crop loans can be extended under tie-up arrangements with corporate for production of high quality produce with stable marketing arrangements provided – and only, provided – the price setting mechanism for the farmer is appropriate and fair.

Agri Service Centre – Rabo India

• Rabo India Finance Pvt Ltd. has established agri-service centres in rural areas in cooperation with a number of agri-input and farm services companies. The services provided are similar to those in contract farming, but with additional flexibility and a wider range of products including inventory finance. Besides providing storage facilities, each centre rents out farm machinery, provides agricultural inputs and information to farmers, arranges credit, sells other services and provides a forum for farmers to market their products.

Non Traditional Markets

• Similarly, Mother Dairy Foods processing, a wholly owned subsidiary of National Dairy Development Board (NDDB) has established auction markets for horticulture producers in Bangalore. The operations and maintenance of the market is done by NDDB. The project, with an outlay of Rs.15 lakh, covers 200 horticultural farmers associations with 50,000 grower members for wholesale marketing. Their produce is planned with production and supply assurance and provides both growers and buyers a common platform to negotiate better rates.

Apni Mandi

• Another innovation is that of The Punjab Mandi Board, which has experimented with a 'farmers' market' to provide small farmers located in proximity to urban areas, direct access to consumers by elimination of middlemen. This experiment known as "Apni Mandi" belongs to both farmers and consumers, who mutually help each other. Under this arrangement a sum of Rs. 5.2 lakh is spent for providing plastic crates to 1000 farmers. Each farmer gets 5 crates at a subsidized rate. At the mandi site, the Board provides basic infrastructure facilities. At the farm level, extension services of different agencies are pooled in. These include inputs subsidies, better quality seeds and loans from Banks. Apni Mandi scheme provides self-employment to producers and has eliminated social inhibitions among them regarding the retail sale of their produce.

Conclusion:

Micro credit and microfinance have received extensive recognition as a strategy for poverty reduction and for economic empowerment. Microfinance is a way for fighting poverty, particularly in rural areas, where most of the world's poorest people live. Accessing small amounts of credit at reasonable interest rates give poor people an opportunity to set up their own small business. Many studies show that poor people are trustable, with higher repayment rates than conventional borrowers. When poor people have access to financial services, they can earn more, build their assets, and cushion themselves against external shocks. Poor households use microfinance to move from everyday survival to planning for the future: they invest in better nutrition, housing, health, and education. Most poor people cannot get good financial services that meet their needs because there are not enough strong institutions that provide such services. Strong institutions need to charge enough to cover their costs. Cost recovery is not an end in itself. Rather, it is the only way to reach scale and impact beyond the limited levels that donors can fund.

Afinanciallysustainableinstitutioncancontinueandexpanditsservicesoverthelongterm.A chievingsustainability means lowering transaction costs, offering services that aremore useful to the clients, and finding new ways to provide banking services to the poor.At the end it should be mentioned that Poor people with no income or means of repayment need other kinds of support before they can make good use of loans. In many cases, other tools will alleviate poverty better—for instance, small grants, employment and training programs, or infrastructure improvements. Where possible, such services should be coupled with building savings. It shows that access and efficient provision of micro credit can enable the poor to smooth their consumption, better manage their risks better, gradually build their assets, develop their micro enterprises, enhance their income earning capacity and enjoy an improved quality of life. Microfinance services can also contribute to the improvement of resource allocation, promotion of markets, and adoption of better technology; thus, micro finance helps to promote economic growth and development.

References:

1. Benchmarks (2005). Microfinance Information Exchange, Inc. (MIX).
2. Dunford, Christopher and Vicki Denman. November 2000. The Case for Credit With Education: A Promising Title II Microfinance Strategy for Cost Effective and sustainable Impact on Chronic Food Insecurity and Malnutrition. Freedom from Hunger. www.fantaproject.org/downloads/ pdfs /cwe .pdf.

3. *Dunford, Christopher. 2001. Building Better Lives: Sustainable Linkage of Microfinance and Education in Health, Family Planning, and HIV/AIDS Prevention for the Poorest Entrepreneurs. http://www.microcreditsummit.org/papers/papers.htm.*
4. *Lapenu C, ZellerM(2001). "Distribution, Growth and Performance of Microfinance Institutions in Africa, Asia and Latin America," Food Consumption and Nutrition Division Discussion Paper No.114, Int. Food Policy Res. Ins. June 2001*
5. *Meyer (2002). An earlier helpful survey published by ADBI. This draws out some of the methodological problems in assessing impact and surveys a number of important studies available at the time of the writing (around 2001).*
6. *Microfinance Information Exchange Inc (2005). Bench marks. All observations are medians. India observations draw from panel data for MFIs in 2004-05 Benchmarks.*

Websites:
- www.ifmr.ac.in
- www.google.com
- www.microfinanceinsight.com
- www.investopedia.com
- www.books.google.com
- www.seepnetwork.org
- www.forbes.com
- www.nationmaster.com

CHAPTER-6

OPEN SOURCE MIS FOR MICROFINANCE IN INDIA: TRENDS AND CHALLENGES

D. Vijaya Geeta
* Associate Professor,
Department of Operations,
GITAM University

ABSTRACT

In recent times, open source markets are gaining popularity in the world of computing. Attributing to features like free or inexpensive licensing terms and availability of cloud services, open source markets has reached varied fields, comprising simple to complex applications. Initiatives such as Microfinance Open Architecture Project (MOAP) supports the cause of enforcing standards for building open source MIS for microfinance institutions. In this context, the paper studies the current scenario of development of MIS for microfinance in India especially in the area of open sourcing. The paper discusses the challenges faced in Indian microfinance institutes and proposes possible solutions to face them.

Keywords: Microfinance; MIS; Open Source; Microfinance Open Architecture Project; MiFOS

INTRODUCTION

Microfinance, which is sometimes referred to as "banking for the poor," is a source of financial service for small scale entrepreneurs who lack access to banking and other related services. Microfinance helps the poor people in securing loans comprising very meager amount, which is not possible in traditional banking system. The microfinance institutes or MFIs provides such loans to the needy people and helps them in establishing small scale businesses. It is not only an alternative to banks but also helps in achieving financial inclusion and equality [1].

The concept of microfinance was taken up by NABARD in India by following the example of "Grameen Bank" which was set by Mohammad Yunus in Bangladesh. In India, a link was established between Self Help Groups (SHGs), NGOs and Banks to carry out the microfinance operations[2]. Not only loans but also other benefits like saving accounts and insurance facilities are provided to the poor people to help them in improving their standard of living. The primary objective of Microfinance Institutions is to reach poorest section of society and fight global poverty.

Concerns for Microfinance

In spite of microfinance being a good concept, there are certain concerns especially in India which has seen cases where microfinance acted as a bane rather than a boon for the borrowers. The growing concerns are [2] Financial illiteracy, Inability to generate sufficient funds, Dropouts and migration of group members, Cluster Formation – Fight to grab established market, Transparent pricing, Multiple Lending and Over-indebtedness .

Out of all these concerns, the most sensitive one is multiple lending and over-indebtedness. In the brink of competition, MFIs are ending up giving multiple loans to the borrowers, which leads to over-indebtedness for the borrowers. This leads to lower recovery for MFIs and in case of borrowers, the loan amount taken exceeds his/her repayment capacities, which may lead the borrower to go into depression and sometimes force them to commit suicide. Another main concern is non-transparent pricing where MFIs shields the actual price and interest rates from the borrowers and thus confine their bargaining power. If not all, however, some of the concerns related to microfinance can be addressed with proper usage of technology. Technology not only will help in reducing the operating costs but also enhance the productivity of an MFI by providing efficient solution. One such solution is Management Information System (MIS).

Management Information Systems

Management Information Systems is defined as "An integrated user-machine system for providing information to support the operations, management analysis, and decision making functions in an organization." MIS plays a vital role in communicating the events that are happening in the organization. Its objective is to capture the data, store the information, process the data to create information and disseminate the same to the user. Entire information related to the employees, customers, policies, procedures and transactions are available through MIS. In fact, MIS helps in providing right information to right people at right time to ensure that effective decision-making takes place.

Microfinance and MIS

Usage of MIS in microfinance institutions (MFIs) provides lots of benefits. Apart from the various required reports, MIS will help in providing detail information on a client and his business activities. This information will help the MFIs in estimating the impact the microcredit had on the client's business. Computerization of microfinance activities will help in performing different tasks like loan approval, disbursements, repayments, deposits, withdrawal and money transfer in much faster and efficient manner with zero or minimal errors.

MIS will help in identifying the Key Performance Indicators (KPIs) based on which timely adjustments can be made for the efficiency and effectiveness of business procedures. MFI services can be made more interactive and transparent. With the burden of clerical drudgery shifted to the information system, productivity of staff will increase thus enabling them to serve more customers in less time. With information at hand, customized solutions or products can be designed for the customer by keeping in view their profile and need.

Concerns of MFI with MIS

Even with the large benefits rendered by MIS, not all the MFIs have adopted information system to leverage their operations. There are primarily three types of system, which are in place [3]:

Manual System: Records are maintained in the form of ledgers and paper documents. These are basically small micro-credit programmes or NGOs.

Semi automated System: Majority of MFI operates in semi automated mode where spreadsheets like MS Excel is used along with the manual system or a basic MIS application. Most of the non regulated MFIs follows such type of system.

Fully Automated System: A few MFIs have adopted fully automated system and utilized the full benefits of the system by integrating the MIS with the business operation of the organization.

One primary reason that can be attributed to the low adoption of MIS in MFIs is the cost involved in building such system. Usually building a customized MIS application is a time taking process that involves different overheads related to the resource utilization in terms of time, money and human resources.

In this context, it is understood that there is a requirement for a system that is standardized to address the transparency issues, customized to be flexible and inexpensive to cater even the small and medium level MFIs.

Open Source MIS

A system that can provide standardization with flexibility in terms of low cost and less time is open source software. Open source software are gaining popularity in recent times can also prove beneficial in the area of microfinance. Open source software as per Wikipedia is defined as "software which is liberally licensed to grant the right of users to study, change, and improve its design through the availability of its source code".

Benefits of open source are as follows [1]:

Open source system calls for community participation. The entire microfinance industry and the surrounding technology ecosystem surrounding can suggest improvements and help in building new features. Besides this, With entire community participation, thorough testing takes place by different experts which helps in maintaining the quality of the system.

Being a shareware, open source system acts like a standard system that will help in maintaining the transparency in the procedures adopted in the system. The open source software can be extended and localized as per the organization needs and by using feedback and discussion forums with the entire community, a collaborative effort in building a better system is possible.

The open source software provides liberty of modifying the system according to the needs and specifications of the organization. It thus gives the benefits of customized application. With the addition of new and local knowledge, new and innovative products can be suggested and designed which will prove beneficial to different categories or sections of society.

.

Table 1 compares open source MIS with the available technologies. From table 1, it is demonstrated that Excel or any spreadsheet, even though inexpensive, fails miserably in other desired features of software. Whereas custom made system has all the qualities desired by a software system but are expensive and consumes more time in building process. Open source MIS fulfills all the desired features of a software system with less cost and development time.

Table 1: Comparison of Open MIS with other technologies

	Low Cost	Data Reliability	Scalability	Data Exchange Capability	Design Flexibility
Excel/Spreadsheet	Yes	No	No	Neutral	No
Traditional Accounting and portfolio Software	Neutral	Neutral	Neutral	No	No
Specialized Vendor Package	Neutral	Yes	Neutral	No	Neutral
Custom Made	No	Yes	Yes	Neutral	Yes
Open Source MIS	**Yes**	**Yes**	**Yes**	**Yes**	**Yes**

Already few initiatives in the direction of open source MIS has taken place such as Microfinance Open Architecture Project (MOAP) which was taken up by Grameen Foundation USA and Grameen Technology Center, MiFOS, an industry wide initiative to address the microfinance industry's information management challenge and Open Source with Cloud which provides SaaS (Software as a Service). With SaaS, MFI need not buy the software but gain access to the software through provider's online cloud.

Open Source MIS in India
Open source MIS are slowly gaining ground in India with the initiative taken by MiFOS. MiFOS provides open source system to four variants of customers: cloud, community, consortium and on-site. Some of the Indian MFIs who have successfully adopted MiFOS are [4]:

Customer Type: Cloud

Adhikar: Adhikar is an NBFC serving more than 150,000 clients across Orissa, India. They are extending innovative financial services through remittances, microfinance, and self-help groups.
Number of Clients: 167,229
Number of Branches: 65

Nirantara: Nirantara established operations in 2006 as Nirantara Community Services. In 2010 it formally took over Shri ShivGayatri Infin Private Limited, an NBFC. Nirantara's mission is to deliver sustainable and need-based financial services at door-step level and at a high customer value to eradicate poverty throughout Karnataka state in India.
Number of Clients: 6,075
Number of Branches: 7

Oraitha Human Services Organization: Oraitha Human Services Organization is an NGO operating in several rural districts throughout Assam. Since 2005 they have carried out microfinance activities which now reach more than 500 clients who primarily practice agricultural activities like animal husbandry and farming. All services are funded by internal contributions from members. Oraitha Human Services Organization is developing additional programs related to sanitation, agriculture, and healthcare. They went live on Mifos in December of 2012 with support from Conflux Technologies and hosting in the Amazon EC2 cloud.
Number of Clients: 500

Customer Type: Community

ASOMI: ASOMI is an NBFC serving more than 40,000 clients throughout the Assam region in Northern India. Guided independently by their internal IT team, ASOMI extended Mifos through several customizations to better support their portfolio and daily loan collections.
Number of Clients: 40,449
Number of Branches: 52

dMatrix Development Foundation: dMatrix Development Foundation is a Section 25-registered company providing microcredit to the economically active poor segment of the Wardha Disrict in India. Their mission is to improve the livelihood of the underserved poor through cost effective doorstep financial and technical support services delivered in a sustainable manner.
Number of Clients:
500

Customer Type: Consortium

Grameen Koota: Grameen Koota played a pioneering role in the Mifos Initiative as the first Mifos implementation. Grameen Koota has been running Mifos fully in production since October 2007. Since deploying Mifos, Grameen Koota has continued their rapid growth and expansion - officially becoming a Non-Banking

Financial Corporation (NBFC) as of March 2008 and continuing to rapidly open new branches with 120 in total.
Number of Clients: 450,567
Number of Branches: 141

Customer Type: On-Site
SEED: SEED Federation is a 100% community-run Self Help Group (SHG) aiming to promote savings amongst its community members. SEED's vision is "Of the Women, by the women, and for the women." They are actively involved in leading a monthly awareness program for the Campaign for Women and Child Rights. SEED Federation began working with Conflux in March of 2011 to implement Mifos to guide their operations.
Number of Clients: 280

Shakti Swasahaya Mahila Mandal (SMM): SMM is a Self Help Group Federation based in Firozabad, India. SMM is providing financial inclusion to poor women through the formation of Self Help Groups. SMM's model slightly differs from normal MFI operations with a great stress on savings. SMM required some creative workarounds and technology and process enhancements to address the painful delay in gathering information at the head office. Information flow was far from real-time with connection sheets being submitted to the office one to weeks after the transactions had already taken place. With Mifos, the head office is now accessing data from the SHGs in near real time. Conflux sought out another open source solution to reduce this lag in data entry. Innovatively, they decided to use Frontline SMS to send meeting and transaction data from the SHG meeting via SMS to the branch office. It then gets entered into Mifos for head office staff to view.
Number of Clients: 300
Number of Branches: 1

Challenges faced by Open Source MIS
Inspite of benefits posed by open source MIS, there has not been much adoption of open source system by MFIs. The challenges in adoption of MIS can be broadly listed as follows [5]:

- Lack of Awareness: Open source systems are often guided by misconceptions. The popular feeling among most of the people is if it is free or inexpensive, it may not be of good quality and thus there will be reluctance to adopt such a system.

- Lack of donor support for software development activities: Donors may fund capacity development or infrastructure projects, but are much reluctant to fund for the salaries of the software engineers who develop the system.

- Lack of computer engineering skills: Successful implementation of MIS in the organization requires an internal staff member who is technically qualified to maintain the system. The current staff members may not be technically qualified.

- Difficulties to adapt management strategies: Open source systems being a shareware or community based system may not able to adopt all the management strategies formulated by the organization.

- Reluctance to commit initial investment: Initial development of open source system requires some investment to bring out the first version of the software. Not many people may come forward to invest.

Measures in addressing the challenges

The challenges posed by open source system can be mitigated by following certain measures. Some suggested measures are:

- Create awareness to all the stakeholders: The first and foremast task that need to be done is to create awareness among all the stakeholders of MFIs on the benefits of Open Source Systems and remove the misconceptions associated with it. This can be done by conducting workshops or seminars where awareness as well as knowledge related to usage of such systems are imparted.

- Government Support / Government Funding: Since the purpose of microfinance is to help the poor and to enhance financial inclusion. The Government bodies or agencies should come forward in supporting and funding open source MIS projects.

- Imparting Skills to the staff / Appointment of technical person: The MFIs should either train the existing staff or appoint a technically qualified person to take care of MIS. Managing open source system requires knowledge of the source programming language and few computing concepts that can be instilled into a staff member with little training.

- Management must become flexible to adopt open source MIS: Instead of system adopting the management strategies, management itself should adopt open source system and formulate strategies.

- Large Companies can invest into Open Source MIS as a CSR activity: Corporates are required to take up community service as part of corporate social responsibility (CSR). Even initiating or funding an open source MIS for microfinance can be taken up as CSR activity since ultimately it benefits the community especially the poor.

- Regulators can open up cloud services to support smaller MFIs: Smaller MFIs who cannot afford to manage the MIS system can make use of cloud service. Regulators through SaaS can provide cloud services to MFIs such that without making any physical procurement, services of MIS can be used from the web.

- Mobile MIS: Another innovative concept would be mobile MIS which requires only procurement of a internet enabled phone and the overheads associated with desktop infrastructure is minimized. Mobile device will help in establishing MIS services in remote areas with space and money constraints.

Conclusion

Microfinance is a useful tool with good intention of helping the poor and thus improves their standard of living. With features like microcredit and offering of other financial services for meager sum, it reaches even poorest of poor, a trait which is not possible with traditional banking system. Microfinance thus helps in achieving financial inclusion with primary objectives being outreach and sustainability. However, microfinance system in India did not achieve much success owing to different factors like non-transparency and over-indebtness of the borrowers. Technology such as MIS can help in answering some of the concerns expressed by MFIs and a system like open source MIS will help in achieving the objectives of microfinance with less cost, time and community support.

References

[1] "Management Information System for Microfinance Institute" [online], available at: http://www.confluxtechnologies.com/1/post/2010/06/management-nformation-system-for-microfinance-institute.html

[2] "MicroFinance – Current Status and Growing Concerns in India"[online], Available at: http://www.iitk.ac.in/ime/MBA_IITK/avantgarde/?p=475

[3] Ali Ahmad, "Management Information Systems (MIS) for Microfinance",[online], available at: http://www.bwtp.org/pdfs/arcm/5Ahmad.pdf

[4] "Whos using MiFOS", [online], available at: http://mifos.org/community/whos-using-mifos

[5] Britta Augsburg, "Free and Open source Software for Microfinance",[online], available at: https://smartech.gatech.edu/bitstream/handle/1853/35354/Britta%20Augsburg.pdf

CHAPTER-7
FINANCIAL SUPPORT FOR ECONOMIC DEVELOPMENT

Pandu Ranga Rao, B
Assistant Director ,
KL University,

In a labour abundant and capital short economy like India there is a severe budgetary constraint for funds and the pressing need for higher investment in the frontiers of social development. Hence the people have to come forward to engage themselves in predictive activities by starting their own industrial of business ventures rather than depending on some employer for employment and livelihood when more and more persons come forward to state their own enterprises small it may be and run the enterprise efficiently the productivity of the nation automatically improves as the process of economic development involves improvement in the Gross National product and depends on the utilization of physical natural resources by the human resource to realise the productive potential of the nation It requires increase in production and consumption.

Revitalization of the agrarian economy and the rural society has a Major plank in the economic planning ever since the country embarked on planned development. However the success achieved in this regaled until recently is not in tune with gigantic size of the problem. The task of rural development is a stupendous one . apart form the fact that India being the second largest country in terms of population and as more than 75 percent of India s population live in its six lakh villages and half of them are still in abject poverty Under those circumstances it is unrealistic to hope to achieve all round economic development in the country unless attempts are made to improve the living conditions of the rural poor.

Prof D.T.Lakadawala in his presidential address at the 11th Indian Labor Economic development in the Conference aptly observed that "Discussion about economic development in aggregate terms have limited relevance as against more relevant view point of reduction of unemployment or reduction in number and percentage of people below poverty line which indicates economic welfare of the people" .

In India, capital is scarce while capital is scarce ,the optimum use of available capital resources in terms of employment and productivity mist therefore become one of the main goals of economic planning. Large industries require huge amounts of capital and their gestation period is long . If we invest the scarce capital in MSME sector the returns are quick and hence the generated returns may again form capital. MSME can thereby save, for production purposes, capital expenditure .Therefore , as MSME need less capital , yield quick returns with less risk, investment in these is preferable in India, a country where capital is relatively scarce.

According to the latest research done by the World Bank, India is home to almost one third of worlds poor. Though many central government and state government poverty alleviation programmes are currently active in India. Micro

Finance plays a major contributor to financial inclusion. In Bangladesh Micro credit model of Mohammed younus's Grameen Bank has proved to be very successful every year 5 percent of people are coming out of poverty with the participation of Micro Finance schemes of Grameen Bank. It was also revealed that the micro credit was useful to the participant in increasing (a) Per capita expenditure (b) Net worth (c) Children schooling and at village level, borrowing had a positive impact on (a) Production (b)Income (c) Employment (d)Wages (e)School enrollment (f)Fertility.

India, there is a wide disparity in wealth and income of people One of the important objects of planning is the reduction of inequalities. it is possible to reduce these inequalities, to some extent, by providing opportunities to have-nots to take up cottage or micro enterprise for their living .V.K.R.V.Rao has said that the a micro enterprise and cottage industries have this in their favor that , with proper safeguards they will result in a large and more widely distribution sharing of the production function and therefore , a more equitable distribution of the produce of industry further micro enterprise apart from playing a dominant part in our economy serve as a means by which there can be an equitable distribution of national wealth.

Among the different types of industry the heavy industries, due to high automation and other reasons are unable to generate more number of employment opportunities whereas the microenterprise will generate more opportunities to unemployed youth by not only self but also wage employment. According to study by SIDO a lakh of investment in fixed assets in microenterprise sector can employ four members Hence the Government have no other alternative for alleviation of unemployment and eradication of poverty .In the present age of Modernization, Globalization and Privatization the microenterprises can be developed only under the protective umbrella of the Government. Historically a large part of the policy frame work for small and microenterprises has been promotion based like reservation of products to small sector lower interests on loans and subsidies. In spite of all the efforts the Indian microenterprise sector suffered the lack of growth and development .The developing Asian countries realized the importance of microenterprises formulated the policies and implemented effectively and enjoying the fruits. The developed countries like U.S.A and Britan have adopted the policies on microenterprises in their countries in due recognition of success of microenterprises in developing countries. Japan the home of microenterprises. Japan is an outstanding example of those countries which have achieved rapid industrialization and development through the microenterprises   The London economist observed commenting on industrial productivity " The Japanese work more entrepreneurs in small teams components flow into many tinny mini firms which operate under the big factory s financial umbrella along the automated production line , the factory's permanent workers in teams of six or seven are responsible for jointly checking each product as it passes their station, at the end of the line the completed product may be backed by a separate 5-10 employee Micro Enterprises ".

Small- and micro-sized enterprises are a vital even dominant component of most MENA economies: In Egypt, for example, small- and micro-sized enterprises provide an estimated 80% of private-sector value-added, employ two-thirds of the entire labor force, and constitute 99.7% of the total number of non-agricultural private enterprises (Ministry of Economy [Egypt] 1998). Statistics on the small- and micro-sized enterprises sector in other countries are less reliable, but in Jordan the "informal" sector is believed to employ 35% of the work force, and in Yemen 45% of it (ERF 1998). Similar ratios are likely to hold true in Morocco and Lebanon, with slightly lower levels for Algeria, Syria, and Tunisia. In spite of this obvious importance, small- and micro-sized enterprises confront a range of obstacles to growth, as well as numerous handicaps to improving competitiveness in the rapidly Globalizing world marketplace. Access to credit is one problem. In Egypt, 94% of industrial Credit is directed to the 2% of enterprises with over 50 employees and despite the existence of some 40 micro-credit programs in the country, 95% of potential beneficiaries have not reached. Micro-credit experts in Morocco believe there are as many as 1.5 million potential clients for their services, which currently reach less than 20 000 customers.

The programme for the development of Micro Enterprise and Small Industries has been accorded a high place in India .Ever since the days of Gandhiji the small industry movement had been largely regarded as a vehicle for uplifting the weaker sections of the population by providing self employment and After independence when the problem of regional imbalances began to appear, small scale cottage and micro enterprises sector was considered as the natural vehicle for redressing such imbalances more recently when the problem of unemployment has began to take an acute form, the ability of micro enterprises to provide jobs at a comparatively lower cost became an attractive proposition for the planner and administration. Hence the micro enterprises assumed importance in plans and policies. The implementing procedures of the existing Small Scale Industries are refined when the Small Scale Industries preceded the Micro Enterprises as a part of strategy of Govt to distribute the scarce capital to more number of first generation entrepreneurs and to have more accountability in the form of return on loans. Promotional schemes for Micro Enterprises so far as the Govt. of India's policies and schemes in respect of Micro Enterprises are concerned enough. The banking and developmental institutional set up in our country is perhaps the largest in the world and well knit with over 63000 branches of banks operating in the country apart from state level corporations with their own micro credit schemes for almost every segment of society

Micro credit has been hailed as "One of the most significant innovations in development policy of the past twenty five years". If we examine weather Micro credit can bring an underdeveloped economy to full development, the key to micro credit's long run effects is the "Graduation rate" that is the rate at which the self employed build up enough wealth to graduate in to the entrepreneurial class. Kamal (1991) noted "That the higher rates of per capita income among Micro credit programme borrowers compared to those who did not borrow". Choudhary et al.(1991) "Asserted that women (and men) participating in BRAC sponsored activities have more income (both in terms of amount and source) own more often gainfully employed than non participants"

Cost effectiveness: Cost and prospects for sustainability. An advantage of microfinance is that donor investment is recycled and reused (Wright 2000). Direct comparisons done by Khandker (1998) show that microfinance can be a more cost-effective developmental tool than alternatives including formal rural financial intermediation, targeted rural infrastructure development projects. More over, unlike many other interventions, Microfinance compares favorably to other interventions particularly with regard to cost-effectiveness food interventions, and rural infrastructure development projects. More over, unlike many other interventions, costs for microfinance tend to diminish with the scale of outreach (Rhyne 1997; Christen et al 1996)

Sustainability: Few, if any, other development tools have the potential to become sustainable such that, after initial start-up grants, new inputs are not required for every future client. There need not be a trade-off between reaching the poorest and attaining financial sustainability. Although there are no rigorous econometric models to substantiate it, there is ample evidence that MFIs targeting the poorest can fare as well financially as those that don't (Gibbons and Meehan 2000; Churchill 2000)There is also ample anecdotal evidence that MFIs that target poorer clients can achieve substantially higher repayment rates than those that target richer clients (Pro Mujer vs. BancoSol; Grameen/BRAC vs. traditional banking system in Bangladesh) It should be noted that emphasizing financial sustainability above all else can have the practical effect of excluding the poorest because of the widespread misperception that the poorest are a greater credit risk and the reality that the unit costs of small loans tend to exceed the unit costs of larger loans.

In developing countries, financing to the rural poor through formal financial services failed to meet the credit requirements of the rural poor people. The main reason of failure was absence of any recognised employment and hence absence of collateral with the poor. The high risk and the high transaction costs of banks associated with small loans and savings deposits are other factors which make them non-bankable. The lack of loans from formal institutions leaves the poor with no other option but to borrow money from local money-lenders on huge interest rates. In different countries including India, efforts have been made by their governments to deliver formal credit to rural areas by setting up special agricultural banks/rural banks or directing commercial banks to provide loans to rural borrowers. Financial assistance schemes for micro enterprises have liberal features like reduced promoters contribution and training and escort service support. The smaller among the small entrepreneurs always been a preferred category "Microcredit allows the poor household to take advantage of opportunities, that is, to assume risks it could not otherwise take, in order to obtain higher returns" (Dunn et al, 1996). However, these programmes have also not worked well due to various reasons. The common reasons found by many researchers are the political difficulty for governments to enforce loan repayment and the selection of relatively wealthy and influential people, rather than the poor, for bank loans (Adams et al., 1984; Adams and Vogel, 1986; World Bank, 1989). Women's World Banking (1995) estimated that in most developing countries, the formal financial system reaches to only top 25 per cent of the economically active population. This leaves the bottom 75 per cent without access to financial services apart from those provided by money-lenders and family. Thus, the inability of formal credit institutions to deal with the credit 58 requirements of poor effectively has led to emergence of microfinance as an alternative credit system for the poor.

Microfinance scheme provides a wide range of financial services to people who have little or nothing in the way of traditional collateral. It helps them to build up assets, survive crises and to establish small business to come out of poverty. Except extending small loans (micro-credit), microfinance programme provides various other financial and non-financial services such as savings, insurance, guidance, skill development training, capacity building and motivation to start income generating activities to enhance the productivity of credit. This innovative programme is reaching the poor people especially women and has an impact on their socio-economic development as well as their empowerment. This programme is becoming popular and emerging as a powerful instrument for poverty alleviation in many countries of Asia, Africa, Europe and America.

Qinghai Community Development Project (QCDP), China: The programme provides microfinance services to extremely poor households. "The program now has over 50,000 members and is growing strongly with a delinquency rate of about 4%. Nearly everyone takes the most flexible option, i.e., a loan in which the principal does not have to be returned until the end of the loan term. Interestingly, most clients repay before their loans fall due."

Since 1993, UNICEF (1996b) has supported a number of microcredit schemes in poorer regions of Lower Egypt and in some urban slum areas. In Alexandria, a microcredit scheme run by a local NGO combines credit for women with efforts to combat child labour. Each borrower group comprises five women, two of whom have working children. The condition for the women's loans is that all the children should go to school. This scheme, in an area with adequate access to basic education, showed that microcredit could reduce child labour and improve school attendance while at the same time improving the income levels of the participating families. It also showed that parents are willing to send their children to school once the economic condition of the family improves.

The concept of providing financial services to low income people is very old. Many informal credit groups have been operating in many countries for several years like the *susus* in Nigeria and Ghana, *chit funds* and Rotating Savings and Credit Associations (ROSCAs) in India, *tontines* in West Africa, *pasanaku* in Bolivia, *hui* in China, *arisan* in Indonesia, *paluwagan* in Philippines etc. It is believed that initially, the informal financial institutions emerged in Nigeria dating back in the fifteenth century. Such type of institutions started establishing in Europe during the eighteenth century when in 1720 the first loan fund targeting poor people was founded in Ireland (Seibel,2005).

In 1847, some credit co-operatives were created in Germany which served 1.4 million people by 1910. In 1880s the British controlled government of Madras in South India tried to use the German experiment to address poverty in India. This effort resulted in membership of more than nine million poor to credit co-operatives by 1946. During the same time the Dutch colonial administrators constructed a co-operative rural banking system in Indonesia which eventually became Bank Rakyat Indonesia (BRI), now one of the largest Microfinance Institutions (MFIs) of the world (Schwiecker, 2004). In the 1970s, a paradigm shift started to take place. The failure of subsidized government or donor driven institutions to meet the demand for financial services in developing countries led to several new approaches. Bank Dagan Bali (BDB) etablished in Indonesia in 1970, was the earliest bank to institute commercial microfinance (Schwiecker, 2004). In 1973, ACCION International, a USA based NGO, disbursed its first loan in Brazil at commercial interest rate to start a micro-enterprise. One year later in 1974, the Self-Employed Women's Association of India (SEWA) started a bank to provide loans to poor women. In a SEWA BANK study, the proportion is about 40% compared with 50% and 62% of saver only and non-client households, respectively. The median income is 30% and 61% higher than for a saver-only and non-client household, respectively. Borrower and saver-only enrollment rates (both 58%) were both greater than the rate for non-client households (52%). Average daily expenditure on food is 21% higher than in non-client households. In contrast, saver only households enjoy only a small dietary margin over non-client households. Average daily expenditure on food is only 5% higher than in non-client households. The average number of income sources was 2.7 for client households compared with 2.5 for both saver-only and non-client households. It is interesting to note that the net impact of the wide-spread closure of large textile mills in Ahmedebad City appears to be that the borrower households suffered greater setbacks (more jobs lost and less compensation paid) but were able to recover more quickly (more laid-off workers are currently economically active) than saver-only and non-client households. Interestingly, fewer other household members in borrower households (60%) than saver-only (73%) or non-client (74%) households took on additional work.   In 1976, Muhammad Yunus, a professor of Economics at Chittagong University, Bangladesh initiated an experimental research project of providing credit to the rural poor. He gave a small loan of 856 Taka ($27)from his pocket to 42 poor bamboo weavers and found that small loans radically changed the lives of these people and they were able to pay back the loans with interest. The success of this idea led Yunus to establish Grameen Bank in 1983 in Bangladesh. This programme showed astonishing growth rates in Bangladesh, particularly during the 1980s and 1990s. It encouraged social innovators and organisations all over the world to begin experiments with different microfinance delivery methods to bring financial services to the poor. It is now adopted worldwide in the countries of different continents. Many international NGOs, such as Foundation for International Community Assistance (FINCA), Americans for Community Cooperation in Other Nations (ACCION), Freedom from Hunger, Opportunity International, Co-operative for Assistance and Relief Everywhere (CARE), Consultative Group for Assisting the Poor (CGAP), etc. are promoting microfinance programme for creating new businesses and combating poverty in a sustainable way. Over the past few decades, microfinance has been experimented in many developing countries. Bank Rakyat Indonesia (BRI) in Indonesia, Bancosol in Bolivia, Bank for Agriculture and Agricultural Co-operatives (BAAC) in Thailand, Grameen Bank, and Bangladesh Rural Advancement Committee (BRAC) of Bangladesh, NABARD in India, Amannah Ikhtiar Malaysia (AIM) of Malaysia, Agriculture Development Bank of Nepal (ADBN), K-Rep in Kenya and Mibanco in Peru have yielded encouraging results in alleviating poverty and empowering the poor through microfinance.

In India, the first initiative to introduce microfinance was the establishment of Self-Employed Women's Association (SEWA) in Gujarat. SEWA was registered as a trade union of self-employed women workers of the un-organised sector in 1972. This trade union established their bank known as SEWA Bank in 1974. To establish this bank four thousand union members contributed Rs. 10 each as share capital. Since then this 60 bank is registered as a co-operative bank and has been providing banking services to poor women and has also become a viable financial venture. In the midst of the apparent inadequacies of the formal financial system to cater to the financial needs of the rural poor, the first major effort to reach these rural poor was made by NABARD in 1986-87, when it supported and funded an action research project on 'Saving and Credit Management of Self-Help Groups' of Mysore Resettlement and Development Authority (MYRADA). For this purpose, a grant of Rs. one million was provided to MYRADA. The encouraging results were yielded. In 1988-89, NABARD undertook a survey of 43 NGOs spread over eleven states in India to study the functioning of the SHGs and possibilities of collaboration between the banks and SHGs in the mobilisation of rural savings and improving the credit delivery to the poor. Encouraged by the results of field level experiments in group based approach for lending to the poor, NABARD launched a pilot project of linking 500 SHGs with banks in 1991- 92 in partnership with non-governmental organisations (NGOs) for promoting and grooming self-help groups of socio-economically homogeneous members. In order to meet their credit requirements, in July 1991 RBI issued a circular to the commercial banks to extend credit to the SHGs formed under the pilot project of NABARD. During the project period different NGOs like Association of Sarva Seva Farms (ASSEFA), Madras; People's Rural Education Movement (PREM), Berhampur; Professional Assistance for Development Action (PRADAN), Madurai; and Community Development Society (CDS), Kerala promoted hundreds of groups. The results were very encouraging. In February 1992, the launching of pilot phase of the SHG- Bank Linkage Programme (SHG-BLP) could be considered as a landmark development in banking with the poor.

In order to further promote this programme RBI issued instructions to banks in 1996 to cover SHG financing as a mainstream activity under their priority sector-lending portfolio. The programme acquired a national priority from 1999 through Government of India budget announcements. With the support from both the government and the Reserve Bank of India, NABARD successfully spearheaded the programme through partnership with various stakeholders in the formal and informal sector. Since the time of its origin, NABARD provides policy guidance, technical and promotional support mainly for capacity building of NGOs and SHGs. Realising the potential in the field of microfinance, the government allowed various private players to provide microfinance in61 the country. These private microfinance providers, commonly known as MFIs, are various NGOs, Non-banking Financial Companies (NBFCs) and other registered companies. Many state governments amended/passed their State Co-operative Acts to use co-operative societies for providing microfinance. These days many public and private commercial banks, regional-rural banks, co-operative banks, co-operative societies, registered and unregistered NBFCs, societies, trusts and NGOs are providing microfinance by using their branch network and through different microfinance delivery models.

Legal legislation: The Asian Development Bank (2000) defines microfinance as the provision of broad range of services such as savings, deposits, loans, payment services, money transfers and insurance to poor and low income households and their micro-enterprises. This definition of microfinance is not restricted to the below poverty line people but it includes low income households also. The Task Force I (A group of senior Government officials and prominent microfinance practionars constituted by NABARD) terms microfinance as the provision of thrift, credit and other financial services and products of very small amounts to the poor in rural, semi-urban or urban areas for enabling them to raise their income levels and improve living standards. The Task Force II emphasizes that microfinance will cover not only consumption and production loans, but also loans for other credit needs such as housing and shelter . The Micro Financial Sector (Development and Regulation) Bill, (2007) defines microfinance as the provision of financial assistance and insurance services to an individual or an eligible client either directly or through a group mechanism for an amount, not exceeding rupees fifty thousand in aggregate per individual for small and tiny enterprise, agriculture, allied activities (including for consumption purposes of such individual); or an amount not exceeding rupees one lakh fifty thousand in aggregate per individual for housing or other prescribed purposes. The eligible clients which may get financial assistance under this scheme may be landless laborers and migrant laborers; artisans and micro-entrepreneurs; disadvantaged cultivators of agricultural land including oral lessees, tenants, and share croppers; and farmers owning not more than two hectares of agricultural land.

Credit with Education: The academic studies show that: "Microfinance programs face unusual challenges in making sure their services reach even the poorest of economically active households. A major obstacle is a set of assumptions of the community of academics, donors and practitioners supporting microfinance programming. They assume that the design of microfinance, especially poverty oriented, group-based microfinance, creates a desirable bias toward the poor (or more accurately, against the not-so-poor). The small loan size, high interest rate, short loan duration (too short for many kinds of investment, especially for most types of production agriculture), the frequent repayments (initially weekly in most programs), and dependence on mutual guarantees are all factors assumed to make the program unattractive to people who have other sources of easier credit. It is assumed that the poor, with few, if any, other options (because they lack collateral and distinct businesses), will tolerate these unattractive features, while the not-so-poor, for whom easier options are available, will tap more attractive sources of credit

"A few years ago an influential book that included case studies of 12 MFIs in Asia, Africa, and Latin America argued that MFIs working with the poorest would experience a trade-off with IFS. Specifically, it concluded that, "at a given point in time [MFIs] can either go for growth and put their resources into underpinning the success of established and rapidly growing institutions, or go for poverty impact…and put their resources into poverty-focused operations with a higher risk of failure and a lower expected return" (Hulme & Mosley, 1996, p.20666). Despite the influence of Hulme and Mosley's study, it is now recognized among many that the alleged trade-off is not inevitable (Christen, 1997; Christen and others, 1995; and Gulli, 1998, p. 28). A study of 11 successful microfinance programs in three continents found that, "Among high-performing programs (current authors' emphasis), no clear trade-off exists between reaching the very poor and reaching large numbers of people" (Christen and others, 1995, p. viii70), and concluded that their results showed that, "…full self-sufficiency can be achieved by institutions serving the very poor…." (Christen and others, 1995).Thus it is not the clientele served that determines an MFI's potential for IFS, but the degree to which its financial services program is well-designed and managed." (p. 4)

This study examined three MFIs: The Center for Agriculture and Rural Development (CARD) a Garmeen Bank replication/adaptation based in the Philippines (Operating Self-sufficiency—OSS—of 102.2%; Institutional Financial Self-sufficiency—IFS—of 95.9%; sample found that 53% of those who joined before CARD became a bank and 63% of those who entered after the bank had been established lived in the poorest houses..Average labor productivity in enterprises was 34% higher than the market wage rate.Rate of return on capital was 117% compared to 46% (effective) rate of interest charged by CARD

Credito con Educacion Rural (CRECER) a Freedom from Hunger Credit with Education affiliate and village-banking program based in Bolivia (OSS—93.8%; IFS—85.0%--due to aggressive expansion plan; and approximately 49% of clients are 'extremely poor')

The Foundation for International Community Assistance (FINCA Uganda), a village banking program based in Uganda (OSS—105.5%; IFS—79.7%--due to failure of Co- Operative Bank of Uganda with which they held 30% of cash and in which 80% of clients kept their savings; 67% of clients enter in severe poverty defined as a daily per capita income or DPCI of less than US$1 with an average of US$0.56. 22% were 'moderate poor' with an average DPCI of US$1.39)"So it is clear that MFIs serving and benefiting substantial numbers of the poorest clients in their countries can be at or near operational self-sufficiency, not too far from IFS, and making progress toward both. They need not experience a trade-off between working with the poorest and institutional financial sustainability." (Christen1996)

"Several authors, including Hulme and Mosley (1997) have noted that "Worryingly, both BRACRDP and Grameen Bank recently appear to be moving away from working with significant proportions of the hard core poor and focusing their activities on the middle income and upper poor, rather than the most desperate." This generally attributed to the increasing emphasis on institutional sustainability which Hulme and Mosley (1996, 1997) and Rogaly (1996) see as "Furthermore as Rhyne (1994); Christen et al. (19967) and many others point out, the greater the Microfinance institution's outreach, (i.e. the more clients it serves) the more cost effective and sustainable it becomes. In most development initiatives, the more people you serve, the greater the cost becomes; with Microfinance initiatives, the opposite is true ." (p. 35) "It is clear that, in these days of dwindling development budgets, the cost-effectiveness and sustainability of interventions is one of the most important criteria for programming funds. It is here that Microfinance has a particular advantage over almost (and probably) all other interventions...." (p. 39)

Macroeconomic policies linked to structural adjustment processes, although subsequently oriented in ways that tended to limit or minimize social problems, could hardly bring about a lasting solution. Such policies support the traditional approach, in which poverty is deemed to be alleviated by top-down money transfers initiated by the State in the direction of the poor. Yet public money transferred to the poor can provide only short-term relief to their situation simply because nowhere is public (or donor) money in infinite supply. In the short- and medium term, macroeconomic policies are bound to work in zero-sum-game environments where money transferred to the poor is necessarily taken from other segments of the economy, a decision always difficult to take at the government level. Furthermore, and of greater importance, the example of developed countries clearly showed that more money allocated to poverty by the government did not necessarily mean less poverty or less exclusion in society, even in the short term. On the contrary, the permanence of public transfers to some categories of people often created frozen situations where none of the actors involved in the poverty struggle had any incentive to move or change .
....At a time when governments are incurring heavy budget deficits, the question arises as to whether the cost of the anti-poverty effort should be shared further by the poor and by the private sector at large.

The income-generating approach described in the preceding paragraphs already allows part of that effort to be shared by the poor themselves. Credit, combined with the effort and skills of the entrepreneurial poor, can create the conditions necessary for the development of income-generating activities. Scarce public money earmarked for poverty eradication is then leveraged through credit are unlikely to create programs suitable for and focused on that group The sustainability and profitability of micro-credit programs in the developing world are achievable. Empirical indications are that the poorest can benefit from microfinance from both an economy and social well-being point-of-view, and that this can be done without jeopardizing the financial sustainability of the MFI. While there are many biases presented in the literature against extending microfinance to the poorest, there is little empirical evidence to support this position. However, if microfinance is to be used, specific targeting of the poorest will be necessary. Without this, MFIs which and the rate at which sustainability is achievable is a function of the goals of the program, the target population, etc. There are examples that serving the poor can be sustainable.

Microfinance is not for everyone. Most importantly, entrepreneurial skills and ability are necessary to run successful microenterprise and not all potential customers are equally able to take on debt. while these points will be true globally across all strata of poverty. It is assumed that they will have a greater effect on the very poorest. The sick, mentally ill, destitute etc. who form a minority of those living the below poverty line are typically not good candidates for microfinance. Most researchers agree that this group of people would be better for direct assistance. More optimistically, microfinance can be effective for a broad group of clients, including those who are living in the bottom half of those below a country's poverty line

Reference :

1. Haynes, S.S.,Planning for Third World Countries Mc Grew Hill, New York, 1991,p.7.
2. Lakadawala D.T., Growth, unemployment and poverty (Presidential Address) All India Labor Economic conference, Sri Venlateswara University, Tirupathi January 12,19977,p.3.
3. Hossain,M.1998,Credit for Alleviation of Rural Poverty: The Grameen Bank, in Bangladesh.
4. Hulme,D.and P.Mosley.1996 . Finance against poverty
5. Kabeer.N.and RK Murthy.1996.Compensating for Institutional Exclusion: Lessons from Indian Government and Non Government Credit Interventions for the poor.IDS Discussion paper 356.IDS.Brighton
6. Johnson,S.and B.Rogaly.1997.Microfinance and Poverty Reduction, Oxfam. Oxford.
7. Ghate.P.E.Ballon   and   V.Manalo.1996.Poverty   Alleviation   and   Enterprise Development: The need for a Differential Approach. Journal of International Development 8(2) P.163-178.
8. Ghate.P.(2008)Microfinance in India: A state of the Sector Report.2007,MFI Publication ,New Delhi.
9. Satish.P.(2005)." Mainstreaming of Indian Microfinance " Economic and Political weekly Vol 40.No 17.P.1733
10. Lipton.M.1996.Success in Antipoverty. International Institute of Labor Studies. Geneva.

CHAPTER-8
MICROFINANCE: EMPOWERING RURAL MASSES IN INDIA

Srinivas Vissapragada
Assistant Professor & Research Scholar
K L University Business School
K L University
Vaddeswarm,Guntur District
Andhra Pradesh

Abstract

Microfinance is not a magic sky-hook that reaches down to pluck the poor out of poverty. It can, however, be a strategically vital platform that the poor can use to raise their own prospects. In India more than 70% of the population lives in rural areas and most of these villages are deprived of basic enmities and underdeveloped. Indian financial system strives hard to empower rural people economically. Implementation new schemes and strategies in the rural areas can eradicate poverty, create employment opportunities and generate economic growth. Microfinance can be a critical element of an effective poverty reduction strategy. Improved access and efficient provision of savings, credit, and insurance facilities enable the poor to augment their consumption, manage their financial risks better, build their assets gradually and develop their micro enterprises. One of the major hindrances in the growth of the microfinance sector is the financial illiteracy of the people. This makes it difficult in creating awareness of microfinance and even more difficult to serve them as microfinance clients. Most microfinance institutions conduct educational training and awareness programmes for the benefit of the rural people. For many years, microfinance was considered as a panacea for poverty. However, since 2010, the sector has been damaged by various localized crises (competition among MFIs). In order to revert to the original social assignment of microfinance, a special legislative frame work and innovative economic models are required for effective delivery of microfinance.

Keywords: microfinance, poverty, financial literacy, economic model, employment

I. Introduction:

The term "Microfinance" pertains to the lending of extremely small amounts of capital to poor entrepreneurs in order to create a mechanism to eradicate poverty by providing the poor and destitute with resources that are available to the wealthy, albeit at a smaller scale. This particular form of lending has existed in the world for quite some time, though formalized by Mohammed Yunus in Bangladesh during the 1970's. Yunus won the Nobel Peace prize in 2006 for his sheer efforts in combating poverty and providing resources to the poor via the Grameen Bank and the microfinance model.[29]. "Microfinance is the provision of financial services to low-income clients or solidarity lending groups including consumers and the self-employed, who traditionally lack access to banking and related services."Microfinance sector has grown rapidly over the past few decades. Banks have also leveraged the Self-Help Group (SHGs) channel to provide direct credit to group borrowers. With financial inclusion emerging as a major policy objective in the country, Microfinance has occupied centre stage as a promising conduit for extending financial services to unbanked sections of population. At the same time, practices followed by certain lenders have subjected the sector to greater scrutiny and need for stricter regulation. Microfinance Institutions (MFIs), irrespective of legal forms, seek to create social benefits and promote financial inclusion by providing financial services to clients of financially un-served and underserved households. Over time, the Microfinance Sector has become an integral part of the financial infrastructure for the vulnerable sections of society in India.

Government, NGOs and other financial institutions have introduced various welfare schemes and activities to reduce poverty. Microfinance, by providing small loans and savings facilities to those who are excluded from commercial financial services has been developed as a key strategy for reducing poverty throughout the world. In India, a substantial microfinance system based on self help groups (SHGs) was developed. It allows poor people to protect, diversify and increase their sources of income, the essential path out of poverty and hunger. As a developmental and economic tool it has caught the imagination of banks, financial institutions and NGOs in India.[30] Although the microfinance sector is having a healthy growth rate, there have been a number of concerns related to the sector, like grey areas in regulation, transparent pricing, low financial literacy etc. In addition to these concerns there are a few emerging concerns like cluster formation, insufficient funds, multiple lending and over-indebtedness which are arising because of the increasing competition among the MFIs. On a national level there has been a spate of actions taken to strengthen the regulation of MF sector including, enactment of microfinance regulation bill by the Government of Andhra Pradesh, implementation of sector-specific regulation by Reserve Bank of India and most recently, release of Draft Microfinance Institutions (development and regulation) Bill, 2011 for comments. Microfinance is not just about giving micro

---

[29] Term Paper Submitted To Dr. Kimberly Leonard-Kempf In Partial Fulfillment For Research Design I School Of Economic, Political And Policy Sciences Political Economy And Public Policy By Sheheryar Banuri Richardson, Texas, November 2006

[30] Micro Finance : A Poverty Reduction Tool by Sangeeta Mohanty, Rashmi Ranjan Mohapatra & Sashikanta khuntia

credit to the poor rather it is an economic development tool whose objective is to assist poor to work their way out of poverty. It covers a wide range of services like credit, savings, insurance, remittance and also non-financial services like training, counseling etc.

Salient features of Microfinance are:

- Borrowers are from the low income group
- Loans are of small amount – micro loans
- Short duration loans
- Loans are offered without collaterals
- High frequency of repayment
- Loans are generally taken for income generation purpose

Meaning and Function of Microfinance

The Asian Development Bank (2000) defines microfinance as the provision of broad range of services such as savings, deposits, loans, payment services, money transfers and insurance to poor and low income households and their micro-enterprises. This definition of microfinance is not restricted to the below poverty line people but it includes low income households also.

The Micro Financial Sector (Development and Regulation) Bill, (2007) defines microfinance as the provision of financial assistance and insurance services to an individual or an eligible client either directly or through a group mechanism for an amount, not exceeding rupees fifty thousand in aggregate per individual for small and tiny enterprise, agriculture, allied activities (including for consumption purposes of such individual); or an amount not exceeding rupees one lakh fifty thousand in aggregate per individual for housing or other prescribed purposes. The eligible clients which may get financial assistance under this scheme may be landless labourers and migrant labourers; artisans and micro-entrepreneurs; disadvantaged cultivators of agricultural land including oral lessees, tenants, and share croppers; and farmers owning not more than two hectares of agricultural land.

II.   Literature Review

Microfinance as an industry evolved in all the third world countries almost at the same time span. The world over, it was getting widely recognized that improving income levels of low-income community is essential to improve their well-being – besides the state sponsored welfare programmers. During the 1970s and 1980s, the microenterprise movement led to the emergence of Non- Governmental Organizations (NGOs) that provided small loans for the poor. In 1990s, across the world, a number of these institutions transformed themselves into formal financial institutions in order to access and on-lend funds, thus enhancing their outreach. Microfinance has enjoyed a wealth of literature in the past, and is quite often seen as one of the most significant tools developed (in recent history) to combat poverty at the grassroots level. Today the important concern is sustainability of microfinance enterprises, specifically because of the nature of the lending itself. Loans are constantly being made to high-risk low income individuals, with unique and innovative methods being utilized to create re-payment incentives. Thus, the most significant concern at the moment is whether the formal microfinance institutions are actually impacting poverty in a significant manner. Microfinance is an emerging phenomenon that opens access to capital for individuals previously shut out from financial services. In its direct engagement with the poor, microfinance represents a new way for financial capital to potentially stimulate economic growth in developing countries. However, microfinance is poorly understood, and it remains unclear whether it delivers on its promises. Microfinance is now promoted as a means to solve the crushing poverty that faces at least a third of the world's population. "Microfinance spans a range of financial instruments including credit, savings, insurance, mortgages, and retirement plans, all of which are denominated in small amounts, making them accessible to individuals previously shut out from formal means of borrowing and saving. The most widespread micro financing instrument is microcredit or micro lending, which is the issuance of small, unsecured loans to individuals or groups for the purpose of starting or expanding businesses. Micro financing aims to alleviate poverty by stimulating economic growth through entrepreneurial initiative".[31]

Gaps in Financial System and Need For Microfinance

According to the latest research done by the World Bank, India is home to almost one third of the world's poor (surviving on an equivalent of one dollar a day). Though many poverty alleviation programs are currently active in India, microfinance plays a major contributor to financial inclusion. In the past few decades it has helped out remarkably in eradicating poverty. Reports show that people who have taken microfinance have been able augment their income and standard of living.

About half of the Indian population still doesn't have a savings bank account and they are deprived of all banking services. Poor also need financial services to fulfill their needs like consumption, building of assets and protection against risk. Microfinance institutions serve as a supplement to banks and in some sense a better one too. These institutions not only offer micro credit but they also provide other financial services like savings, insurance, remittance and non-financial services like individual counselling, training and support to start own business and the most importantly in a convenient way. The borrower receives all these services at her/his door steps and in most cases with a repayment schedule of borrower's convenience. But all this comes at a cost and the interest rates charged by these institutions are higher than commercial banks and vary widely from 10 to 30 percent. Some claim that the interest rates charged by some of these institutions are very high.

Modes of Delivery of Microfinance

Micro Finance Institutions (MFIs) around the world follow a variety of different methodologies.
The focus of such service is women rather than men for the reason women are more judicious
and economical to men. The following are major methodologies employed by MFIs for delivery
of financial services to low income families.

---

[31] Microfinance: Creating Opportunities for the Poor? by Susanna Khavul is an Assistant Professor of Strategic Management and Entrepreneurship in the Department of Management, University of Texas at Arlington.

- **Self Help Groups(SHGs)**

The Self Help Groups (SHGs) is the dominant microfinance methodology in India. In this case the members of Self Help Group pool their small savings regularly at a prefixed amount on daily or weekly basis and SHGs provide loan to members for a period fixed. SHGs are essentially formal and voluntary association of 15 to 20 people formed to attain common objectives. People from homogenous groups and common social back ground and occupation voluntarily form the group and pool their savings for the benefit of all of members of the groups. External financial assistance by MFIs or banks augments the resources available to the group operated revolving fund. Saving thus precede borrowing by the members. NABARD has facilitated and extensively supported a program which entails commercial banks lending directly to SHGs rather than via bulk loan to MFIs. If SHGs are observed to be successful for at least a period of six months, the bank gives credit usually amounting 4 times more than their savings.

- **Individual Banking Programmes**

In Individual Banking Programmes (IBPs) there is provision by Microfinance institutions for lending to individual clients though they may sometimes be organized into joint liability groups, credit and saving cooperatives. This model is increasingly popular through cooperatives. In cooperatives, all borrowers are members of organization directly or indirectly by being member of cooperative society. Credit worthiness and loan securing are a function of cooperative membership in which member's savings and peer pressure are assumed to be key factors.

- **Grameen Model**

Grameen Model was pioneered by DR Mohammed Yunus of Grameen Bank of Bangladesh. It is perhaps the most well known and widely practiced model in the world. In Grameen Model the groups are formed voluntarily consisting of five borrowers each. The lending is made first to two, then to the next two and then to the fifth. These groups of five meet together weekly, with seven other groups, so that bank staff meets with forty clients at a time. While the loans are made to the individuals, all in the group are held responsible for loan repayment. According to the rules, if one member ever defaults, all in the group are denied subsequent loans.

Self Help Groups (SHGs) model is more popular in India. There are three models of SHGs. The salient features are given below:-
 i) SHGs-Bank Linkage model:-This model involves the SHGs financed directly by the Commercial Banks viz. CBs (Public Sector and Private Sector), RRBs, and Cooperative Banks.
 ii) MFI-Bank Linkage model:-This model covers financing of micro Finance Institutions (MFIs) by banking agencies for on ward lending to SHGs and other small borrowers.
 iii) NGOs-Bank Linkage Model:-Under this model NGOs promote the linkage between banks and SHGs for savings and credit.

III.   INDIAN MICROFINANCE SECTOR

Indian microfinance sector is expected to grow nearly ten times by 2011 to a size of about Rs250 billion from the current market size of Rs27 billion, at a compounded annual growth rate of 76%. Microfinance in India started evolving in the early 1980s with the formation of informal Self Help Group (SHG) for providing access to financial services to the needy people who are deprived of credit facilities. National Bank for Agriculture and Rural Development, the regulator for microfinance sector, and Small Industries Development Bank of India are devoting their financial resources and time towards the development of microfinance. Microfinance has enormous growth potential as half the world's population earns less than US$2 per day, which is insufficient to meet their basic needs. One of the fastest growing sectors of India, microfinance is spearheading intense competition among the largest players. By the end of March 2009, microfinance institutions expanded their outreach to 50 million households and about 38 million borrowers. These institutions are organized under three models: SHG, Grameen model/Joint liability groups and Individual banking groups as in cooperatives. As of March 2009, both SHG bank linkage and MFIs have collectively disbursed US$3.9 billion to the poor.

State- wise position of MFIs

Name of the State	No of MFIs	Share %
Andhra Pradesh	484	62
Bihar	44	6
Gujarat	8	1
Jharkhand	1	0
Karnataka	20	3
Kerala	18	2
Madhya Pradesh	14	2
Maharashtra	15	2
Maharashtra	15	2
Orissa	28	4
Rajasthan	18	2
Tamil Nadu	101	13
Uttar Pradesh	5	1
West Bengal	30	4

Sources: NABARD

Conclusion:

Offer incentives to MFIs for opening branches in unbanked villages, so as to increase rural penetration. Also MFIs be encouraged to offer complete range of products to their clients. Transparent pricing and technology implementation to maintain uniformity and efficiency are among the others which these institutions should adopt. Inability of MFIs in getting sufficient funds is a major hindrance in the microfinance growth and so these institutions should look for alternative sources of funds. Some of the alternative fund sources include outside equity investment, portfolio buyouts and securitization of loans which only a few large MFIs are currently availing. Lending to the poor through microcredit is not the end of the problem but beginning of a new era. If effectively handled, it can create miracle in the field of poverty alleviation. But it must be bundled with capacity building programs. Government cannot abdicate its responsibility of social and economic development of poor and down trodden. In absence of any special skills with the clients of microcredit, the fund is being used in consumption and procurement of non-productive assets. Hence it is very important to provide skills development training program like handicraft, weaving, carpentry, poultry, goat rearing, masonry, bees farming, vegetable farming and many other agricultural and non agricultural training. Government has to play proactive role in this case. People with some special skills have to be given priority in lending microcredit. These clients should also be provided with post loan technical and professional aid for success of their microenterprises. If government and MFIs act together then microcredit can play a great role in poverty alleviation.

References:

1. Planning Commission, Approach Paper to the Tenth Five Year Plan (2002-07), New Delhi, 2001
2. Planning Commission, Report of the Working Group on Agricultural Credit, Co-operation and Crop Insurance for the Tenth Five Year Plan (2002-07), New Delhi, 2001.
3. Ministry of Finance, Task Force on Revival of Cooperative Credit Institutions (Draft Report), New Delhi, 2004.
4. Ministry of Finance, Expert Committee on Consumption Credit (Chairman: B. Shivaraman), New Delhi, 1976. [5] Ministry of Rural Development (GoI), Annual Report (2004-05), New Delhi, 2005.
5. Crisil Rating India Top 50 Microfinance Institutions
6. NABARD Report on Status of microfinance in India,2012
7. Microfinance as a Poverty Reduction Tool—A Critical Assessment, DESA Working Paper No. 89

CHAPTER-9

ROLE OF MICRO-FINANCE IN RURAL INDIA

Dr. L.SRINIVAS REDDY,
Global Education Centre
(School of Business Management)
Hyderabad. INDIA

Abstract

India falls under low income class according to World Bank. It is second populated country in the world and around 70 % of its population lives in rural area. 60% of people depend on agriculture, as a result there is chronic underemployment and per capita income is only $ 3262. This is not enough to provide food to more than one individual. The obvious result is abject poverty, Low rate of education, low sex ratio, and exploitation. The major factor account for high incidence of rural poverty is the low asset base. According to Reserve Bank of India, about 51 % of people house possess only 10% of the total asset of India .This has resulted low production capacity both in agriculture (which contribute around 22-25% of GDP) and Manufacturing sector. Rural people have very low access to institutionalized credit.

Key words: Micro finance Institutions, Rural population , poverty

Introduction
Micro-finance economically disadvantaged segments of society, for enabling them to raise their income levels largest in term of population after China. India's GDP ranks among the top 15 economies of the world. However, around 300 million people or about 80 million households are living below the poverty line, i.e. less than $2 per day according to the World Bank and the poorest are which earns $1 per day. It is further estimated that of these households, only about 20% have access to credit from the formal sector. Out of these 80 million house hold, 80% takes credit from the informal sources i.e. local Zamidars, Chit Funds etc. With about 80 million households below MFIs include non- governmental organizations (NGOs), credit
unions, non-bank financial intermediaries, and even a few commercial banks.
Microfinance:

Microfinance refers to a variety of financial services that target low-income clients, particularly women. Since the clients of microfinance institutions (MFIs) have lower incomes and often have limited access to other financial services, microfinance products tend to be for smaller monetary amounts than traditional financial services. These services include loans, savings, insurance, and remittances. Microloans are given for a variety of purposes, frequently for microenterprise development. The diversity of products and services offered reflects the fact that the financial needs of individuals, households, and enterprises can change significantly over time, especially for those who live in poverty. Because of these varied needs, and because of the industry's focus on the poor, microfinance institutions often use non-traditional methodologies, such as group lending or other forms of collateral not employed by the formal financial sector.

Microfinance [MF] broadly envisions a world in which low-income, poor and the poorest households have permanent and reliable access to a range of better quality financial services at affordable price to finance their income generating activities, build assets, smoothen consumption and protect against risks. A harsh aspect of poverty is that income is often irregular and undependable. Access to micro-credit helps poor smoothen cash flows and avoid periods when access to food, clothing, shelter or education is lost. Micro-credit makes it easier to manage shocks like sickness, emergencies, natural disasters etc. When women participate in MF program they are self-empowered to take informed decisions in their family and social life. In developing countries clients' demand confirm that poor people value MF services.

Banks in India have been providing micro-credit through a credit delivery model, viz. SHG-Bank Linkage Program [SBLP] since 1992.Since 2000-01 bank credit has fueled significant and rapid growth of SHGs including Government program " Swarnjayanti Gram RozgarYojana[SGSY] and covering large number of women as on end-March 2012. However, unsatisfactory recovery performance of banks' loan to SHGs in past few years resulted in Non-Performing Assets [NPA] and decelerated growth. This paper attempts to analyze agency-wise and region-wise banks' performance under the SBLP as on end-March 2012 in all its aspects including exclusive women SHGs, NPAs and suggests strategy to accelerate growth and contain NPAs

Need of the study
• The need of microfinance arises because the rural India requires sources of finance for poverty alleviation, procurement of agricultural and farms input.
• Micro finance is a programme to support the poor rural people to pay its debt and maintain social and economic status in the villages.
• As we know that India is agriculture based economy so microfinance may be a tools to empower the farmers and rural peoples to make agriculture profitable.
• So the researchers are interested to find out the scopes of microfinance in rural India. This research paper is highlighting a picture rural India as a profitable segment for microfinance institutions.

Objective of the study
• To study the importance and role of microfinance in poverty alleviation in india and profitable agriculture activities
• To analyze the growth of microfinance sector developed in India and see potential for the microfinance institutions, NGOs, SHGs in the market.
• To analyze the structure and pattern of microfinance programme in rural Indian by the MFIs, NBFCs.
• To understands the marketing of microfinance products in rural market..

Research Methodology
This is a descriptive research paper based on secondary data. Data have been find out by googling in different websites research paper and magazines.

Legal and Regulatory Framework for the Microfinance Institutions in India:
Societies Registration Act, 1860:
NGOs are mostly registered under the Societies Registration Act, 1860. Since these entities were established as voluntary, not-for-profit development organizations, their microfinance activities were also established under the same legal umbrella. Main purpose is:
• Relief of poverty
• Advancement of education
• Advancement of religion
• Purposes beneficial to the community or a section of the community.

Indian Trusts Act, 1882:
Some MFIs are registered under the Indian Trust Act, 1882 either as public charitable trusts or as private, determinable trusts with specified beneficiaries/members.

Not-For-Profit Companies Registered Under Section 25 Of Companies Act, 1956:
An organization given a license under Section 25 of the Companies Act 1956 is allowed to be some of the provisions of the Companies Act, 1956. For companies that are already registered under the Companies Act, 1956, if the central government is satisfied that the objects of that company are restricted to the promotion of commerce, science, art, religion, charity or any other useful purpose; and the constitution of such company provides for the application of funds or other income in promoting these objects and prohibits payment of any dividend to its members, then it may allow such a company to register under Section 25 of the Companies Act.

A Profile of Rural India
• 350 million Below Poverty Line
• 95 % have no access to microfinance.
• 56 % people still borrow from informal sources.
• 70 % don't have any deposit account.
• 87 % no access to credit from formal sources.
• Annual credit demand is about Rs.70,000 crores.
• 95 % of the households are without any kind of insurance.
• Informally Microfinance has been in practice for ages.

Rural India and Microfinance
Micro financing has become important since the possibility of a sub-Rs 1,000 mobile handset has been ruled out in the near future. Rural India can generally afford handsets in the price range of Rs 1,500-2,000. To succeed in India, agribusiness must empower the farmer by making agriculture profitable, not by expropriating him foe this particular purpose the farmer should be
funded for their basic and small needs. Micro finance is expected to play a significant role in poverty alleviation and development. The need, therefore, is to share experiences and materials which will help not only in understanding successes and failures but also provide knowledge and
guidelines to strengthen and expand micro finance programmers. The development process through a typical micro-finance intervention can be understood with the help of the following Chart The ultimate aim is to attain social and economic empowerment. Successful intervention is therefore, dependent on how each of these stages has been carefully dealt with and also the capabilities of the implementing organizations in achieving the final goal, e.g., if credit delivery takes place without consolidation of SHGs, it may have problems of self-sustainability and recovery. A

number of schemes under banks, central and state governments offer direct credit to potential individuals without forcing them to join SHGs

Performance:

Aggregate performance as on end-March 2012 is as under.

- Saving-linked 79.60 lakh SHGs [estimated 103 million members] had savings of Rs.6,551.41 crore with Banks.
- Saving-linked exclusive women SHGs [62.99 lakh] with savings of Rs.5,104.33crore with banks accounted for 79.1% and 77.9% respectively of the total.
- Share of women SHGs [36.49 lakh] and loan outstanding [Rs.30,465.28crore] was 83.8% each in the total.
- Under SGSY, SGSY-saving-linked 22.23 lakh SHGs with savings of Rs.1,395.25 crore. Accounted for 26.7% and 21.3% respectively of the total
- Share of SGSY-SHGs [12.16 lakh] and loan outstanding [Rs.8,054.83crore] was 27.9% and 22.2% respectively of the total.
- According to NABARD, SHGs have mobilized estimated savings of over Rs.22,000crore of which nearly 70% [Rs.15,400 crore] was used for internal lending. During 2011-12 alone, 11.48 lakh SHGs availed loan of Rs.16,534.77crore from Bank sand as on end-March, 2012, 43.54 lakh SHGs had outstanding credit of Rs.36,340 crore. Thus, the total pooled resources outstanding at members' level would be Rs.51,740crore. Credit availed by SHGs along with their internal savings is revolved many times within the groups for shorter durations which makes the multiplier effect larger than the figures reported by banks.
- With the increase of NPAs the percentage of NPAs to outstanding loan shot up from 2.94% as on end-March 2010 to 4.72% and 6.09% in following two years.

Success Factors of Micro-Finance in Rural India

Over the last ten years, successful experiences in providing finance to small entrepreneur and producers demonstrate that poor people, when given access to responsive and timely financial services at market rates, repay their loans and use the proceeds to increase their income and assets. This is not surprising since the only realistic alternative for them is to borrow from informal market at an interest much higher than market rates. Community banks, NGOs and grass root savings and credit groups around the world have shown that these micro enterprise loans can be profitable for borrowers and for the lenders, making microfinance one of the most effective poverty reducing strategies.

A. For NGOs

• The field of development itself expands and shifts emphasis with the pull of ideas, and NGOs perhaps more readily adopt new ideas, especially if the resources required are small, entry and exit are easy, tasks are (perceived to be) simple and people's acceptance is high – all characteristics (real or presumed) of microfinance.

• Canvassing by various factors, including the National Bank for Agriculture and Rural Development (NABARD), Small Industries Development Bank of India (SIDBI), Friends of Women's World Banking (FWWB), Rashtriya Mahila Kosh (RMK), Council for Advancement of People's Action and Rural Technologies (CAPART), Rashtriya Gramin Vikas Nidhi (RGVN), various donor funded programmes especially by the International Fund for Agricultural Development (IFAD), United Nations Development Programme (UNDP), World Bank and Department for International Development, UK (DFID)], and lately commercial banks, has greatly added to the idea pull. Induced by the worldwide focus on microfinance, donor NGOs too have been funding microfinance projects. One might call it the supply push.

• All kinds of things from khadi spinning to Nadep compost to balwadis do not produce such concrete results and sustained interest among beneficiaries as microfinance. Most NGO-led microfinance is with poor women, for whom access to small loans to meet dire emergencies is a valued 0outcome. Thus, quick and high 'customer satisfaction' is the USP that has attracted NGOs to this trade.

B. For Financial Institutions and banks

• Microfinance has been attractive to the lending agencies because of demonstrated sustainability and of low costs of operation. Institutions like SIDBI and NABARD are hardnosed bankers and would not work with the idea if they did not see a long term engagement – which only comes out of sustainability (that is economic attractiveness).On the supply side, it is also true that it has all the trappings of a business enterprise, its output is tangible and it is easily understood by the mainstream. This also seems to sound nice to the government, which in the post liberalization era is trying to explain the logic of every rupee spent. That is the reason why microfinance has attracted mainstream institutions like no other developmental project. Perhaps the most important factor that got banks involved is what one might call the policy push. Given that most of our banks are in the public sector, public policy does have some influence on what they will or will not do. In this case, policy was followed by diligent, if meandering, promotional work by NABARD. The policy change about a decade ago by RBI to allow banks to lend to SHGs was

initially followed by a seven-page memo by NABARD to all bank chairmen, and later by sensitization and training programmers for bank staff across the country. Several hundred such programmers were conducted by NGOs alone, each involving 15 to 20 bank staff, all paid for by NABARD. The policy push was sweetened by the NABARD refinance scheme that offers much more favorable terms (100% refinance, wider spread) than for other rural lending by banks. NABARD also did some system setting work and banks lately have been given targets. The canvassing, training, refinance and close follow up by NABARD has resulted in widespread bank involvement.

Marketing of Microfinance Products

Contract Farming and Credit Bundling
• Banks and financial institutions have been partners in contract farming schemes, set up to enhance credit. Basically, this is a doable model. Under such an arrangement, crop loans can be extended under tie-up arrangements with corporate for production of high quality produce with stable marketing arrangements provided – and only, provided – the price setting mechanism for
the farmer is appropriate and fair.

Agri Service Centre – Rabo India
• Rabo India Finance Pvt Ltd. has established agri-service centre's in rural areas in cooperation with a number of agri-input and farm services companies. The services provided are similar to those in contract farming, but with additional flexibility and a wider range of products including inventory finance. Besides providing storage facilities, each centre rents out farm machinery, provides agricultural inputs and

information to farmers, arranges credit, sells other services and provides a forum for farmers to market their products.

Non Traditional Markets

• Similarly, Mother Dairy Foods Processing, a wholly owned subsidiary of National Dairy Development Board (NDDB) has established auction markets for horticulture producers in Bangalore. The operations and maintenance of the market is done by NDDB. The project, with an outlay of Rs.15 lakh, covers 200 horticultural farmers associations with 50,000 grower members for wholesale marketing. Their produce is planned with production and supply assurance and provides both growers and buyers a common platform to negotiate better rates.

Apni Mandy

• Another innovation is that of The Punjab Mandy Board, which has experimented with a 'farmers' market' to provide small farmers located in proximity to urban areas, direct access to consumers by elimination of middlemen. This experiment known as "Apni Mandy" belongs to both farmers and consumers, who mutually help each other. Under this arrangement a sum of Rs. 5.2 lakh is spent for providing plastic crates to 1000 farmers. Each farmer gets 5 crates at a subsidized rate. At the Mandy site, the Board provides basic infrastructure facilities. At the farm level, extension services of different agencies are pooled in. These include inputs subsidies, better quality seeds and loans from Banks. Apni Mandy scheme provides self-employment to producers and has eliminated social inhibitions among them regarding the retail sale of their produce.

Findings

• Considerable gap between demand and supply for all financial services.

• Majority of poor are excluded from financial services. This is due to, interlayer, the following reasons:

• Bankers feel that it is risky to finance poor people's because of their creditworthiness.

• High transaction costs

Conclusion

The potential for growing micro finance institutions in India is very high. Major cross-section can have benefit if this sector will grow in its fastest pace. Annual growth rate of about 20 % during the next five year. The loan outstanding will consequently grow from the present level of about 1600 crores to about 42000 crores. This suggests need for evaluating district-wise SHGs completing three years on an annual basis so as to assess poverty penetration and impact in respect of increase in asset creation, average annual net income, savings, employment generated per household, repayment performance, reduction in availing multiple loans and loans from informal sources with higher interest rates, degree of social empowerment of women in terms of self-confidence, participation in decision-making in matters related to family welfare, economic activities.

References

1. www.ifmr.ac.in
2. www.google.com
3. www.microfinanceinsight.com
4. www.investopedia.com
5. www.books.google.com
6. www.forbes.com
7. www.nationmaster.com
8. www.thaindian.com
9. www.authorstream.com
10. www.indiamicrofinance.com
11. www.gdrc.org
12. www.accion.org
13. Research paper by Vishal Sehgal
14. Presentation by N. Srinivasan

CHAPTER-10

The Importance and Role of Micro Finance in Poverty Alleviation and Profitable Agriculture Activities in India.

K.Madhava Rao
Assistant Professor
Department of Management Studies
Baba Institute of Technology and Sciences (BITS)
P.M.Palem, Visakhapatnam – 48

Abstract:
India falls under low income class according to World Bank. It is second populated country in the world and around 70 % of its population lives in rural area. 60% of people depend on agriculture, as a result there is chronic underemployment and per capita income is only $ 3262. This is not enough to provide food to more than one individual. The obvious result is abject poverty, low rate of education, low sex ratio, and exploitation. The major factor account for high incidence of rural poverty is the low asset base. According to Reserve Bank of India, about 51 % of people house possess only 10% of the total asset of India .This has resulted low production capacity both in agriculture (which contribute around 22-25% of GDP) and Manufacturing sector. Rural people have very low access to institutionalized credit (from commercial bank).

Key words: *Agriculture, Reserve Bank of India, production capacity, Rural people, Commercial bank.*

Introduction

Micro-finance economically disadvantaged segments of society, for enabling them to raise their income levels largest in term of population after China. India's GDP ranks among the top 15 economies of the world. However, around 300 million people or about 80 million households are living below the poverty line, i.e. less than $2 per day according to the World Bank and the poorest are which earns $1 per day. It is further estimated that of these households, only about 20% have access to credit from the formal sector. Out of these 80 million house hold, 80% takes credit from the informal sources i.e. local Zamidars, Chit Funds etc. With about 80 million households below MFIs include non- governmental organizations (NGOs), credit unions, non-bank financial intermediaries, and even a few commercial banks.

Need of the study

- ➤ The need of microfinance arises because the rural India requires sources of finance for poverty alleviation, procurement of agricultural and farms input.
- ➤ Micro finance is a programme to support the poor rural people to pay its debt and maintain social and economic status in the villages.
- ➤ As we know that India is agriculture based economy so microfinance may be a tools to empower the farmers and rural peoples to make agriculture profitable.
- ➤ So the researchers are interested to find out the scopes of microfinance in rural India. This research paper is highlighting a picture rural India as a profitable segment for microfinance institutions.

Objective of the study

- ✓ To study the importance and role of microfinance in poverty alleviation and profitable agriculture activities.

- ✓ To analyze the growth of microfinance sector developed in India and see potential for the microfinance institutions, NGOs, SHGs in the market.
- ✓ To analyze the structure and pattern of microfinance programme in rural Indian by the
- ✓ MFIs, NBFCs.
- ✓ To understands the marketing of microfinance products in rural market.

Research Methodology

This is a descriptive research paper based on secondary data. Data have been finding out by googling in different websites research paper and magazines.

Legal and Regulatory Framework for the Microfinance Institutions in India:
Societies Registration Act, 1860:

NGOs are mostly registered under the Societies Registration Act, 1860. Since these entities were established as voluntary, not-for-profit development organizations, their microfinance activities were also established under the same legal umbrella. Main purpose is:

- ✓ Relief of poverty
- ✓ Advancement of education
- ✓ Advancement of religion
- ✓ Purposes beneficial to the community or a section of the community.

Indian Trusts Act, 1882:

Some MFIs are registered under the Indian Trust Act, 1882 either as public charitable trusts or as private, determinable trusts with specified beneficiaries/members.

Not-For-Profit Companies Registered Under Section 25 Of Companies Act, 1956:

An organization given a license under Section 25 of the Companies Act 1956 is allowed to be some of the provisions of the *Companies Act, 1956.*

For companies that are already registered under the Companies Act, 1956, if the central government is satisfied that the objects of that company are restricted to the promotion of commerce, science, art, religion, charity or any other useful purpose; and the constitution of such company provides for the application of funds or other income in promoting these objects and prohibits payment of any dividend to its members, then it may allow such a company to register under Section 25 of the Companies Act.

A Profile of Rural India

- ✓ 350 million Below Poverty Line
- ✓ 95 % has no access to microfinance.
- ✓ 56 % people still borrow from informal sources.
- ✓ 70 % doesn't have any deposit account.
- ✓ 87 % no access to credit from formal sources.
- ✓ Annual credit demand is about Rs.70, 000 crores.
- ✓ 95 % of the households is without any kind of insurance.
- ✓ Informally Microfinance has been in practice for ages.

Rural India and Microfinance

Micro financing has become important since the possibility of a sub-Rs 1,000 mobile handset has been ruled out in the near future. Rural India can generally afford handsets in the price range of Rs 1,500-2,000.

To succeed in India, agribusiness must empower the farmer by making agriculture profitable, not by expropriating him foe this particular purpose the farmer should be funded for their basic and small needs.

Micro finance is expected to play a significant role in poverty alleviation and development. The need, therefore, is to share experiences and materials which will help not only in understanding successes and failures but also provide knowledge and guidelines to strengthen and expand micro finance programmes.

The development process through a typical micro-finance intervention can be understood with the help of the following Chart The ultimate aim is to attain social and economic empowerment. Successful intervention is therefore, dependent on how each of these stages has been carefully dealt with and also the capabilities of the implementing organizations in achieving the final goal, e.g., if credit delivery takes place without consolidation of SHGs, it may have problems of self-sustainability and recovery. A number of schemes under banks, central and state governments offer direct credit to potential individuals without forcing them to join SHGs. Compilation and classification of the communication materials in the directory is done based on this development process.

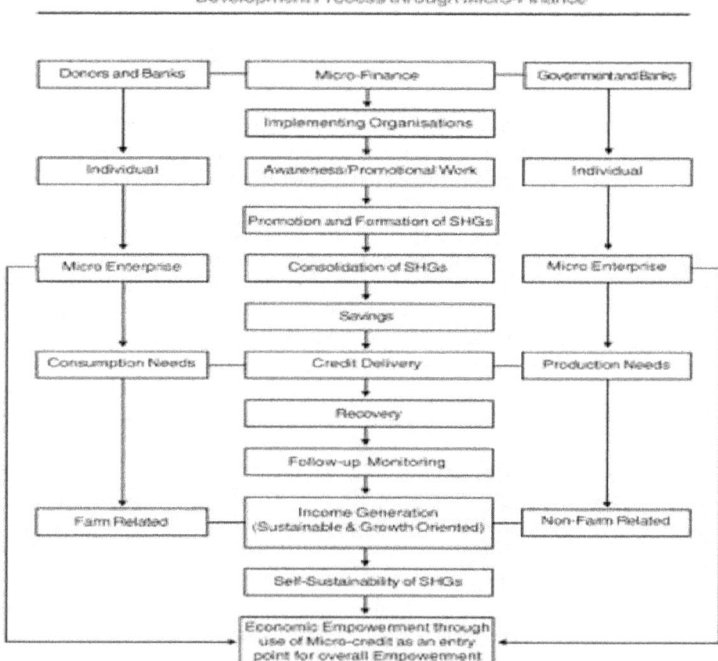

Development Process through Micro-Finance

Success Factors of Micro-Finance in Rural India

Over the last ten years, successful experiences in providing finance to small entrepreneur and producers demonstrate that poor people, when given access to responsive and timely financial services at market rates, repay their loans and use the proceeds to increase their income and assets. This is not surprising since the only realistic alternative for them is to borrow from informal market at an interest much higher than market rates. Community banks, NGOs and grass root savings and credit groups around the world have shown that these micro enterprise loans can be profitable for borrowers and for the lenders, making microfinance one of the most effective poverty reducing strategies.

A. For NGOs

The field of development itself expands and shifts emphasis with the pull of ideas, and NGOs perhaps more readily adopt new ideas, especially if the resources required are small, entry and exit are easy, tasks are (perceived to be) simple and people's acceptance is high – all characteristics (real or presumed) of microfinance.

Canvassing by various factors, including the National Bank for Agriculture and Rural Development (NABARD), Small Industries Development Bank of India (SIDBI), Friends of Women's World Banking (FWWB), Rashtriya Mahila Kosh (RMK), Council for Advancement of People's Action and Rural Technologies (CAPART), Rashtriya Gramin Vikas Nidhi (RGVN), various donor funded programmes especially by the International Fund for Agricultural Development (IFAD), United Nations Development Programme (UNDP), World Bank and Department for International Development, UK (DFID)], and lately commercial banks, has greatly added to the idea pull. Induced by the worldwide focus on microfinance, donor NGOs too have been funding microfinance projects. One might call it the supply push.

All kinds of things from khadi spinning to Nadep compost to balwadis do not produce such concrete results and sustained interest among beneficiaries as microfinance. Most NGO-led microfinance is with poor women, for whom access to small loans to meet dire emergencies is a valued outcome. Thus, quick and high 'customer satisfaction' is the USP that has attracted NGOs to this trade.

B. For Financial Institutions and banks

Microfinance has been attractive to the lending agencies because of demonstrated sustainability and of low costs of operation. Institutions like SIDBI and NABARD are hard nosed bankers and would not work with the idea if they did not see a long term engagement – which only comes out of sustainability (that is economic attractiveness).On the supply side, it is also true that it has all the trappings of a business enterprise, its output is tangible and it is easily understood by the mainstream. This also seems to sound nice to the government, which in the post liberalisation era is trying to explain the logic of every rupee spent. That is the reason why microfinance has attracted mainstream institutions like no other developmental project. Perhaps the most important factor that got banks involved is what one might call the policy push. Given that most of our banks are in the public sector, public policy does have some influence on what they will or will not do. In this case, policy was followed by diligent, if meandering, promotional work by NABARD. The policy change about a decade ago by RBI to allow banks to lend to SHGs was initially followed by a seven-page memo by NABARD to all bank chairmen, and later by sensitisation and training programmes for bank staff across the country. Several hundred such programmes were conducted by NGOs alone, each involving 15 to 20 bank staff, all paid for by NABARD. The policy push was sweetened by the NABARD refinance scheme that offers much more favourable terms (100% refinance, wider spread) than for other rural lending by banks. NABARD also did some system setting work and banks lately have been given targets. The canvassing, training, refinance and close follow up by NABARD has resulted in widespread bank involvement.

Marketing of Microfinance Products
Contract Farming and Credit Bundling

Banks and financial institutions have been partners in contract farming schemes, set up to enhance credit. Basically, this is a doable model. Under such an arrangement, crop loans can be extended under tie-up arrangements with corporate for production of high quality produce with stable marketing arrangements provided – and only, provided – the price setting mechanism for the farmer is appropriate and fair.

Agri Service Centre – Rabo India

Rabo India Finance Pvt Ltd. has established agri-service centres in rural areas in cooperation with a number of agri-input and farm services companies. The services provided are similar to those in contract farming, but with additional flexibility and a wider range of products including inventory finance. Besides providing storage facilities, each centre rents out farm machinery, provides agricultural inputs and information to farmers, arranges credit, sells other services and provides a forum for farmers to market their products.

Non Traditional Markets

Similarly, Mother Dairy Foods Processing, a wholly owned subsidiary of National Dairy Development Board (NDDB) has established auction markets for horticulture producers in Bangalore. The operations and maintenance of the market is done by NDDB. The project, with an outlay of Rs.15 lakh, covers 200 horticultural farmers associations with 50,000 grower members for wholesale marketing. Their produce is planned with production and supply assurance and provides both growers and buyers a common platform to negotiate better rates.

Apni Mandi

Another innovation is that of The Punjab Mandi Board, which has experimented with a 'farmers' market' to provide small farmers located in proximity to urban areas, direct access to consumers by elimination of middlemen. This experiment known as "Apni Mandi" belongs to both farmers and consumers, who mutually help each other. Under this arrangement a sum of Rs. 5.2 lakh is spent for providing plastic crates to 1000 farmers. Each

farmer gets 5 crates at a subsidized rate. At the mandi site, the Board provides basic infrastructure facilities. At the farm level, extension services of different agencies are pooled in. These include inputs subsidies, better quality seeds and loans from Banks. Apni Mandi scheme provides self-employment to producers and has eliminated social inhibitions among them regarding the retail sale of their produce.

Findings

> ➢ Considerable gap between demand and supply for all financial services.
> ➢ Majority of poor are excluded from financial services.

This is due to, interalia, the following reasons:

- Bankers feel that it is risky to finance poor people's because of their creditworthiness.
- High transaction costs.

Conclusion

The potential for growing micro finance institutions in India is very high. Major cross-section can have benefit if this sector will grow in its fastest pace. Annual growth rate of about 20 % during the next five year. The loan outstanding will consequently grow from the present level of about 1600 crores to about 42000 crores Annual growth rate of about 20 % can be achieved during the next five years.

References
[1] www.ifmr.ac.in
[2] www.google.com
[3] www.microfinanceinsight.com
[4] www.investopedia.com
[5] www.books.google.com
[6] www.seepnetwork.org
[7] www.forbes.com
[8] www.nationmaster.com
[9] www.thaindian.com
[10] www.authorstream.com
[11] www.knowledge.allianz.com
[12] www.familiesinbusiness.net
[13] www.indiamicrofinance.com
[14] www.gdrc.org
[15] www.accion.org
[16] International Review of Business and Finance ISSN 0976-5891 Volume 2 Number 1
(2010),   pp.   29–35   ©   Research   India   Publications
http://www.ripublication.com/irbf.htm
[17] Research paper by Prabhu Ghate
[18] Research paper by Vishal Sehgal
[18] Presentation by N. Srinivasan

Chapter-11
Role Of Bharatiya Mahila Bank (BMB) for Women Empowerment
Through Self Help Groups

*Dr.K.Manjusree Naidu

**Dr.M.Jyothsna

Absract:

The budget 2013-14 is remarkable and innovative for one gender of the population because the Finance Minister announced the setting up of India's first women's bank as a public sector bank with Rs 1,000 crore as initial capital.BMB is a pet project of the Congress-led United Progressive Alliance (UPA) government. Exclusive women bank is defined as: "The bank is going to be run mostly by women and it would provide funds for the entrepreneurial initiatives by women". The announcement of First Women bank in India has received a huge appreciation from the countries around the world. Bharatiya Mahila Bank was inaugurated on 19th November, 2013 .BMB will have at least 25 branches—one each in all state capitals, by the end of this fiscal year.

Experts in the field of banking have expressed their opinion on the need and importance of exclusive women bank in India. At the national and international level there are many women banks which are operating successfully by achieving the objectives for which it has been started. The UPA governments innovative step is to see that India's first Women Bank has to operate in an effective and efficient direction by taking into consideration the experiences of the already existing women banks in India and abroad. What people (men and women) require from banks are **quality services** that meet their needs; based on their gender, age, financial background, these requirements may differ.

Objective of the study: Study the working of the successful women banks in India and abroad and to highlight how BMB can contribute to women empowerment through self help groups. The data below states how bank can empower women in unorganized sector by providing micro finance to self help groups.

Introduction:

The budget 2013-14 is remarkable and innovative for one gender of the population because the Finance Minister announced the setting up of India's first women's bank as a public sector bank with Rs 1,000 crore as initial capital.BMB is a pet project of the Congress-led United Progressive Alliance (UPA) government. Exclusive women bank is defined as: "The bank is going to be run mostly by women and it would provide funds for the entrepreneurial initiatives by women". The announcement of First Women bank in India has received a huge appreciation from the countries around the world. Bharatiya Mahila Bank was inaugurated on 19th November, 2013 .BMB will have at least 25 branches—one each in all state capitals, by the end of this fiscal year.

After the inauguration the Finance minister P.Chidambaram, announced that India's newest public sector bank, is likely to break-even in the next "three to five years" and total business will rise to Rs.60,000 crore by 2020,

Experts in the field of banking have expressed their opinion on the need and importance of exclusive women bank in India. At the national and international level there are many women banks which are operating successfully by achieving the objectives for which it has been started. The UPA governments innovative step is to see that India's first Women Bank has to operate in an effective and efficient direction by taking into consideration the experiences of the already existing women banks in India and abroad. What people (men and women) require from banks are **quality services** that meet their needs; based on their gender, age, financial background, these requirements may differ. According to the recent World Bank study only 26 per cent of women in India have an account with a formal financial institution.BMB can contribute to economic development of women because only 7.3% of the total banking credit is extended to women. BMB should focus on providing micro finance services to self help groups because it empowers women in rural and urban areas.

Dr.K.Manjusree Naidu Associate Professor, GIM, GU, mparuchuru@yahoo.com

** *Dr. M.Jyothsna, Associate Professor, GIM, GU,* jyothsna_mallela@yahoo.co.in

Objective of the study: Study the working of the successful women banks in India and abroad and to highlight how BMB can contribute to women empowerment through self help groups. The data below states how bank can empower women in unorganized sector by providing micro finance to self help groups.

- 92% of all workers in India are in the unorganised sector.
- 96% of all women workers are in the unorganised sector.
- Women workers are economically active and they are bankable.

The methodology: The study is based on the secondary and primary sources of data.

Paper presentation: The paper is presented in three sections. Section I: Presents the examples of the successfully operating women banks in the world. Section II: Presents the examples of the successfully operating women banks in India. Section III: Presents the respondents opinion relating to mahila bank and how to empower women through micro finance.

Section I

The concept Women bank isn't altogether new on an international scale. In 1979, Women's World Banking (WWB) was officially incorporated, registered in the Netherlands as Stichting (Foundation) to Promote Women's World Banking, an international nonprofit organization with the objective of providing women entrepreneurs with the capital and information necessary to access the money economy of their own countries and build viable businesses. WWB is governed by a Board of Trustees, made up of representatives from the sectors of banking, finance, business, law, and community organizing. WWB provides the following products and services like savings ,micro finance, housing and home improvement loans ,individual lending, rural finance, advisory and technical assistance etc. The operations of WWB is changing on a massive scale since 1990 on the basis of the extensive research work conducted by WWB. For Example WWB has conducted extensive gender research on household dynamics and the ways in which women's roles and responsibilities impact spending, saving and investment decisions in low-income families.The research findings have led to modifications like simplified loan paperwork and borrowing requirements, which take into account women's lower literacy rates in many countries; changes in the design of MFI branches to accommodate women with small children and housing loans for which women must be placed on the property title for the household to receive the loan.

Banks for women in Islamic Countries: . In Pakistan, <u>First Women Bank</u> was founded in 1989 and strives for the economic empowerment of women. Saudi Arabian women, although not allowed to vote or drive, have the right to control their own finances, and Saudi banks have been devoting extensive resources to 'ladies banking' over the past few years, with separate entrances, distinct product offerings and a staff consisting entirely of women. In 2006 **Masrafy Bank in Bahrain** has been granted a licence to start the first Islamic investment bank for women, aimed at targeting high net worth women across the Gulf region.

Studies and statistics showed that women in the Gulf region have funds worth US$38 billion and there were no credible investment avenues to maximize returns from investing these funds in a professional manner. Masrafy was started hoping that it is capable to bridge this gap because and also the bank will have the strategic advantage of expertise in launching many projects in the region and also give them an opportunity to participate in all investment opportunities in the **region in line with their expectations.**

In Iran Melli is the countries first exclusive women bank where an exclusive female staff will serve the female customers. It was started with the hope that it will be easier for Iranian women to handle their own money in a country that routinely discriminates against them. Only last year women allowed to inherit their husbands land which requires banking services for them .

In Sri Lanka's Women's Bank's was started by Nandasiri Gamage in 1989 it is owned and operated by poor women in Srilanka. Acccording to the founder The Women's Bank has evolved from community savings groups into a very critical savings mechanism and lending institution that works well for low-income communities in Sri Lanka," he said. The interesting feature in case of Srilanka is Gamage a man could deeply understand the problems of poor women in banking. The success of the bank is attributed to the unique management structure, unique credit culture and auditing unit etc

Section II: Successful women banks in India

Mann Deshi Mahila Bank licenced Urban Cooperative Bank (UCB) was started in 1997 by Chetna Sinha in Satara in Maharastra with the objective of operating among the poorer sections of the population through micro finance projects. The Bank aims at providing client friendly products and services to the poor women with different flow of income. The bank is also involved in taking up Customer Friendly Innovations services like *B-School for Rural Women*: In December 2006,

Mann Deshi Foundation, in partnership with HSBC Bank, launched the Mann Deshi Udyogini, the business school for rural women. The school provides free business and financial training to poor rural women. One of the outstanding features in the business model of the Mann Deshi is that it uses microfinance and financial literacy as safety nets to increase disaster resilience among the rural poor women. An outcome of this holistic approach is that around 127000 women in the rural Maharashtra have been benefited from the services of Mann Deshi and started controlling the finances, conducting businesses, acquire property rights, and break caste barriers.

In May 1974, the Mahila SEWA Co-operative Bank was registered as a co-operative bank in Ahmedabad under the dual control of The Reserve Bank of India (RBI) and The State Government. The objective of the bank was to provide appropriate banking services to the informal sector women workers. Elaben Bhatt is the founder of SEWA bank and is run by qualified managers, accountable to the board.

Currently, the SEWA bank has eight branches in Gujarat and a network of bank Saathis in the communities that allows adequate decentralization and collection of deposit. Bank account holders are mainly consist of 80% urban and 20% rural self-employed women. These women are mainly engaged in three predominant activities - small trade workers (vendors), daily wage earners and home-based workers. The bank has a turnover of Rs 200 crore and net profit of Rs 2 crore. It has total of two lakh shareholders.

Important areas to focus for the BMB to achieve economic development of women
An institution run by women, for women will definitely make a difference if the focus is on the following areas

Selecting the Objective of the bank: The already existing women banks at national and international level are functioning with specific objectives .For the better prospects of the new bank government should identify the appropriate objective for the short term and long term success. Profit should not be the prime consideration.

Innovative Approach: The innovative approach is to be implemented and the new bank should not be another carbon copy of the public sector banks. The innovativeness should be in providing easy access to basic banking services of savings and credit to women, with a focus on financial inclusion. Credit Frame work for the projects should be designed in a transparent and accountable direction where in borrowers will involved in repayment as per the dead line date. This bank should not follow the footsteps of Regional rural banks which failed to achieve the basic objective of helping the farmers, artisans and agricultural labours in the villages and it became more urban oriented.

Bank Board Members and staff:
The success of the bank exclusively depends on top management consisting of bank board and staff member. Many women CEOs in Indian banks (public and private) made a tremendous effort for the success of their respective banks which has to be extensively

utilized by the new bank for the achievement of its goals. The banks board should preferable consists of eminent women with experience and knowledge of finance, banking, insurance, agriculture, rural and cottage industries and MSMES and they should be familiar the socio-economic milieu of the poor and weaker sections of the women .The services of women CEOs in Indian Banks should also be used as board members so that the new bank can start off with the highly experienced and eminent members.

Table I : Women CEO's in Indian Banks (2009-2012)

Private Sector Banks	Public Sector Banks
Chanda Kochhar	Shubalakshmi Panse
Managing Director &Chief Executive	Managing Director &Chief Executive
ICICI Bank	Allahabad Bank
Appointment :June,2009	Appointment :October ,2012
Shikha Sharma	VR Iyer
Managing Director &Chief Executive	Managing Director &Chief Executive
Axis Bank	Bank OF India
Appointment :May,2009	Appointment :November ,2012
Naina Lal Kidwai	Arundhati Bhattacharya
Country head of HSBC India	Chairman and managing director
	State Bank of India ,2013
	Usha Ananthasubramanian,
	Chairperson and managing director of Bharatiya Mahila Bank

The female employees in the commercial banks can be requested to extend their support and service for the success of the new institution. To run the bank effectively it is essential to have competent, knowledgeable and competent women personal.

As on 31 March 2011, the total employee strength of all scheduled commercial banks in the country is 10,50,885 of which females constitute 1,86,784, or just 17.77% of the total employees. Regional rural banks (RRBs) are having the lowest percentage of female employees, mainly because of low availability of qualified women in rural areas. The new bank should identify the qualified female employees who ready to serve in the rural areas by offering good number of benefits to the existing bank employees.

Table II: Position of employees of all commercial banks as on 31 March 2011

Name of the Bank	Total employees	Female employees	percentage of females
State Bank Group	3,00.628	57,544	19.14
Nationalized banks	4,75.060	78,759	16.58
Private sector banks	1,71,071	38.297	22.39
Regional rural banks	79,886	4,481	5.61
Foreign banks	24,240	7,703	31.78
Total:	10,50,885	1,86,784	17.77

Source: Basic Statistical Returns of SCBs in India, March 2011 (RBI website)

Role Model: The bank being the first of its kind in India Bank should focus on improving financial literacy apart from banking services. The bank should provide customised services according to the needs and demands of the customers.

The customer relationship focal point should be on upgrading the skills of literate women customers by providing entrepreneurial training which includes covering the basics of general, financial and marketing management. Prominence should be given to the basic services of deposit scheme credit, payments and remittances. The bank can handle the income generating agency functions by attracting customers on behalf of the government ,insurance companies and mutual funds for payments and collections. The bank can be role model once all the above services are taken care with utmost prominence and significance.

Branches: If financial inclusion is the basic objective than atleast 50 percent of the branches should be in rural areas. Keeping in view the profile of the customers the branches should be located in residential areas.

Technology: From the day of inception bank should have latest technology ,relevant for financial inclusion. It should also have core banking, smart and biometric cards and **mobile banking.**

Services: Banks should look at all aspects of their customer segment and be prepared to advance diverse kinds of loans for a variety of requirements. Logically, neither the lawyer nor the court needs to be used for recovery of loans.

Section III: Respondents opinion on Mahila bank

Primary data survey report about Mahila Bank : Opinion was collected from fifty self help groups presidents. The summary of respondents opinion on Bharatiya Mahila bank is presented below. Respondents were of the opinion that more focus should be on providing low interest rates for self help groups. Unlike the other public sector banks respondents are expecting customer friendly environment in the bank. To start bank branches in the mandals where number of self help groups are operating. To start incubation centers for self help groups in important branches were there is good scope for starting self help groups.

Bank should concentrate on creating awareness and starting self help groups as a result economic independence and women empowerment can be further strengthened. Self help groups depend on the micro finance facility provide by the banks and financial institutions. The purpose of starting Bharatiya Mahila bank will be fulfilled if the bank concentrates on providing loans to micro, medium and small entrepreneurs on one side and on the other side micro finance loans to self help groups. When women CEO'S of leading private and public sector banks are successfully managed then their services can be utilized to make Bharatiya Mahila Bank as number one bank for women empowerment. The success stories of many self help groups will be a motivating factor for banks to provide loans to women in which loan recovery is highly appreciable. Bank should design a plan to provide loans which is collateral free because women do not generally have property on their own names to get loans from banks.

Conclusion: The relationship between the Bank and borrower is not confined to one transaction. It is a continued relationship of mutual trust. So to make the Mahila Bank more powerful government should initiate steps to encourage more number of women entrepreneurs in urban and rural areas. The services of women CE's from public and private banks can be successfully utilized by appointing them as special invitees.

Is gender-segregated banking the way forward, in all parts of the world? The question has to be answered by analyzing the actual facts and research survey results by well known organizations. Banks should provide micro finance encouragement and support to women entrepreneurs which are highly desirable. The bank should be role model for other banks and this can be achieved by involving the well known women CEO's from public and private banks.

References:

1. Vivek Kumar Tripathi, Microfinance -Evolution, And Microfinance-Growth, Of India,International Journal of Development Research, ISSN:2230-9926, May,2014.

2. Sibghatullah Nasir, Microfinance in India: Contemporary Issues and Challenges, Middle-East Journal of Scientific Research 15 (2): 191-199, 2013,ISSN 1990-9233, IDOSI Publications, 2013.

3.Gupta, M.S. 2008, Micro finance through SHGs – An Emerging Horizon for Rural Development, Indian Journal of Commerce, Vol. 61, No.3, July-Sept.

4.Anil K Khandelwal, "Microfinance Development Strategy for India", Economic and Political Weekly, March 31, 2007.

5.David Raju G, Women in Indian Banking Industry – Their Role in Growth of the Sector, Global Journal for research analysis,2014.

6.Kanwar,G. Kartikeya, R., Kapoor,R and Rajat K. B 2008, Micro finance in Indian Scenario – A study on the existing models, Indian Journal of Commerce, Vol. 61, No. 2, April-June.

7. Anil K Khandelwal, "Microfinance Development Strategy for India", Economic and Political Weekly, March 31, 2007.

8. Basic Statistical Returns of SCBs in India, March 2011 (RBI website)

CHAPTER-12

Micro Finance - The New Found Value in Women Through Self-help Groups.

* Prof. P.Sheela

**Dr. Rajeshwari Panigarhi

Abstract

Access to microfinance through self- help group has been identified as an important means to overcome poverty and has contributed much towards empowerment of women in particular and the society at large. Microfinance institutions have proved that lending to women is much emphasized that women are more reliable and providing them with the credit facilities raises the likelihood of timely payment. Poverty reduction also emphasizes on the well being of their family both economically as well as psychologically. The objective of this research is i) To analyze the value women were able to generate economically, psychologically and socially from being a part in this programme. ii) To analyze the possibilities of freedom women had derived from out of this programme iii) To understand how women were able to effectively utilize the financial benefits iv) To understand the involvement of women in making the decision on taking loan v) To offer suggestions for their better performances in the future. This research was focused in the rural areas of Visakhapatnam districts, covering sixteen groups who are actively participating in the microfinance finance programme and two groups who had discontinued from the programme. Both primary and secondary data was used in this research. The method used for data collection was through semi- structured interviews with focus group discussion (FGDs), informal conversations and observations were noted while interacting with the respondents. The outcome of the study had shown that there was a gradual increase in the all the three dimensions such as their economic, social and psychological status. The members in this study have expressed their deep satisfaction over the interaction with the other members within the group and with the officials at the microfinance institution. They have strongly considered the space provided to them through this programme is safe and they could share and learn better from each other's experiences, which in turn contributed a lot in developing their self confidence. The monitoring system of both the microfinance institutions as well as the leaders of the group focused on the client, repayment rates and loan disbursement was effective but very little focus was made on their social monitoring indicators, which would limit the process of empowerment in women. The members have strongly expressed had the microfinance institutions extend better training opportunities to both the team leaders as well as to all the member, would definitely help them in further enhancing their skills.

* Prof. P.Sheela., Professor, Dept of Fiance. GITAM Institute of Mnagement- GITAM University.
** Dr.Rajeshwari Panigrahi, Associate Professor, Dept of Marketing, GITAM Institute of Mnagement- GITAM University

Introduction

Access to microfinance through self- help group has been identified as an important means to overcome poverty and has contributed much towards empowerment of women in particular and the society at large. Micro finance is a means initiated by the government of India to help the poor in getting financial support from conventional formal financial institutions. It provides opportunities to the unbankables to establish enterprises and strengthen their financial position within the reach of millions of people who are poor to be served by the regular banks. Gert van Maanen, Microcredit: Sound Business or Development Instrument, Oikocredit, 2004 have emphasized that banks are for the people with money, but not for people without. Based on the premise that poor has the skills but those are unrealized or underutilized. So the ultimate goal of microfinance is to provide the poor an opportunity to become self-sufficient by encouraging them to save for their future, borrow for their well being and protecting them from the risk in the form of insurance.

Generally majority of the beneficiaries through this programme are women, today they are contributing equally to the family income and became productive members of the economy. This effort by women helps the family to experience an increase in the consumption pattern, standard of living and enhancing the education standard of the family. In such a situation microfinance is considered as an effective tool to alleviate poverty and empower the women. Women are yet to open up and participate actively in the economic activity. Microfinance will provide women the financial support to start their entrepreneurial initiatives which in turn provides them the opportunities to participate in the economies economic activities. Such participation would definitely enable women to develop the confidence on their abilities, improves their status and make them more effective in their decision making process.

Most of the microfinance institutions across the globe have been focusing on women. Research across have proved that women beneficiaries of microfinance programme are of small credit risk, they are very prompt in repaying their loans and they efforts are always structured towards the families well being. In other words microfinance programme are giving more opportunities to women in the socioeconomic ways and is reducing the gender differences.

Accordingly to a recent report of the world bank confirms that economies that discriminate gender pays the cost of high rate of poverty, low economic growth, lower purchasing power, poor governance and a lower living standards for all people. Women are more in unemployment rate and they constitute the bulk of those who need financial support. Providing microcredit to women would definitely generate multiple benefits for the microfinance institutional activities   for generations together.

This paper is focused to study the extent to which the goals of empowerment approach initiated by the microfinance institutions are being realized and if so, to what extend the access to microfinance programme enabled the participants translate opportunities into their economical, psychological and social relationships. In good olden days women were restricted to take part in any social or economic activities. This situation was even worse in the rural areas. Today this situation is even better but only to a certain extend. Today more women are given the opportunities to participate in income generating activities. This was because microfinance institutions are coming forward in providing microfinance to the deprived poor women through the self help group concept. The primary objective of microfinance is to empower. This gained the attention of the researcher to study the influence of microfinance programme on women and investigate if it created a new found value economically, socially and psychologically in them after joining the programme.

Objective of the research is as follows

i) To analyze the value women were able to generate economically, psychologically and socially
   by associating in this programme.
ii) To analyze the possibilities of freedom women had derived from out of this programme
iii) To understand how women were able to effectively utilize the financial benefits
iv) To understand the involvement of women in their day to day decisions and
v) To offer suggestions for their better performances in the future.

Research Methodology

Sources for data: This research was focused in the rural areas of Visakhapatnam districts, covering sixteen groups who are actively participating in the microfinance finance programme and two groups who had discontinued from the programme. Both primary and secondary data was used in this research.

Sampling method: cluster and area sampling was used. Since the number of groups was large, the groups were randomly selected. The data collected was analyzed and interpreted by using Simple correlation coefficient, paired T test, cross tabulation and percentage. A semi-structured interview was prepared with focus group discussion (FGDs), informal conversations and observations were made while the research was being carried out.

II. Review of Literature

There exists a body of literature on the impact of microfinance on women. A great deal of literature focuses on the influence and impact of microfinance and its importance, but this study does not delve in those areas, rather than focus on the impact of the economic, psychological and social aspects which would enhance the standard of living not only the members but their family.

Good many studies have argued that microfinance can be used as an effective tool to fight poverty (e.g. Hulme & Mosley, 1996, Latifee, 1997), few are less optimistic about the potential impact of microfinance sometimes has (Rogaly, 1996). This section in turn looks at each areas where impact as been identified. A key objective of many microfinance interventions is to empower women. (Mosedale 2003, p.1) states that if we want to see people empowered it means we currently see them as being disempowered.

The founder of Grameen Bank (Muhammud Yunus) has quoted that microfinance is a strong vehicle in reducing poverty though the virtuous cycle comprising: low income, low credit and low investment to more income, more credit opportunity and more investment (Hulme & Mosley, 1996). Good number studies, have found that well designed lending programmes can improve the lives of the poor above the official poverty line (Hulme & Mosley, 1996, Mosley, 2001). Several studies have found evidence that impact of loan on the borrowers income is directly related to the level of income, with the 'middle' and 'upper' poor are more likely to benefit than the 'core' poor (ibid.).

(Littlefield, Murduch and Hashemi ,2003, p.4) state that access to MFIs can empower women to become more confident, more assertive, more likely to take part in family and community decisions and better able to confront gender inequities.

Few studies have found evidence of diversification of income sources among poor clients (Mosley, 1996), while others have found that clients tend to specialize in more productive activities (Montgomery et al., 1996). One theory posits that poorer clients seek to diversify in order to protect their income while clients who are better off are better able to assume the risks associated with specialization (Sebstad & Chen, 1996).

Studies have found evidence of increased incomes leading to asset accumulation among program participants (Sebstad & Chen, 1996). In a study conducted in Bangladesh it was found that successive loans led to a build-up of assets over time, and that the structure of assets tends to favour productive assets, suggesting an emphasis among borrowers on securing income (Montgomery et al.,1996).

Many research has been carried out focusing on the empowerment related to the process internal change (Mayoux 1998) and capacity building of women and right to make decision (Kabeer 2001). Micro finance is being promoted as an entry point in context of a wider strategy for women's economic power and sociopolitical empowerment (Kessey2001).(Ranjula bali swaina and Fan Yang Wallentin 2009) their strongly indicate that SHG members are empowered by participating in the micro finance programme in the sense they have a greater propensity to resist existing gender and cultural norms that restricts there ability to develop and make decision.

(M.Sangeetha.2013) Microfinance is playing a vital role in the success of the SHGs: particularly in the entry of rural women into the micro enterprises will be encouraged and aggravated.(S.Sarumathi and Dr.K.Mohan. 2011) micro finance has bought economical, psychological and social impact on women participants through SHG. (Nobel Laureate Amartaya Sen. 1993) in their research had emphasized that the freedom to lead different types of life is reflected in the
person's capability .The capability of a person depends on a variety of factors, including personal characteristics and social arrangements.

(Malhotra 2002) through their research developed the most commonly used dimensions of women's empowerment, drawing from the frameworks developed by various authors in different fields of social sciences. These frameworks suggest that women's empowerment needs to occur along multiple dimensions including: economic, socio-cultural, familial/interpersonal, legal, political, and psychological. According to (Krishna 2003) empowerment means increasing the capacity of individuals or groups to make effective development and life choices and to transform these choices into desired actions and outcomes. It is by nature a process and/or outcome.

(Ranjula Bali Swain ,2007) through their research concluded many strides have been made in the right direction and women are in the process of empowering themselves and microfinance institutions that provide support in financial services and specialized training, have a greater ability to make a positive impact on women empowerment.

(Susy Cheston, Lisa Kuhn) in their research concluded Microfinance has the potential to have a powerful impact on women's empowerment.(Dr. K. Mohan) found that microfinance brought psychological and social empowerment than economic empowerment. Impact of micro finance is appreciable bringing confidence, courage, skill development and empowerment. (Mr. Nikhil) considered that the microcredit movement has proved that it is possible to deliver financial services to poor people living in rural areas at a large scale, free from any reliance on subsidies.

(Otero.1999) illustrates the various ways in which "microfinance, at its core combats poverty. Her research states that microfinance creates access to productive capital for the poor, which together with human capital, addressed through education and training, and social capital, achieved through local organisation building, enables people to move out of poverty.

(Simanowitz, 2001).Emphasis that impact assessment of microfinance interventions is necessary, not just to demonstrate to donors that their interventions are having a positive impact, but to allow for learning within MFIs so that they can improve their services and the impact of their projects

(Wright,1999) argues that by increasing the income of the poor, MFIs are not necessarily reducing poverty. It depends what the poor do with this money. The focus needs to be on helping the poor to "sustain a specified level of well-being. (Hulme and Mosley 1996) in a comprehensive study on the use of microfinance to combat poverty, argue that well-designed programmes can improve the incomes of the poor and can move them out of poverty.

(Hulme and Mosley .1996) show that when loans are associated with an increase in assets, when
borrowers are encouraged to invest in low-risk income generating activities and when the very poor are encouraged to save; the vulnerability of the very poor is reduced and their poverty situation improves.

We have seen that poverty and livelihood security consist of economic and social conditions, therefore, when analyzing the impact of microfinance, social impact must be assessed.(Kabeer 2003). Microfinance interventions have also been shown to have a positive impact on the education of clients' Children (Littlefield, Murduch and Hashemi 2003).

(Robinson,2001) in a study of 16 different MFIs from all over the world shows that having access to microfinance services has led to an enhancement in the quality of life of clients, an increase in their self-confidence, and has helped them to diversify their livelihood security strategies and thereby increase their income.

Data Analysis

Table 1: Brief Profile of the members in the Self- help groups

Sr. No	Particulars	% (standard deviation)
1	Average age of the members (Yrs)	28.04 (10.64)
2	Married	92
3	illiterate	58
4	Edication upto 7th standard	28
5	Education upto 10th Standard	14
6	Members belonging to the lower social class	56
7	Average number of family members	5.2 (1.62)
8	Average number of earners in the family	2.60 (0.87)
9	Average family income	Rs. 6800.50 (4864.58)
10	Average number of years of association with the group	4.98 (2.91)

(Figure in the brackets shows the standard deviation)

The socio- economic profile shows that majority of the members come from the lower social class group. The study clearly states that the beneficiaries of the programme belong to the lower to the lower income group. More than half of the respondents are illiterates and there is very little scope for them to be employed. The number of years of association with the group varies from two to five or seven years. The income levels of the family members ranges between Rs. 4005 to Rs.8000 per month.

Table 2. **Expressing the feeling and opinions of the participants freely**

Sl.No	Expressing their feeling and opinions freely by the participants in the programme			Expressing their feeling and opinions freely by the non-participants		
	Options	frequency	Per cent	Options	frequency	Per cent
1	Yes	156	97.5	Yes	7	35
2	No	4	2.5	No	13	65
	Total	160	100	Total	20	100

156(97.5%) participants out of 160 who are the members of the self help group have expressed that they have developed confidence and is taking active participation in their day to day decision regarding family matters and is able to initiate discussions at the group level activities and they feel that there opinions are being considered. When compared to the group who left the programme mid way, these members have expressed that they still depend upon their spouses for decisions as far as there family matters are concerned and they hardly find scope to express their opinions.

Table 3. **Moving Independently**

Moving Independently						
Participants				Non- participants		
Sl.No	Options	Frequency	Per cent	Options	frequency	Per cent
1	Yes	158	98.75	Yes	3	35
2	No	2	1.25	No	17	85
	Total	160	100	**Total**	20	100

158(98.75%) participating members have expressed that they could carry out both their family as well as their group related matters such as paying their current bills, making their monthly payments at the bank, visiting government offices for either payment or to represent matters of their colony concerns, visiting political offices for representing the neighbors problems and requesting for schemes for their development. They accompany their children's school to enquire their educational performance etc. where as 85 per cent of the non participants have expressed that they depend on others for any requirements.

Table 4. **The purpose of taking the Loan**.

The purpose of taking the Loan			
Sl.No	Purpose of loan	Frequency	Percent
1	House hold Requirements	35	21.8
2	To start a business	52	32.5
3	To expand the existing one	37	23.1
4	Health purpose	28	17.5
5	Easily available	8	5
	Total	160	100

More than 50 per cent of the respondents have taken loan for their business purpose. This numbers speak the right direction into which this programme is spear heading. More over the outcome of this is contributing toward the economic well being of the members and their family. This also tells the way women are being empowered in taking decisions. The second reason for taking loan was towards their household requirements; it was found that women were able to renovate their house which was given through them by the government. This also indicates their improvement in the standard of living. 5 percent of the respondents had expressed that they took loan since it is easily available and they used the amount to repay the loans they have taken from the money lenders who was charging them a high rate of interest.

Table 6. Correlation between reduce in poverty and improvement of standard of living.

Variables		Reduce in poverty level	Improvement in the standard of living
Reduce in poverty level	Pearson Correlation	1	.357**
	Sig. (2-tailed)		.000
	N	160	160
Improvement in standard of living	Pearson Correlation	.357**	1
	Sig. (2-tailed)	.000	
	N	160	160

Table 6 shows a positive correlation between reduce in the poverty level and in improvement of the standard of living. Reduction in poverty level might not lead to the increase in the income at this point of time due to the rising prices experienced.

PAIRED t- TEST

Ho: there is no difference in the mean income of the respondents before and after joining the group.

Table 7.Paired t test table

Income	Mean	N	Standard Deviation	Std. Error Mean
Income of the respondents before joining the group	1050	160	740.37	55.301
Income after joining the group	1623.74	160	901.426	72.364

Table 7.1

Mean	SD	Std. Error Mean	t	df	sig. value
-573.74	720.467	53.425	-9.742	160	.000

The probability value is 0.000 ($p < 0.01$). We reject the null hypothesis and conclude the mean salary after joining the group is significantly greater than the mean salary before joining the group. This statistics clearly states that the microfinance has significantly increased the income of the members.

Table 8 . Cross tabulation of psychological variables with different age groups between the respondents from participant and non participant groups.

		Age of the respondents in the participating Group					Age of the respondents in the non- participant group				
		20-30		30-40		Total	20-30		30-40		Total
		Yes	No	Yes	No		Yes	No	Yes	No	
V A R I A B L E S	Self Confidence	103	2	49	6	160	5	14	4	2	20
	Improvement in courage	98	7	51	4	160	3	9	3	3	20
	Skill improvement	103	2	52	3	160	0	14	1	5	20
	Development in literacy levels	67	38	34	21	160	2	12	1	5	20
	Awareness of children's educational requirements	73	32	42	13	160	3	11	2	4	20
	Awareness of issues related to the environment	86	19	43	12	160	2	12	1	5	20
	Unity and peace at home	102	3	53	2	160	3	11	0	6	20
	Respect in the family and society	104	1	52	3	160	2	12	1	5	20

It is evident from table 8 that microfinance has bought tremendous psychological well being among the members of the self help group. It is observed and the data did prove that majority of the members in the programme fall in the age group 20-30 years and the outcome of the micro finance progamme had a great impact on them psychologically, economically and socially. They are proud to express that they hold a special identity both within their family as well as in the society. Being young in age proves that there is an ample opportunity for these members in the programme to grow economically and take a lead in motivating many more young members to join the programme in the near future.

Observations and finding

Micro finance has proved as a important vehicles for the empowerment of women and a means for more effective participation in the self help group programme. The members of the self help group had acknowledged the importance of the space that the programme had provided to them to learn from each other and their unity both within the family as well as in the group did enhance their efficiency. The respondents did express how their informal gathering had enhanced their confidence to know things they have never heard before from the officials either at the bank or in government offices. They have expressed the informal gathering created a kind of competitive environment either on the repayment front or in their savings of their earning. Their were happy to share their experience with the other members of the group or better interact with the bank officials which consequently gained self confidence and courage from each other, they also expressed that they were in a position to motivate and attract new members. At times they were advised by their leaders to convene meeting for the non members mentioning the advantages they could derive from out of the programme.

When enquired from their spouses, they expressed very positive about the advantages their wife derived and had no objection to them. Forming and maintaining group, however, is not that easy a task. Often there are times when some members delay in making their payment on time, which then leads to tension among the group. At times these problems are intensified by the pressure of financial sustainability, which has encouraged the leader to explore ways to facilitate timely repayment and strengthen the group dynamics.

The research found out that there was an expansion in the range and location of women activities and micro finance programme had enhances the scope of the women activities beyond the house hold domain and in their occupations. Men still continue to work outside the home while women engage in activities like vegetables, clothes sales at home, livestock rising, Kirana stores, pickles and grocery sales at their respective houses.

The most important changes witnessed by women after the access to microfinance are an increase in their sense of self worth. Their contribution toward the welfare of the family had given them a space of monetary value which has resulted in them a sense of value amidst the family members. In few cases the monetary benefits derived from out of the micro finance programme is contributed towards their husbands already existing business. The research also paved way in finding out women's contribution to improve their families economic well being, which is a source of increasing the respect they have been receiving, from both the family and from others in their community more widely. Few of them have expressed over their discussion that they are quoted as smart women either by their spouse, their in-laws or by there neighbors. Few have expressed that other women in their community frequently refer them as one who has bought a major change in their family, considering them has the most effective decision maker in the family, more control over money and full authority in the house. Such statement made by the other women, makes them feel highly respected in the community.

Majority of the respondents had expressed that participating in the microfinance programme gave them a lot of weight in decision making which is an important outcome of empowerment. Majority of them over the discussion had expressed that they had a choice over how many children they preferred to have, decisions on the families welfare initiatives, the children's education, health concern, saving and control over the family earned money are all the assertive in voicing their opinions.

Women members regarded their association with the self help group articulated their desire to attend groups where they can collectively learn and develop skill and is in a position to share those skills with others. Majority of the respondents expressed that their awareness about environment improved after taking part in micro finance programs actively. Maximum number of respondents accepted that microfinance has brought economic development directly and indirectly in them and created a sense of happiness and peace in the family.

Members have expressed their literacy is not the only thing that has changed these women's lives. New-found numeracy skills have empowered members to better manage their money. More than 95 per cent have expressed that they have become economically and socially empowered after joining the SHG. Majority of the respondents have reported that they have experienced a reduction in the poverty level specially those members who have received financial benefits more than three times.

The worrying part was the members who withdrew from out of the programme had expressed the following are the reasons for backing out of the programme i) few of them expressed that men started utilizing the money earned by them to drink more and neglected the family, ii) so repayment of the loan derived was an add-on stress to the women. iii)Few of them had expressed that participation in the programme added stress and health problems and more over they felt that they could not spare time over meetings, iv) more over their were put on severe strains on women's existing networks & repayment became a problem v) above all debt lead them to severe impoverishment, abandonment and put serious strains on networks with other women.

Conclusion

To conclude the study has clearly states that the self help group members are doing pretty well with the support of the microfinance programme. The programme did positively influence on the psychological and social aspects of the members and empowering them economically. The Impact of micro finance is appreciable in bringing confidence, courage, skill development and in taking prompt decision not only in their incentives but also in the welfare of their family members specially in the development of their children's career. The confidence gained by members is enabling them to move freely and participating in various social welfare activities both with the group and the society with good cooperation. Over the interaction with the members it was understood that the monitoring system of both the microfinance institutions as well as the leaders of the group focused on the clients, repayment rates and loan disbursement which was effective but very little focus was made on their social monitoring indicators, which would limit the process of empowerment in women. While interacting with the members it was noticed that majority of the members are unaware about the training needs and were on the opinion that they are not eligible for such an opportunity due to their poor literacy level. When they were being informed about the benefits of training outcomes, the members have strongly expressed for such an exposure. So there is every need for microfinance institutions to extend better training opportunities to both the team leaders as well as to all the members, which would definitely help them in further enhancing their skills. All they need is a way to develop their skills and talents by participating in various training programs.

References

Ackerley, B. (1995). Testing the Tools of Development: Credit Programmes , Loan Involvement and Women's Empowerment. World Development, 26(3), 56-68.

Anderson, C. L., L. Locker, et al. (2002). "Microcredit, social capital, and common pool resources." World Development 30(1): 95-105.

Bai, Chengyu & Ge Youli, (1997). 'Poverty Alleviation, Microfinance & Sustainable Development - An Introduction to UNDP's Integrated Poverty Alleviation Projects in China', In: Rural Microfinance in China, edited by Du. X, Liu W., Zhang B. & Sun R., pp. 161-166, Beijing: China Economics Publishing House.

Bhatt, N. (1997). "Microenterprise development and the entrepreneurial poor: including the excluded?" Public Administration and Development 17(4): 371-386.
Cheston, S. and L. Kuhn. (2002). "Empowering women through microfinance." Draft 7/8/02, sponsored by UNIFEM.

Cheng, Enjiang, (1997). 'Credit for Poverty Alleviation and Links with Formal and Informal Financial Institutions in China - A preliminary Study of Results from Surveys of Five Provinces in China', In: Rural Microfinance in China, edited by Du. X., Liu W., Zhang B. & Sun R., pp. 320-331, Beijing: China Economics Publishing House.

Chowdhury, A. & Abbas Bhuiya, (2002). 'The Wider Impacts of BRAC Poverty Alleviation Programme,' Imp-Act Programme Document No. 15, pp. 13-14.

Egger, P. (1986). "Banking for the Rural Poor - Lessons from Some Innovative Savings and Credit Schemes." International Labour Review 125(4): 447-462.

Greeley, M. (2003). "Poverty reduction and microfinance - Assessing performance." Ids Bulletin-Institute of Development Studies 34(4): 10

Fisher, Thomas and M.S. Sriram ed., 2002, Beyond Micro-credit: Putting Development Back into Microfinance, New Delhi: Vistaar Publications; Oxford: Oxfam.

Kabeer, Nailer, (2002). 'Micro-finance, Wider Impacts and Social Change: Processes and Outcomes', in Imp-Act Programme Document No. 15, pp. 8-10.

S. P. Gupta (2009) -"Statistical methods", Thirty eight revised Editions, Sultan Chand & Sons Publishers,
New Delhi.

C.R Kothari (2007) - Research Methodology Methods & Techniques, Second Edition, New age International
publishers, New Delhi.

Manjula Bolthajjira Chengappa. "Micro-Finance and Women Empowerment: Role of Nongovernment Organizations".

Matin, I. and D. Hulme (2003). "Programs for the poorest: Learning from the IGVGD program in Bangladesh." World Development 31(3): 647-665.

Nanda, Priya, (1999). 'Women's participation in rural credit programmes in Bangladesh and their
demand for formal health care: is there a positive impact?', Health Economy, Vol. 8, No. 5, pp.
415-428.

K. Rajendran and R.P. Raya (2010) Impact of Micro Finance - An empirical Study on the Attitude of SHG
Leaders in Vellore District (Tamil Nadu, India). 'Global Journal of Finance and Management'- ISSN 0975 -6477 Volume 2, Number 1, pp. 59-68,

Khandker, S. R. (2005). "Microfinance and poverty: Evidence using panel data from Bangladesh." World Bank Economic Review 19(2): 263-286.

Quinones, B. R. and H. D. Seibel (2000). "Social capital in microfinance: Case studies in the Philippines." Policy Sciences 33(3-4): 421-433.

Ranjula Bali Swaina and Fan Yang Wallentin (September 2009) Does microfinance empower womenEvidence from self-help groups in India, 'International Review of Applied Economics' Vol. 23, No. 5, , 541

Rankin, K. N. (2002). "Social capital, microfinance, and the politics of development." Feminist Economics 8(1): 1-24.

Servon, L. J. and T. Bates (1998). "Microenterprise as an exit route from poverty: Recommendations for programs and policy makers." Journal of Urban Affairs 20(4): 419-441.

Shaw, J. (2004). "Microenterprise occupation and poverty reduction in microfinance programs: Evidence from Sri Lanka." World Development 32(7): 1247-1264.

Sharif, N. R. (2004). "Microcredit programs and women's decision-making status: Further evidence from Bangladesh." Canadian Journal of Development Studies-Revue Canadienne D Etudes Du Developpement 25(3): 465-480.

S.Sarumathi and Dr.K.Mohan, "Role of Micro Finance in Women's Empowerment", Journal of Managementand Science, Vol. 1, No.1, Sep 2011, pp. 1-10.

Chapter-13
A Review of the Recent Developments in Micro Finance Literature

*Rajeshwari Panigrahi
**P.Sheela

Abstract

Purpose-Micro finance is India can trace its origins back to the early 1970s when the self employed Women's association SEWA of the state of Gujarat formed an urban cooperative bank, called Shri Ahila SEWA Sehkari Bank with the objective of providing banking services to poor women employed in the unorganised sector since then there has been continuous effort both from the government and non government sector taking initiatives to provide thrift finance to rural people. This subject has also gained lots of research interest thus, this study in intended to understand and explore the various dimension of search done in this area.

Design and Methodology -This study is a review of the studies taken place in the area of Microfinance to understand various dimensions of Micro-finance which have been researched and understand the trends of research undertaken in this area.

Introduction

Microfinance in India can trace its origins back to the early 1970s when the Self Employed Women's Association ("SEWA") of the state of Gujarat formed an urban cooperative bank, called the Shri Mahila SEWA Sahakari Bank, with the objective of providing banking services to poor women employed in the unorganised sector in Ahmedabad City, Gujarat. In 1980s this concept has evolved around SHGs (Self Help Groups), informal bodies that would provide the clients the much needed savings and credit facilities. This sector has grown significantly over the years and become a multi Billion dollar Industry with bodies such as the Small Industries Development Bank of India and the National Bank for Agriculture and Rural Development devoting significant financial resources to microfinance. Today, the top five private sectors MFIs reach more than 20 million clients in nearly every state in India and many Indian MFIs have been recognized as global leaders in the industry.

Market and Government both failed to provide saving and credit facility to rural people and this failure provided an opportunity for Microfinance Institutions which aimed to meet the small savings and credit requirements enabling them to rise their income levels and improve standards of living.

Micro Finance may be defined as "provision of thrift, the wide network of the organized banking system which provides credit and other financial services and products to rural areas. According to United Nations microfinance institutions can be broadly defined as provider of small scale financial services such as savings credit and other financial services to poor and low income people. The term "microfinance institution" now refers to microfinance institutions (MFIs) in India and finally a wide range of organizations dedicated to providing these services and includes NGOs, credit unions co-operatives, private commercial banks, NBFCs and parts of State-owned banks.

*Associate Professor GITAM Institute of Management GITAM University
** Professor, GITAM Institute of Management GITAM University

According to estimates provided by Reserve Bank of India there are over 450 million "unbanked people" (People who have no access to formal financial services) and most of these stay in rural areas. This group largely depends on informal providers of finance, Money lenders and family sources. Access to finance is essential for enabling individuals and communities to come out of the vicious circle of poverty and money lenders charge huge amount of interest and are the root cause for increasing Poverty in rural areas. Therefore, Indian Government and RBI have a policy of financial inclusion as a policy initiative. Government has directed Indian banks to lend money to priority sectors and rural development is termed as priority according to government regulations. Banks have welcomed this Policy because until recently banks used to lend to MFIs and they woud lend funds to poor women across rural India MFIs used to charge 12-13% rate of interest and benefitted from 100% repayment rates now by lending to MFIs banks have been able to meet the priority sector lending requirements with what historically amounted to risk free and profitable.

Need and Objective of the study-Microfinance is a niche area which provides lot of scope for research this study intends to examine the amount and dimensions of research done in this area and identify future opportunities and intends to explore the research carried out in this area.

Design and Methodology -This study is a review of the research done in the area of Microfinance to understand various dimensions of Micro-finance which have been researched and understand the trends of research undertaken in this area.

Studies and Dimensions in Microfinance

"**Microfinance regulation influence on small Firms' financing in Tanzania**" a study Published in *Journal of financial regulation and compliance* (2003) authors Andrew Satta T through case study of a Microfinance industry in Tanzania argued that regulating microfinance operations and activities is likely to strengthen institutions (MFIs) Financial stability and in turn could provide an important source of finance to small firms. The paper aimed at moving the microfinance regulation debate forward by generating a number of relevant inputs towards the formulation of a regulatory framework.

"**Financial Services for the Poor: Assessing Microfinance Institutions**" Published in the Journal *"Managerial Finance"* (2004) authors Koveos P and Randhava J studied the framework within which microfinance institutions (MFIs Deliver their service and provide an assessment of their operations and financial management. Authors examined the institutions because of their current importance to a special group of consumers, primarily poor and disenfranchised in the developing world and their future promise as an economic development solution the manner of assessment of these institution is different from the other banks and financial institutions because of their unique objective and their efficiency is hence judged by economic (or Financial) dimension as well as the social dimension. It was found that the MFIs have demonstrated considerable ingenuousness and innovation and their credit portfolios outrank the best managed portfolios at large multinational banks, group surveillance and incentive –compatibility between lenders and borrowers are instructive ,there is considerable heterogeneity among MFIs, but on the question of sustainability there is broad consensus, the advantages for the beneficiaries are manifold , economies of scale and scope as the institution's grow in size, the ability to tap private funds as their long-term profitability becomes evident, the huge unfulfilled demand for funds.

Megicks Phillp etal, *"Published in international Journal of Bank Marketing*(2005) **"studied "Enhancing Micro finance outreach through market oriented new service development in Indian regional rural bank"** measured effectiveness on Indian microfinance institutions in achieving their economic and social goals have largely identified have largely identified only limited success. Critics of Indian regional rural bank have argued that a market approach to the new service development is responsible for their inadequate performance which the banks and financial institutions do not bring in anything new in terms of a service product to address the financial requirement of this section of the population. Authors found that the behaviour of managers along with institutional characteristics are identified as influences on market orientation, service innovation, customer satisfaction and outreach performance within RRBs. Thus, the study indicates the importance of designing the right type of product for the people in the rural area who look for such small investments and credits.

"Role of Microfinance in disaster mitigation" a study intended to examine the suitability of using microfinance for natural disaster risk reduction at the household and community level, and also of delivering it in the wake of a natural disaster published in the journal *"Disaster Prevention and management"* (2005) authors Anand Kumar T.S and Newport Jayant K found that microfinance should be recognized as one of a series of measures within a disaster risk management strategy. Along with eco-friendly farming it can help overcome poverty in developing countries.

Jones Linda etal., in their study **"The Double X factor: Harnessing Female Human Capital For Economic Growth"** published in *International Journal of Emerging Markets* (2006) Presents   MEDA(Mennonite Economic Development Associates) programs in small enterprise development value chain and microfinance projects to illustrate that the human capital of even hard to reach women can be harnessed for a community's and even a nation's economic growth .The authors found that Working with disadvantaged populations that have been relegated to the bottom of the socio-economic heap has challenges. Program design must overcome a host of constraints including illiteracy and innumeracy, lack of technical and business skills, and the psycho-social consequences of Generations of disenfranchisement. Yet, case after case has proven that these seemingly intractable obstacles diminish with appropriate project interventions.

"An Egyptian case study: Financial services for young people who work" Published in *International Journal of Emerging Market*(2006)Authors Caroline Hossein etal examined the innovativeness of the methods of loans disbursement intended to help micro-finance institutions diversify their portfolios and reach a young and viable market. The study finds that the young people market has been rarely researched in the MF sector. Children and youth like many other groups face a host of issues especially unemployed and poor ones.

"The Uganda rural farmers Scheme: Women's accessibility to Agricultural credit" A study published in Agricultural Finance Review fall (2006) Binuma M.Abaru etal investigated factors related to loan approval, Disbursement repayment and loan rationing among 1012 Farmers in rural farmers scheme in Uganda between 1987 and 1995. Results of this study indicate that women have a higher loan approval rate and loan repaid/loan borrowed ratio than man but lower actual disbursement levels. Loan rationing among men and women are not statistically different and no justification was found for microfinance institutions discriminating against women in giving loans based on repayment rates. There is a wide gap between loan approved and disbursed.

Katchova Anil.L etal, In their study "A dynamic Model of Individual and group lending in developing countries' Published in Agriculture Finance Review(Fall 2006) Examined the contract design problem of microfinance institutions seeking to maximise outreach to the poor while remaining financially sustainable a dynamic model of group lending is developed that shows how optimal interest rates depends on information regarding moral hazard and adverse selection problems, correlated project risks and strategic default. Relative to traditional static model the results indicate a dynamic model better explains the current experience with individual and group lending in developing countries.

In a paper "Institutional Preparedness and Sustainability of Microfinance institutions during post disaster scenario" published in the *Journal Disaster Prevention and management*(2007) author Anand Kumar T.S tried to show the contribution of microfinance in poverty reduction and strengthening the risk management capacity of the poor and found that it is essential for MFIs to prepare a strategy for maintaining liquidity in a disaster situation, especially keeping disaster loan funds (DLFs) in reserve to help affected households.

"The Impact of capital structure on the performance of micro finance institutions" a paper by Anthony and Coleman Published in the journal of Risk Finance (2007) examined the impact of capital structure on the performance of Microfinance institutions and found that Most of the microfinance institutions employ high leverage and finance their operations with long-term as against short-term debt. Also, highly leveraged microfinance institutions perform better by reaching out to more clientele, enjoy scale economies, and therefore are better able to deal with moral hazard and adverse selection, enhancing their ability to deal with risk.

Chantal McPhee and Annettein their paper "Case Study Al Amana of Morocco" Published in Journal of enterprising Communities: People and Places in the Global Economy (2009) examined the internal and external factors that contributed the success of Al Amana which is a successful Microfinance institution in Morocco .The results of the research provide a case study of a successful Micro Finance Institution that is contributing to the development of entrepreneurs in its region and also highlights the specific organisational factors as well as key elements in the enabling environment that have facilitated the success of Al-Amana

"Role of microfinance saving in Cameroon: a neo-structuralist analysis" Published in International Journal of development issues (2009)Author Tche Jacob aimed to establish an original data base from the field work on microfinance institutions in Cameroon. The statistical analysis carried out indicates that microfinance savings are associated to variables other than rate of interest. The paper supports, therefore, the neo-structuralist analysis of financial development where microfinance institutions are an important structural feature of financial systems in many developing countries.

Nasrin Shahinpoor in her paper "the link between Islamic banking and micro financing" Published in International Journal of Social economics (2009) showed the link between Islamic Banking and Micro finance and found that Islamic religious leaders usually dismiss micro financing because micro financing requires high-interest rate which is against Islamic law. This paper finds that it is possible to combine the two practices and to convince Islamic religious leaders that Islamic banking could be applied to micro financing.

Glemain Pascal in his study "The French Context of Microfinance" studied the system of solidarity based finance actors (Social finance institutions) supply banking products and services to those who are excluded from access to the banking system and the possibility of having an alternative financial system that is socially responsible in articulation with public and private sector. Published in International Journal of Social Economics (2009) this study found that social and solidarity-based economy needs are to be recognized by contemporary economics and Solidarity-based finance shows that another sustainable development model is possible.

"Evaluating Impacts of Microfinance institutions using Guatemalan Data" published in Managerial Finance (2009) Authors James C Brau etal investigated micro lending outcomes among Latin American non-governmental organizations (NGOs), specifically microfinance institutions (MFIs).While there is a growing movement of non-profit ventures channelizing small loans to the poor worldwide, assessments of their impacts are lacking. It was found that MFIs do produce a measure of improvement in the lives of microfinance clients but this improvement is concentrated along the social dimensions of housing health and client empowerment.

Mark Schreiner in his paper "Statistical audit sampling for portfolio-at-risk in microfinance" Published in Managerial finance (2009) provided a rigorous, statistically correct, and low-cost way to audit sample a lender's loan portfolio, be they a micro lender or other type of lender. No other paper applies this method to loan portfolios, even though it is a high demand application. The paper finds statistical audit sampling for a lender's loan portfolio is simple, rigorous, and inexpensive.

Bangladesh is a very poor country and needs a strong foundation and continuous effort to uplift these poor and microfinance can play an important role. Ahmed Salehuddin in his study "Microfinance Institutions in Bangladesh: Achievements and challenges" Published in Managerial Finance (2009) reviewed the Bangladesh experience with Microfinance popularly known as micro Credit. The Success of microfinance in Bangladesh has generated immense interest in other countries of the world. The paper emphasized the role of autonomous national microfinance fund and analyses the efficiency of microfinance delivery mechanism in Bangladesh and also examined the new realities /Challenges faced by the microfinance movement in Bangladesh.

"Leveraging Donor funds: the switch to commercial Funding" is a study by Biekpe.N and Kieweu Joseph Published in Managerial Finance(2009) M highlighted important factors that influence funding decisions from the perspective of commercial lenders, and suggest commercialization of microfinance as a source of alternative development finance. The study finds that specific critical success factors define minimum pre-conditions for microfinance institutions considering commercial funding as an alternative source of finance. The study reveals that the three most important considerations for lending evaluation are transparency in financial reporting, sound financial management, and previous history of borrowing.

In a study "A model of Microfinance with adverse selection loan default and self financing" Published in Agricultural Finance Review (2010) Batabyal.A.A and Beladi.H Analysed a Market of Microfinance in a region of a developing nation in which all projects are either of high or low quality. There is an adverse selection because only borrowers know whether their project is of high or low quality but the micro finance institutions MFIs do not. MFIs are found to be competitive, risk neutral and they offer loan and contracts specifying amount to be repaid only if a borrower's Project makes a profit. Otherwise this borrower defaults on his contract and the some of the important findings indicate that in the pooling equilibrium, a borrower with a low-quality business project will obtain positive expected profit. In contrast, this borrower will obtain zero expected profit in the separating equilibrium. Second, for small enough values of the probability p that a business project is of high quality, MFIs will not finance any business project in the pooling equilibrium. Third, the cost of sending a signal is not too high and hence a separating equilibrium exists. Finally, under some circumstances, self-financing can be used to mitigate adverse selection related problems

Rehman M.M and Ahmed.F In their paper "Impact of microfinance of IBBL on the rural poor's Livelihood in Bangladesh: An empirical Study" Published in International Journal of Islamic and Middle Eastern Finance and Management (2010) described a scheme which aims to alleviate rural poverty by providing small and micro investment to the agricultural and rural sector for generating employment and to raise the income of the rural poor and found that that household income, productivity of crops and livestock, expenditure, and employment had increased significantly due to the influence of invested money. Results of the Logit-model showed that clients' socio-economic factors like age, number of family members in farming, total land size and clients' ethics and morals had a positive and significant influence on household income.

"Islamic Microfinance an ethical alternative to poverty alleviation" a study published in *Humanomics* (2010) authors Rahim and Rehman assessed the potential of Islamic financing scheme for micro financing purposes and found that Islamic finance offers various ethical schemes and instruments that can be advanced and adapted for the purpose of microfinance. Comparatively, qardhul hasan, murabahah, and ijarah schemes are relatively easy to manage and will ensure the capital needs (qardhul hasan), equipments (murabahah) and leased equipments (ijarah) for potential micro-entrepreneurs and the poor. Participatory schemes such as mudarabah and musharakah, on the other hand, have great potentials for microfinance purposes as these schemes can satisfy the risk sharing needs of the micro entrepreneurs.

Kamukama.N etal., in their study "Intellectual capital and performance: Testing interaction effects" published in Journal of Intellectual Capital (2010) intended to examine the interaction effect of intellectual capital elements and how they fuse to affect financial performance in micro finance institutions and explored the major mix of intellectual capital elements that explains the source of value creation hence performance in microfinance institution and found that The magnitude effect of human capital on performance depends on any of structural or relational capital; hence the assumption of nonadditivity is met. However, no significant interaction effects were established between relational and structural capital

"Micro Finance and gender Considerations in developed countries in developed countries The case of Catalonia" published in Management research review(2010) authors Estape.G and Consol. T focussed on the role played by microfinance institutions (MFI) in the improvement of women's micro-entrepreneurship in economically developed countries. In the context of Catalan MFIs, and also studied the allocation of resources to business projects led by women; and analyzed the main features characterizing both women's personal traits and their business initiatives. This study also compared the Microcredit programs compared by gender.

Alam M.N in a study "Cost Minimisation through interest free micro-credit to micro entrepreneurs–A Case of Bangladesh" published in World Journal of Entrepreneurship (2010) through an institutional-network theoretical approach studied the phenomenon of the system and the extent to which interest free microfinance to micro entrepreneurs contributes in minimising different costs of both the lender and the borrowers. The study indicated that that interest free micro credit by Islamic banks minimise different costs of both the lender and the borrowers and the entire loan giving policy of the bank saves both money and time for micro entrepreneurs and these entrepreneurs wish have maximum returns on investment. The study also reveals the existence of skills with rural micro entrepreneurs and the need of proper guidance in utilising the borrowed funds in a productive way minimise cost and maximise earnings with proper utilisation of these funds.

Nixon.K etal examined the mediating effect of competitive advantage in the relationship between intellectual capital and financial performance in Uganda's microfinance institutions in their study "Competitive advantage: Mediator of intellectual capital and performance" which was published in Journal of intellectual capital (2011).The findings indicate that there is a competitive advantage is a significant mediator in the association between intellectual capital and financial performance by 22.4 Percent in Uganda micro finance institutions and also confirmed a partial type of mediation between the intellectual capital ,competitive advantage and financial performance

"Commercialization and changes in capital structure in microfinance institutions" Published in Managerial finance (2011) authors Hoque.M and Chisty.M examined the impact of commercialization on capital structure, mission and performance of microfinance institutions (MFIs).Results of the study indicate leverage decreases the relative level of outreach to the very poor. This is expected as increases in cost of capital leads to higher cost of borrowing, higher default rate and increased risk. Increased use of commercial debt and equity financing lowers productivity for client-maximizing MFIs through lower conversion of savers to borrowers or the yield rate.

"Micro Finance and women entrepreneurs in Pakistan" a study by Samia Mahmood Published in International Journal of Gender and entrepreneurship (2011) intended to understand the influence and impact of micro-finance on women's entrepreneurship and empowerment within developing countries such and Pakistan and found that microfinance institutions are providing credit to women for staring their business however,62 percent of the women borrowers established their own business from microfinance loan and 38 percent did not use it for the said purpose and the lack of training by microfinance institutions is considered to be a contributing factor in very less number of women starting new business from microfinance loan. Thus, this study suggests that just not the fiancé would enable women to start their business ventures but also training is equally essential.

"Financial institutions' social responsibility in developing country a framework of analysis" published in African Journal of Economic and Management Studies(2012) author Ogola Fredrick provided a framework for analyzing the social responsibility (SR) of financial institutions (FIs) in developing countries (DCs), especially in Sub-Saharan Africa (SSA), with regard to their contribution to development The study identified seven indicators for the social responsibility of financial institutions: low interest on loans; small loans; micro-savings; income equality; marketing equality; geographical equality; and unbiased financial education. These groups of indicators reflect the different areas that are relevant for assessing the SR of FIs.
Rouf K.A Published a paper in Humanomics (2012) titled "Green microfinance promoting Green enterprise development" The paper examined microcredit & renewable energy programs for green development and the findings showed a positive indication towards environmental sustainable development.

"Why does the micro credit borrowing rate differ across countries? A cross country study" by Pereira.S & Mourao P published in International journal of social economics (2012) examined the socio economic variables that influence the number of micro-credit projects worldwide and also studied the socio-economic variables that led to a higher default rate. The results showed green cases (Characterised by a lower probability of default) are increased when the collateral value is required and the case is not in Africa.

Murty S. K& Nkubito.K in their study "Is value chain financing a solution to the problems and challenges of access to finance of small-scale farmers in Rwanda?" Published in Managerial Finance (2012) tried demonstrating the relationship between value chain financing and access to finance of small scale farmers in Rwanda. The authors proposed two models of access to finance and their correlation with improves productivity and therefore, profit for producers was to obvious. Value chain financing in one of the southern regions improved the life of small scale farmers tremendously. It was also evident that impact of the access to value chain financing products had a direct link to the levels of profit and production.

"Investigating causal relationship between social capital and micro finance" a study by Published in the International journal of social economics (2013) Akram .S and Rautray J.K investigated the causal link between social capital and micro finance by testing the role of social capital in explaining the household's to access to microcredit under the group based lending approach. It was found that participation in local organisations heterogeneity of associations and level of both generalised and institutional trust were identified as the key dimensions of structural and cognitive social capital to influence households' access to credit on the other hand when these dimensions were combined in a single social capital index , the result indicated that social capital index has no significant effect on microfinance participation. This result provides support to the argument that grouping all the dimensions of social capital into one index may run the risk of losing the explanatory power of social Capital.

"Profiting from poverty: ethics of microfinance in BOP" Published in South Asian Journal of Global Business Research (2013) authors Sama .M.L and Casselman .M examined the ethical Dilemmas that emerge when offering microfinance services to BOP markets and found that
In many of the key dilemmas represent themselves in the extreme poverty segment of the BOP where commercial business models have the least traction.

Arup Roy and Chandana Goswami, in their study "A scientometric analysis of literature on performance assessment of microfinance institutions (1995-2010)"which was a literature review of the studies on micro finance for fifteen years from 1995 to 2015 proposed a conceptual model which focussed on the performance of MFIs .The study also documented the various dimensions of the performance measurement of the MFIs that were done till than and in turn attracted the attention of microfinance researchers, microfinance practitioners and various rating agencies to the to the various dimensions affecting the overall assessment of microfinance institutions.

Nutshell view of the Research done so Far

1. Regulation of MFIs
2. Microfinance Institution framework
3. Product Development in MFIs
4. Suitability of microfinance disaster reduction at household and community level
5. Improvement of Human capital through Microfinance
6. Innovative methods of loan disbursement in MFIs
7. Impact of capital structure on performance of MFIs
8. Contribution of Micro Finance in poverty reduction and strengthening the risk management capacity of the poor.
9. Internal & External factors that contributed the success of an MFI
10. Study investigated the factors related to loan approval, Disbursement & repayment & loan rationing.
11. Contract Design Problem of microfinance institutions seeking to maximise the outreach to the poor.
12. Factors influencing the microfinance savings.

13. Link between Islam Banking and microfinance.
14. System of solidarity based finance actors and the Possibility of having an alternative financial system.
15. Investigation of Micro Lending outcomes.
16. Tool to Audit sample a lenders Loan Portfolio.
17. Bangladesh Experience of Micro Finance.
18. Important factors influencing the funding decisions.
19. Study of Micro Finance Projects and important Lending considerations.
20. Micro Finance Scheme in a country need to alleviate poverty.
21. Potential of Islamic financial Scheme for micro finance purposes.
22. Examination of the interaction effect of intellectual capital elements.
23. Role Played by microfinance in women entrepreneurship.
24. Impact of Commercialisation.
25. Phenomenon of the system and the extent to which interest free microfinance to micro entrepreneurs contributes in minimising different costs of both the lender and the borrowers.
26. Micro Finance as social responsibility.
27. Microcredit & renewable energy programs for green development.
28. Socio economic variables that influence the number of micro-credit projects worldwide and also studied the socio-economic variables that led to a higher default rate.
29. Relationship between value chain financing and access to finance of small scale farmers.
30. Causal link between social capital and micro finance.
31. A literature review proposing a conceptual model focussing on the performance of MFI.
32. ethical Dilemmas that emerge when offering microfinance services to BOP markets

Findings and Conclusion
This paper is an effort to explore the various area of research done in the area of microfinance. Total 32 articles were reviewed published in various international journals and the Important Heads under which the existing research is carried can be grouped in to the areas as follows

    (a) Microfinance a tool for poverty alleviation and women empowerment and as funding tool for farmers and small businesses, Improvement of human capital.

    (b) System of microfinance functioning-Institutional regulation, Loan disbursement, Factors influencing funding decision, lending considerations.

    (c) Micro financing system & Product development.

    (d) Microfinance capital structure and projects funded by MFIs

    (e) Ethics and CSR in Microfinance

The studies clearly show that there is still a vast scope and potential of growth for MFIs and large area still remains unexplored only study which is done in Bangladesh exhibits the model which they adopted and how it contributed to the human development and standards of living. None of the other studies have touched any model pertaining to a country.

Largely it's found that microfinance is new concept and is gaining importance throughout the world but there not research done in citing the success stories and the models adopted across different countries

Majority of the country use the Microfinance for poverty alleviation and providing finance to small business enterprises and farmers.

Some studies prove that Microfinance is a good alternative to provide small loans and encourage thrift savings and one of the study in Bangladesh also proves Microfiance as successful and achieved its results,

Future Research

1. *Types of Microfinance products and their success stories across the world.*
2. *Important models which are successful and their possible application in other areas.*
3. *The reach of microfinance and its impact on Rural development, Poverty alleviation and women empowerment.*

References

1. Alam M.N.(2010) "Cost Minimisation through interest free micro-credit to micro entrepreneurs –A Case of Bangladesh", World Journal of Entrepreneurship, Management and Sustainable Development, Vol. 6, No. 3, pp247-256.

2. Anand Kumar T.S and Newport Jayant K (2005) Role of Microfinance in disaster   mitigation Disaster Prevention and Management Vol. 14 No. 2, 2005 pp. 176-182

3. Anthony.K and Coleman (2007) "The Impact Of Capital Structure on The Performance of Micro Finance Institutions" journal of Risk Finance Vol 8 No 1 pp 56-71.

4. Batabyal.A.A and Beladi.H (2010), A model of Microfinance with adverse selection loan default and self financing" Agricultural Finance Review Vol. 70 No. 1, pp. 55-65.

5. Biekpe.N and Kieweu (2009),Managerial Finance, Leveraging Donor funds: the switch to commercial Funding, Vol. 35 No. 12, pp. 1011-1026.

6. Chantal McPhee and Annettein (2009) "Case Study Al Amana of Morocco" Journal of Enterprising Communities: People and Places in the Global Economy, Vol. 3 No. 1, pp. 59-70.

7. Estape.G.D and Consol. T.M (2010) Micro Finance and gender Considerations in developed countries in developed countries Management Research Review Vol. 33 No. 12, pp. 1140-1157.
8. Glemain Pascal(2009) The French Context of Microfinance , International Journal of Social Economics, Vol 36 No.12 pp1118-1132.
9. Hoque.M and Chisty.M (2011) Commercialization and changes in capital structure in microfinance institutions, Managerial Finance Vol. 37 No. 5, pp. 414-425.
10. James C Brau etal(2009) Evaluating Impacts of Microfinance institutions using Guatemalan Data, Managerial Finance ,Vol. 35 No. 12, 2009 pp. 953-974.
11. Jones Linda etal (2006) "The Double X factor: Harnessing Female Human Capital For Economic Growth" International Journal of Emerging Markets, Vol 1 No.4 pp 291-304.
12. Kamukama.N etal. (2010) "Intellectual capital and performance: Testing interaction effects" Journal of Intellectual Capital Vol. 11 No. 4, pp. 554-574.
13. Katchova Anil.L etal (Fall 2006), A dynamic Model of Individual and group lending in developing Countries, Agriculture Finance Review,pp251-265.
14. Koveos peter & Dipinder Randhawa (2004), Financial Services for the Poor: Assessing Microfinance Institutions "Managerial finance", volume 30 Number 5 pp-70-95
15. Kyereboah.A and Coleman (2007) The Impact of capital structure on the performance of micro finance institutions" The Journal of Risk Finance Vol. 8 No. 1, pp 56-71
16. Mark Schreiner(2009) Statistical audit sampling for portfolio-at-risk in microfinance, Managerial finance Managerial Finance Vol. 35 No. 12, pp. 990-998.
17. Megicks Phillip etal, (2005) "Enhancing Micro fiancé outreach through market oriented new service development in Indian regional rural bank" International Journal of Bank Marketing Vol. 23 No. 1, pp. 107-125.
18. Microfinance and Its Delivery Models. Experiences, options and future. Journal of StudyMode.com. Retrieved 08, 2007, from http://www. study mode.com/essays/Microfinance- Its-Delivery-Models-119718.html.
19. Nixon.K etal(2011) Competitive advantage: Mediator of intellectual capital and performance Journal of Intellectual Capital Vol. 12 No. 1, 2011 pp. 152-164.
20. Rahim and Rehman (2010) Islamic Microfinance an ethical alternative to poverty alleviation" Humanomics Vol. 26 No. 4, pp. 284-295.
21. Rehman M.M and Ahmed.F(2010), Impact of microfinance of IBBL on the rural poor's Livelihood in Bangladesh: An empirical Study" International Journal of Islamic and Middle Eastern Finance and Management Vol. 3 No. 2, pp. 168-190.
22. Salehuddin Ahmed (2009) Microfinance Institutions in Bangladesh: Achievements and challenges, Managerial Finance Vol. 35 No. 12,   pp. 999-1010.
23. Samia.M (2011) Micro Finance and women entrepreneurs in Pakistan, International Journal of Gender and entrepreneurship, Vol. 3 No. 3, 2011 pp. 265-274.

24. Shahinpoor Nasrin (2009) the link between Islamic banking and micro financing, International Journal of Social economics,Vol36 No.10 pp 996-1007

25. Tche Jacob (2009) "Role of microfinance saving in Cameroon:A neo-structuralist analysis" International Journal of Development Issues ,Vol. 8 No. 1, pp. 48-60.

26 Tche Jacob (2009) Role of microfinance saving in Cameroon: a neo-structuralist analysis International Journal of development issues, Volume 8 number 1 pp 48-60.

26. Tenaw, S. and K.Z. Islam,(2009) Rural financial services and effects of microfinance on agricultural productivity and on poverty. University of Helsinki Department of Economics and Management Discussion Papers series), 1: 28.

27. **Ogola Fredrick(2012)** Financial institutions' social responsibility in developing country a framework of analysis, African Journal of Economic and Management Studies, Vol. 3 No. 1, pp. 116-136.

28. Rouf K.A (2012), Green microfinance promoting Green enterprise development, Humanomics, Vol.28 No.2 pp-148-161.

29. Pereira.S & Mourao P (2012) Why does the micro credit borrowing rate differ across countries? A cross country study International journal of social economics, International Journal of Social Economics Vol. 39 No. 8, pp. 536-550.

30. Murty S. K & Nkubito.K(2012), Is value chain financing a solution to the problems and challenges of access to finance of small-scale farmers in Rwanda?" Managerial Finance Vol. 38 No. 10, pp. 993-1004.

31. Murty S. K& Nkubito.K (2012), Is value chain financing a solution to the problems and challenges of access to finance of small-scale farmers in Rwanda, Managerial Finance, Vol. 38 No. 10, 2012 pp. 993-1004.

32. Akram .S and Rautray J.K(2013),Published in the International journal of social economics, International Journal of Social Economics Vol. 40 No. 9, pp. 760-776.

33. Arup Roy and Chandana Goswami,(2013) "A scientometric analysis of literature on performance assessment of microfinance institutions (1995-2010)"International Journal of Commerce and Management Vol. 23 No. 2, pp. 148-174.

34. Linda M. Sama and R. Mitch Casselman (2013) Profiting from poverty: ethics of microfinance in BOP Global Business Research Vol. 2 No. 1, pp. 82-103

Links

http://www.legatum.org/attachments/MicrofinanceCrisis.pdf

CHAPTER-14
Evaluation and Impact of Micro finance in Coastal Andhrapradesh

* Dr. Shaik Shamshuddin
** Dr. Haniefuddin S
*** Dr. Shaik Khadar Baba

ABSTRACT

This paper evaluates the aspects relating to microfinance in coastal Andhrapradesh, this study will be useful to accelerate economic growth, maintain political order, reduce poverty and adapt to climate change. The term microfinance is widely used to refer to institutions governing savings, credit, insurance and financial payments by relatively poor people, including those regulated by both official laws and comfortable norms. Analysis of microfinance is widely framed as a purely micro issue, centered on the motivation and behavior of specific users and providers. However, such analysis is almost invariably located whether explicitly or implicitly in a wider view of how the state, markets and society institute poverty.

These SHGs are mainly formed and managed by women and this has become an instrument, which has led to women's empowerment and social change. Most of the microfinance institutions in India attempt to go beyond savings and credit groups to provide microfinance services in the form of savings and insurance.

This paper first set out a general well-being regime framework that can be used for this analysis and sketch the role microfinance plays within it.

This paper provides a review of the literature on microfinance and a critical assessment of its effectiveness. It examines the experience of India, which has one of the largest microfinance sectors in the world, and particularly describing the microfinance status in coastal Andhra Pradesh.

Keywords: Microfinance, Microcredit, Self Help Group

* Dr. Shaik Shamshuddin : Asst Professor GIM Gitam University, Visakhapatnam, e-mail : shamshuddin1234@gmail.com.

** Dr. Haniefuddin S : Professor in the department studies, NIST Vizag, cell : +91-9985401439,
email : haniefuddin@rediffmail.com.

*** Dr. Shaik Khadar Baba : Employee Andhra University, e-mail : skkbaba@yahoo.com.

Evaluation and Impact of Micro finance in Coastal Andhra pradesh

Introduction :

Microfinance is the provision of loans and other financial services to the poor. The microfinance has evolved due to the efforts of committed individuals and financial agencies to promote self-employment and contribute to poverty alleviation and provision of social security. India has been able to develop its own model of microfinance organizations in the form of savings and credit groups known as the Self Help Group (SHGs), which are bank-linked.

Microfinance is one of the ways of building the capacities of the poor who are largely ignored by commercial banks and other lending institutions and graduating them to sustainable self employment activities by providing them financial services like credits, savings and insurance. The reasons of this neglect are many. Often, such credits are just not profitable enough for banks because of economies of scale. By focusing on small amounts, and easing collateral requirements, microfinance institutions are better equipped to target poor individuals or groups who need resources to finance small scale investments.

The microfinance sector is growing and attracting banks and private equity (PE) investors again, says India Ratings & Research (Ind-Ra). However, this time the growth is much lower than the over 100% annual growth seen during FY06-FY10 and benefits from a tighter supervisory regime. The sector"s outreach increased over 23% yoy and gross loan portfolio grew 42% yoy in FY14. Ind-Ra expects the sector to grow at a CAGR of 24% and require an equity infusion of INR27bn over FY15-FY19.

The Microfinance Institutions (MFI) in Andhra Pradesh is being driven away by the provisions of the APMFI Act and the developments that followed, according to the industry. While the largest and only listed MFI has shifted its base to Mumbai, others like Basix, Spandana, Share and Asmitha are spreading to other States in India and abroad.

The MFIs in the State clocked losses of over Rs. 6,500 crore in Andhra Pradesh following the APMFI Act, 2011 which is intended to control high interest rates, coercive collections and illegal insurance practices by the MFIs. Within a year, the operations of the MFIs in the State have come down to less than 10% besides reduction of over 30,000 staff. Companies that bore the brunt include the first listed MFI SKS and others like Share, Basix and Spandana.

The AP government, based on reports received from district collectors on MFI operations, passed the Andhra Pradesh Micro Finance Institutions (Regulation of money lending) Ordinance 2010. The AP Ordinance (which subsequently became an Act) was aimed at crippling the seemingly haphazard processes followed by MFIs when lending to the poor. MFIs could not recover their loans, make fresh loans without government approvals, and had to provide a list of employees involved in the recovery and lending parts of business. This, coupled with active encouragement to borrowers from local politicians and strongmen to halt repayments, resulted in a contagion effect in the state. The collection efficiencies dropped to below 20% in January 2011 from 99% in September 2010.

Microfinance delivery models:

Microfinance services are provided with different methods in India and elsewhere.

Delivery models can be divided into two broad categories.

I) Group models

II) Individual models

Group models can be divided into three categories.

I) Self-help Groups (SHG)- Bank-linkage

II) The Grameen model

III) Joint Liability Groups (JLG)

Objectives Of The Study :

To study the working of microfinance agencies with particular reference to Costal Andhra Pradesh.

To study the various problems and perspectives of SHGs along with members' perception in the selected area of the study.

Finally, to suggest suitable measures for the effective working of the Self Help Groups in Costal Andhra Pradesh.

Data Collection :

In keeping view of the objectives set for the study, the primary and secondary methods of data collection have been adopted. The primary data are collected from the selected sample SHGs in the selected districts of Andhra Pradesh, with the help of a schedule. Secondary sources of the data were also used and they include records, reports, files and other published and unpublished materials.

The survey interview and questionnaire instrument were designed with close-ended and open-ended questions. Close ended-questions help the respondents to choose the answer or responses that have already been given by the interview questions or the questionnaire. This was used in order to offer both the researcher and respondents the advantage of answering the questions faster and easier.

Sampling of Respondents :

The sample size consists of 200 people in random who are associated to the various MFI's and SHG's operating in the coastal Andhrapradesh. The total no. of respondents is 200.

In India, Andhra Pradesh has been playing a pioneering role in harvesting the potential of microfinance institution (MFI) and self help group (SHG) and therefore drew a lots of research attention. Analyzing the effect of some crucial socio-economic factors such as self help group members' age, education, marital status, members yearly income, type of family, member's husband education, husband income, household income, loan amount and number of meeting attended by members, and size of land promoting employment and income generating activities.

Literature review :

Tara Fleming (2014) "Examining the Influence of Microfinance on Household Conditions in Hyderabad, India " this paper aims to do this by regressing the number of loans that have gone into default during any cycle on a host of measures designed to assess the individual's ability to pay back the loans. The observations have been drawn from a survey of 2,800 households in India. While predicting whether or not a person will default on a loan is nigh unto impossible, modeling the probability that they will incur back-debt by the frequency of missing payments could be a reasonable proxy for this measure.

Mader, P. (2013), Rise and Fall of Microfinance in India: The Andhra Pradesh Crisis in Perspective opined the crisis of microfinance which erupted in 2010 in Andhra Pradesh has complex causes rooted in Indian history.

Prasad Pole et.al, (2014) "A Critical Evaluation of the SKS Microfinance Fiasco" observed crises have hit various players from different parts of the world in the global microfinance industry in the past. In the present study, they critically evaluate the SKS and Andhra Pradesh microfinance crisis in India. SKS established itself as a leader in the microfinance industry in India, and became the first listed microfinance company in the country. The dream run did not continue for long; as the Andhra Pradesh government started putting some regulatory conditions in place researchers critically evaluate the SKS crisis to ascertain whether the cause was purely the government's action or the over-indebtedness amongst the borrowers of the microfinance industry. Further questions on commercialization of the microfinance industry are also discussed.

Taylor, M. (2011), 'Freedom from Poverty is Not for Free': Rural Development and the Microfinance Crisis in Andhra Pradesh, this study examines how the 2010 microfinance crisis in Andhra Pradesh reveals significant fault lines that underlie this narrative. It argues that the crisis of microfinance in Andhra Pradesh needs to be placed within the context of severe agrarian dislocations stemming from the impact of trade liberalization, drought cycles and a transformation of rural social relations.

Prabhjot Kaur (2014) "Outreach and Sustainability of Microfinance Institutions in India in Pre and Post Andhra Pradesh Microfinance Crisis in Context of South Asia", examines Microfinance Crisis, 2010 sustainability and outreach of MFIs in India is doubtful and questionable. Present paper attempts to look into various dimensions of sustainability and outreach of Indian MFIs in the context of other countries in South Asia. Microfinance crisis has hit Operational Sustainability of Indian MFIs very badly, yet, on cost front Indian MFIs seems to be best performer in South Asia

Prabhjot Kaur and Soma Dey (2013) "Andhra Pradesh Microfinance Crisis and its Repercussions on Microfinancing Activities in India", attempts to look into the enabling reasons responsible for spawning the crisis. Further attempt has been made to trace the repercussions of Andhra Pradesh Crisis on the activities of MFIs.

Findings of the Study:

Among the MFIs` and SHGs` studied in coastal Andhrapradesh, it has been observed that generally, SHGs are based on a microfinance model similar to credit and thrift societies identified as Nidhis in South India.

The study data divulges that out of 30.18% SHG households belonging to scheduled castes (SC) category, 32.47% belong to general category, 20.53% belong to schedule tribe (ST) and 12.70% belong to other backward classes category (OBC).

The study reveals that monthly income of 51% SHG households is between Rs.4,000 and Rs.12,000, 55.6% have savings between Rs1,500 and Rs3,000, 56% have their personal bank account and 46% have a PAN card.

More than 84% of SHG households have items like mobile phones, fans TV sets and gas stoves which have become necessities.

The study further indicates more than 46% opined they have low level of income, poverty, lack of basic amenities of life and poor living conditions.

40% of the respondents opined they are unable to bear the expenditure on health.

23.9 % respondents opined that non-repayment by members is responsible for dis-functioning of MFIs`.

45% respondents mentioned interest rates need to reduce.

51 % opined there should be rotation of leadership.

Suggestions :

Identify the ground-level microfinance experience those managing the investments and making decisions.

Smaller groups of five to ten members should be allowed to form an SHG which can lead to better consistency among members.

There should be rotation of leadership so that everyone in the group develops leadership qualities and become more responsible.

There should be some provision to reward the members of SHG members who have never borrowed loan.

Professional help should be provided to SHGs for preparing loan proposals and for chalking out viable business plans.

Micro enterprises started by SHGs can be made viable and sustainable only if they are provided access to markets.

References :

Prabhjot Kaur (2014) "Outreach and Sustainability of Microfinance Institutions in India in Pre and Post Andhra Pradesh Microfinance Crisis in Context of South Asia", Global Journal of Finance and Management, Volume 6, Num ber 6, pp. 569-574

Tara Fleming (2014) "Examining the Influence of Microfinance on Household Conditions in Hyderabad, India " Journal of Business and Economics, Volume 5, No. 8, pp. 1262-1270.

Mader, P. (2013), "Rise and Fall of Microfinance in India: The Andhra Pradesh Crisis in Perspective" .Strat. Change, 22: pp. 47–66.

Prasad Pole et.al, (2014) "A Critical Evaluation of the SKS Microfinance Fiasco" Indian Journal of Finance, 8(6), pp. 7 – 21.

Taylor, M. (2011), 'Freedom from Poverty is Not for Free': Rural Development and the Microfinance Crisis in Andhra Pradesh, India. Journal of Agrarian Change, 11: 484–504.

The Hindu "Rejected in AP, Microfinance Institutions move to other States" September 30, 2013.

Prabhjot Kaur and Soma Dey (2013) "Andhra Pradesh Microfinance Crisis and its Repercussions on Microfinancing Activities in India", Global Journal of Management and Business Studies, Volume 3, Number 7, pp. 695-702.

P. Basu and P. Srivastava, (2005) "Scaling-up microfinance for India's rural poor", World Bank
Policy Research, Working Paper 3646.

PART-II

CASE STUDIES

CASE STUDY -1

ROLE OF MICROFINANCE THROUGH SELF HELP GROUPS AND ITS IMPACT ON THE LIVING STANDARDS OF RURAL POOR - A CASE STUDY IN SELECTED RURAL AREAS OF VISAKHAPATNAM, A.P, INDIA.

* Mr. R.L.N.MURTHY, research scholar, GITAM University, Visakhapatnam
**Professor P. SHEELA, professor, Dept of Finance, GITAM Institute of Management, GITAM University, Visakhapatnam.

Abstract

Microfinance has become increasingly popular as a tool for poverty reduction in developing and transition countries. The major challenge before developing countries is how to improve living standards of the poor. Microfinance has been chosen to shoot this problem. But, the question of how far microfinance is successful in improving living standards of the rural poor is still unanswered. It is in this context a research has been initiated to know the role of microfinance in improving living standards of the rural poor. Microfinance institutions are encouraging the self help groups to mobilize savings and turning the rural poor into income generating entrepreneurs.

This study aims at understanding the role of microfinance in improving living standards of the rural poor through self help groups. A questionnaire using likert type scale has been designed and executed to know whether the living standards have been improved through support of microfinance. The respondents have been selected on random basis covering selected rural areas of Visakhapatnam on all the beneficiary of the microfinance through SHGs. Responses to questions, such as increase in income, increase in savings, access to better health, access to better education, and improved financial position, have been sought to know whether their living standards have improved. Most of the respondents expressed their favorable response and did mention that microfinance through SHGs had helped them to a certain extent and also improved their living standards, the study also explored that few of the respondents were not fully aware the details of the program and is still relying on their group leaders instructions, which seems to be a bottle neck for their future endeavors.

INTRODUCTION

Microfinance is a financial service provided by micro finance institutions to the poor through either directly or group mechanism, the main aim of the microfinance is poverty reduction through empowering the rural poor and women. It offers various services such as providing collateral free micro credit, group lending savings pooling and insurance service. It is often argued that MFIs charge high rate of interest they charge about 28% of interest but the fact is that these MFIs are borrowing from banks at 13 to 14% and 7 to 10% is the operating cost.

However, china, Vietnam, and South Korea achieved fruitful results in bringing down the poverty level through the magical mechanisms of microfinance. Microfinance has gained popularity since professor Mohammed Yunus who is the pioneer of microfinance thought created wonders in uplifting the living standards of the poor in Bangladesh.

Microfinance institution are really playing key role in poverty reduction. These MFIs are the vital sources for the poor to borrow collateral free loans. These loans meant for uplifting of poor by inculcating entrepreneurial ship. In India, microfinance institutions provide their services either directly or group based. Most of the MFIs are encouraging self help groups to provide micro credit. The reason behind the act is to make the members feel group responsibility. By encouraging groups saving mobilization also becomes easy self help groups are such groups mainly dominated by females, that save small amount of money and members can borrow from common pool on a rotating basis these SHGs are sometimes used by MFIs for group lending. Group members are made aware of the purpose of group formation, purpose of lending, repayment duration, terms of repayment, and interest charged. It is usually expected that the members are repaying from the savings generated from their entrepreneurial activity. It is only then the poverty reduction and uplifting of living standards of the poor is possible through microfinance.

In order to examine whether the standard of living improved among the poor there are several indicators that come handy. Increased savings increased income, improved healthcare ,improved education, better decision making are the most vital indicators in examining the impact of the microfinance on the living standards of the poor.

Many countries, developed, developing and transition countries, have embraced the concept of microfinance. MFIs provide wide range of services. The known activity of

MFIs is providing credit to poorer households MFIs are not equally dispersed worldwide. They appear to be especially well developed in certain Asian and Latin American countries, such as Bangladesh, Bolivia, and Indonesia (IMF working paper wp/02/159 "Microfinance institutions and public policy"). This study aims at finding out whether microfinance is really successful in improving living standards of the rural poor through SHGs.

OBJECTIVES OF THE STUDY

- The prime objective of the study is to know the impact of microfinance in improving living standards of the rural poor through SHGs.
- To know whether there exist a relationship between income increase and saving increase after availing micro finance facility.
- To know whether there exists a relationship between income increase and role in decision making process increased after availing microfinance facility.
- To know whether there is a relationship between improved standards of living and increase in income, increase in savings, better access to education, better access to health care and improved financial position of family after availing microfinance facility.
- To know the awareness among the microfinance users about the purpose and terms of micro credit and repayment.

LIMITATIONS OF THE STUDY

- This study mainly conducted in rural areas of Visakhapatnam. Henceforth, the results of this study are applicable to rural areas of Visakhapatnam only.
- This study is mainly based on primary data, which is obtained through a questionnaire. The accuracy is largely dependent on the accuracy of the responses given by the respondents.

METHODOLOGY

Data collection

Data has been collected from primary and secondary sources.

Primary data has been collected by employing a structured questionnaire and administering that questionnaire coupled with face to face interview with the respondents belong to various villages of Visakhapatnam district.

The questionnaire consists of various questions on respondents profile their awareness about the purpose of loan provided, terms of loan repayment duration and interest charged. It also consist questions on their arrangement to repay the loan and their satisfaction with the loan processing by their group leader.

The likert-type scale has been incorporated in the questionnaire which consists 5 points ranging 1 for strongly disagree to 5 for strongly agree with 3 as a neutral point.

Secondary data, about previous studies, and literature review on microfinance has been obtained from various national and international journals and websites.

Sample size

A sample of 120 respondents who availed microfinance facility, has been obtained on random basis coupled with convenience sampling. And the data has been analyzed with SPSS 20.

Literature review

Microfinance is a powerful tool in improving living standards of the rural poor. It encourages savings and inculcates entrepreneurial attitude among the unemployed poor. It encourages group responsibility which helps the poor in achieving economic development. The reserve bank of India (RBI) and national bank for agriculture and rural development (NABARD) define microfinance as "provision of thrift, credit and other financial services and products of very small amounts to the poor in rural semi-urban areas for enabling them to raise their income levels and in improving living standards.

Poor households face many constraints in trying to save, invest, and protect their livelihoods. They take financial intermediation seriously and devote considerable effort to finding workable solutions. Most of the solutions are found in the informal sector, which, so far, offers low- income households convenience and flexibility unmatched by formal intermediaries. The microfinance movement is striving to match the convenience and flexibility of the informal sector, while adding reliability and the promise of continuity, and in some countries it is already doing this on a significant scale. (Jonathan Morduch and Stuart Rutherford April 1, 2003)

Microfinance according to Otero (1999) is "the provision of financial services to low –income poor and very poor self –employed people". The UN declared 2005 as the international year of microcredit. Poverty is a complex issue and is difficult to define as there are various dimensions. (Microfinance Literature Review by Eoin Wrenn 2005)

One of the most important aspects of microfinance is saving mobilization. It has been recognized that the poor people who are capable of coming out of poverty can improve their living standards when right environment and opportunities exist. (Khan and Rahaman)

The question of the role of microfinance in reducing inequality and vulnerability remains valid today. This tool has been adopted in European, American, Asian and African countries as a tool to poverty reduction. (Gerard Tchouassi and Lefi, 2011.)

(Zeller and Johanssen 2006) assumed that Micro Finance Institutions are able to contribute to improving economic conditions at the local, regional and country level and those contributions are higher than the contributions to poverty alleviation.

(Rajasekhar D,2000) conducted a study on "Microfinance Programmes and Women's Empowerment: A study of Two NGO's From Kerala" and found that Microfinance programmes are important institutional devices for providing small credit to the rural poor in order to alleviate poverty.

China, Vietnam, and South Korea have significantly reduced poverty in recent years with little microfinance activity. (Adebiyi Julius and, Bolanle Aminat)

It is widely accepted that micro financing plays a very important role in improving the living conditions of the poor by making it possible for the poor to have access to productive resources with financial services being a key resource. (William Gabriel Brafu-Insaidoo and Ferdinand Ahiakpor)

Microfinance is considered as a tool for socio-economic development. It is one way of fighting poverty in rural areas where the poorest people live. It puts credit, savings, insurance and other basic services within the reach of poor people. (Mrs.T.Chandrabai, Dr.K.Venkata janardhan rao, Mr.Suresh Kandulapati) High-quality microfinance is characterised by services that are easily accessible to the poor, responsive to the full range of their financial needs and reasonably priced.(Kieran Donaghue and Stav Zotalis, AusAID)

SELF HELP GROUPS

Self Help Groups are Group based financial service models have captured the attention of development practitioners around the world. (Social intermediation and microfinance programs.

SHGs had set a new agenda for financial intermediation by banks in the form of micro-credit and infused the dynamism among members to climb up the socio-economic ladder in the development process. (Chintamani Prasad Patnaik)

(Rekha Goankar,2001) in her study concluded that the movement of SHGs can significantly contribute towards the reduction of poverty and unemployment in the rural sector of the economy and the SHGs can lead to social transformation in terms of economic development and the social change.

(Gladis Mary John,2008) found that membership in SHG inculcated a great confidence in the mind of majority of women to succeed in day to day life. Positive change was found in the attitude of relatives and friends towards the women in self help groups. Self help groups develop group responsibility and provide necessary moral and financial support in the process of development.

Against this backdrop of failures of earlier poverty alleviation schemes and the financial institutions to reach the real needy, microfinance schemes using self-help groups (SHGs) were designed and NABARD considered this „SHG-Bank Linkage" model as a core strategy for rural development. Self Help Groups (SHGs) are necessary to overcome exploitation, create confidence for the economic self-reliance of rural poor, particularly among women who are mostly invisible in the social structure. These groups enable them to come together for a common objective and gain strength from each other to deal with exploitation, which they are facing, in several forms. (Dr. B.B. Mansuri) Self-Help Groups [SHGs] have proved to be an effective tool or instrument in India to

address the problem of poverty on the one hand and also empower women on the other. It is not only expected to empower women economically but also socially in terms of say fighting for their rights, fighting against the social evils such as gender bias, child labour, violence against women, secondary status assigned to women, dowry, crimes against women etc.(N. Manimekalai)

Table 1: Profile of Respondents

VARIABLE	MEASURING GROUP	frequency	percentage
	20-30	25	20.80%
	30-40	42	35.00%
	40-50	43	35.80%
	50-60	10	8.30%
age	Total	120	100.00%
	female	73	60.80%
	male	47	39.20%
gender	Total	120	100.00%
	uneducated	11	9.20%
	below SSC	28	23.30%
	SSC	32	26.70%
	intermediate	22	18.30%
	graduated	22	18.30%
	post graduate	5	4.20%
Education	Total	120	100.00%
	married	113	94.20%
	bachelor	7	5.80%
marital status	Total	120	100.00%
	<2	1	0.80%
	2-5	103	85.80%
	>5	16	13.30%
family members	Total	120	100.00%
	daily wage	17	14.20%
	private company	37	30.80%
	small business	47	39.20%
	agriculture	13	10.80%
	unemployed	5	4.20%
	domestic servant	1	0.80%
occupation	Total	120	100.00%
	<1year	6	5.00%
	1-3 years	33	27.50%
	4-6 years	43	35.80%
occupational	>7years	38	31.70%
experience	Total	120	100.00%

Table no 1 provides the information about the demographic profile of respondents. Most of the respondents fall between the age groups of 30-40 and 40-50 years. And these two groups together constitute 70.8% of the total respondents. Most of these are found to be middle aged people. Females are the dominating users of microfinance facility and they are 60.8% and males were 39.2%. Educated people are the prime users of micro credit and they are nearly 91%. Most of the people are having qualification of SSC or less than that. Married people constitute 94.2%. Most of the respondents have 2-5 family members and they constitute 85.8%. It is found that only 39.2% of total respondents are having small business as their occupation. 35.8% of total respondents have the occupational experience of 4-6 years. From these results it is evident that most of the microfinance users are middle aged and married people with SSC qualification.

Graduates and post graduates also there who availed micro credit facility. Graduate are 18.3% and Post graduates are 4.2% and mere 9.2% are then uneducated respondents in all 120 respondents. Married women are the prime users of microfinance.

TABLE NO: 2 LOAN DETAILS

VARIABLE	MEASURING GROUP	frequency	percentage
satisfied with way of loan processed	yes	85	70.80%
	no	34	28.30%
	3	1	0.80%
	Total	120	100.00%
no of times benefits derived	once	12	10.00%
	twice	47	39.20%
	>twice	59	49.20%
	not yet received	2	1.70%
	Total	120	100.00%
amount of loan received	<5000	8	6.70%
	5000-10000	73	60.80%
	>10000	39	32.50%
	Total	120	100.00%
amount spent for the purpose	business	67	55.80%
	household	39	32.50%
	others	14	11.70%
	Total	120	100.00%
arrangements for repayment	business income	57	47.50%
	savings from	36	30.00%
	borrowing from	13	10.80%
	income earned	14	11.70%
	Total	120	100.00%

Table no 2 shows loan details of respondents. Large percentage Respondents are satisfied by way of loan processing and that is 70.8%. Most of the respondents availed microfinance facility for more than twice and they are 49.2% and there is also another largest percentage which shows that 39.2% of respondents availed microfinance facility for exactly two times. This is a clear indication that microfinance is helpful otherwise they would not have come forward to avail micro credit. Staggering 60% of respondents taken 5000-10000 rupees and 32.5% of respondents taken more than 10000. It can be said that nearly 10000 rupees is the requirement to meet their needs. Overwhelmingly 55.8% respondents used the money taken towards small business. But it is also observed that 32.5% people are using microfinance funds for their household requirements. It is not to be encouraged. The purpose can better be served through the commitment of using these funds for income generating activities. Most of the respondents are making their repayment arrangements by way of business income and savings.

TABLE NO 3: RESPONDENTS AWARENESS.

VARIABLE	MEASURING	frequency	percentage
Awareness of duration of repayment	yes	112	93.30%
	no	8	6.70%
	Total	120	100.00%
Awareness of repayment terms	yes	107	89.20%
	no	13	10.80%
	Total	120	100.00%
Awareness of how much interest	yes	111	92.50%
	no	9	7.50%
	Total	120	100.00%
Purpose of micro credit	yes	112	93.30%
	no	8	6.70%
	Total	119	100.00%

TABLE NO 3 shows the awareness of the respondent about purpose of loan, interest charged, and duration of the loan. Few people, though negligible, found that they are unaware. Most of the respondents are aware about the interest charged, duration of the loan, and purpose of the loan. This is a positive sign that people aware about the basics of the micro finance facility.

HYPOTHESES TESTING
RELATIONSHIP BETWEEN THE INCREASE OF INCOME AND THE INCREASE OF SAVINGS
H_{01}: there is no relationship between increase in income and increase in savings after availing microfinance facility
H_{a1}: there is a relationship.

Correlations		The income has	The savings has
The income has increased	Pearson	1	.755**
	Sig. (1-		.000
	N	120	120
The savings has increased	Pearson	.755**	1
	Sig. (1-	.000	
	N	120	120
**. Correlation is significant at the 0.01 level (1-tailed).			

From the above correlation table it is significant with 0.755 at 0.01 level. So, null hypothesis has been rejected and alternative hypothesis is accepted. It means there is a significant relationship existing between increase in income and increase in savings. So, MFIs are successful in saving mobilization.

REGRESSION ANALYSIS BETWEEN INCREASE OF INCOME AND ROLE IN DECISION MAKING PROCESS

H_{02}: there is no relationship between income increased and role in decision making process increase.

H_{a2}: there is a significant relationship

Variables Entered/Removed[a]

Model	Variables Entered	Variables Removed	Method
1	The income has increased[b]	.	Enter

a. Dependent Variable: Role in decision making process increased

b. All requested variables entered.

Model Summary

Mode l	R	R Square	Adjuste d R Square	Std. Error of the Estimat e	Change Statistics				
					R Square Chang e	F Change	df1	df2	Sig. F Chang e
1	.484[a]	.234	.228	1.08516	.234	36.101	1	118	.000

a. Predictors: (Constant), The income has increased

ANOVA[a]

Model		Sum of Squares	df	Mean Square	F	Sig.
1	Regressio n	42.512	1	42.512	36.101	.000[b]
	Residual	138.954	118	1.178		
	Total	181.467	119			

a. Dependent Variable: Role in decision making process increased
b. Predictors: (Constant), The income has increased

Coefficients[a]

Model		Unstandardized Coefficients		Standardized Coefficients	t	Sig.
		B	Std. Error	Beta		
1	(Constant)	4.214	.344		12.242	.000
	The income has increased	-.563	.094	-.484	-6.008	.000

a. Dependent Variable: Role in decision making process increased

From the regression analysis and ANOVA table that shows there exist significant relationship between role in decision making increased and income increased. So, null hypothesis has been rejected and alternative hypothesis accepted. It is a clear indication that microfinance is playing a significant role in empowering the rural poor in decision making process through increase in their income.

RELATIONSHIP BETWEEN THE INCREASE OF INCOME AND THE OPERATINAL AAISTANCE RECEIVED FROM MFI

H_{03}: there is no relationship between operational assistance received from MFIs and income increased.

H_{a3}: there exists a significant relationship.

ANOVA[a]

Model		Sum of Squares	df	Mean Square	F	Sig.
1	Regression	22.363	1	22.363	24.262	.000[b]
	Residual	106.925	116	.922		
	Total	129.288	117			

a. Dependent Variable: The income has increased

b. Predictors: (Constant), Operational assistance received from MFIs was helpful to run the business

Variables Entered/Removed[a]

Model	Variables Entered	Variables Removed	Method
1	Operational assistance received from MFIs was helpful to run the business[b]	.	Enter

a. Dependent Variable: The income has increased
b. All requested variables entered.

Model Summary

Model	R	R Square	Adjusted R Square	Std. Error of the Estimate	Change Statistics				
					R Square Change	F Change	df1	df2	Sig. F Change
1	.416[a]	.173	.166	.96009	.173	24.262	1	116	.000

a. Predictors: (Constant), Operational assistance received from MFIs was helpful to run the business

Coefficients[a]

Model		Unstandardized Coefficients		Standardized Coefficients	t	Sig.
		B	Std. Error	Beta		
1	(Constant)	2.424	.244		9.947	.000
	Operational assistance received from MFIs was helpful to run the business	.380	.077	.416	4.926	.000

a. Dependent Variable: The income has increased

From the above bi-variate regression analysis it is significant at 0.001 level. So, null hypothesis has been rejected and alternative hypothesis is accepted. It means the operational assistance received from MFIs is helpful in improving income level.

MULTIPLE REGRESSION ANALYSIS BETWEEN DIFFERENT VARIABLES RELATED TO STANDARDS OF LIVING

H_{04}: there is no significant relationship between living standards improved and increase in income, increase in savings, better access to health care, better access to education, and financial situation improved.

H$_{a4}$: increase in income, increase in savings, better access to education, better access to health care, and improved financial situation are significantly related to improved living standards.

Descriptive Statistics

	N	Maximum	Mean
The income has increased	120	5	3.5167
The savings has increased	120	5	3.3333
Better access to education	120	5	3.0083
Better access to healthcare	120	5	3.0083
Financial situation improved	120	5	3.4833
Living standards improved	120	5	3.9167
Valid N (listwise)	120		

Variables Entered/Removed^a

Model	Variables Entered	Variables Removed	Method
1	Financial situation improved, Better access to healthcare, The savings has increased, Better access to education, The income has increased^b	.	Enter

a. Dependent Variable: Living standards improved
b. All requested variables entered.

Model Summary

Model	R	R Square	Adjusted R Square	Std. Error of the Estimate	Change Statistics				
					R Square Change	F Change	df1	df2	Sig. F Change

1	.817^a	.668	.654	.61783	.668	45.925	5	114	.000

a. Predictors: (Constant), Financial situation improved, Better access to healthcare, The savings has increased, Better access to education, The income has increased

ANOVA^a

Model		Sum of Squares	df	Mean Square	F	Sig.
	Regression	87.651	5	17.530	45.925	.000^b
1	Residual	43.515	114	.382		
	Total	131.167	119			

a. Dependent Variable: Living standards improved
b. Predictors: (Constant), Financial situation improved, Better access to healthcare, The savings has increased, Better access to education, The income has increased

Coefficients^a

Model		Unstandardized Coefficients		Standardized Coefficients	t	Sig.
		B	Std. Error	Beta		
	(Constant)	.362	.249		1.456	.148
	The income has increased	.279	.105	.282	2.664	.009
	The savings has increased	.130	.086	.128	1.519	.131
1	Better access to education	.160	.085	.144	1.873	.064
	Better access to healthcare	-.026	.070	-.028	-.364	.716
	Financial situation improved	.498	.076	.443	6.569	.000

a. Dependent Variable: Living standards improved

From the above multiple regression analysis it is evident that it is statistically significant (with F=45.925 and probability 0.000). Hence, null hypothesis has been rejected and alternative hypothesis has been accepted. It means increase in income, savings, better access to health care, education and improved financial situation are significantly related to living standards improved.

FINDING AND CONCLUSION

Microfinance is playing a vital role in improving the living standards of the rural poor in rural areas of Visakhapatnam district. SHGs are playing decisive role in outreach of microfinance to rural poor in Visakhapatnam. Most of the microfinance users are married and middle aged women. Microfinance users prefer ten thousand rupees and more for their business purposes. Large number of people found using these micro finance funds to their household requirements and that is not the purpose of loan given. Microfinance users of Visakhapatnam are repaying from their business income and savings. These people found satisfaction with the way loan where being processed. Most of the people are aware the purpose for which the loan was given, the duration and terms of microfinance and very few people were found unaware of the particulars. The operational assistance from MFIs is important in increasing income. Increasing income is also increasing the role in their decision making process within the family there by empowering the women. Increase in income, increase in savings, better access to education, better access to health care and improvement in financial position have a significant relationship with improvement in living standards after availing microfinance facility. Hence, microfinance facilities the institutions can be positively attributed towards the improvement of the members living standards.

REFERENCES

1. David s. gibbons and Jennifer w. meehan,2002, Financing microfinance for poverty reduction

2. Mohammad Arifujjaman Khan, Mohammed Anisur Rahaman.Impact of Microfinance on Living Standards, Empowerment and Poverty Alleviation of Poor People: A Case Study on Microfinance in the Chittagong District of Bangladesh –

3. Gerard Tchouassi and LEFI, 2011.Microfinance, inequality and vulnerability: Empirical analysis from Central African countries –Journal of Development and Agricultural Economics Vol. 3(4), pp. 150-156,

4. Abosede, Adebiyi Julius* and Azeez, Bolanle Aminat , 2011.Microfinance and gender in the context of millennium development goals (MDGs) in Nigeria –Journal of Development and Agricultural Economics Vol. 3(3), pp. 98-106, March 2011

5. William Gabriel Brafu-Insaidoo and Ferdinand Ahiakpor,2011. Understanding the marketing strategies of microfinance institutions within the Accra metropolis of Ghana: Case of selected institutions African Journal of Marketing Management Vol. 3(2), pp. 45-55

6. Rajesh Kumar Shastri, 2009. Micro finance and poverty reduction in India (A comparative study with Asian Countries) African Journal of Business Management Vol.3 (4), pp. 136-140, April, 2009

7. C. O Adebayo, S. A Sanni and L. J. S Baiyegunhi. Microcredit scheme impact and food security status of beneficiaries in Kaduna State, Nigeria: A propensity score matching approach,African Journal of Agricultural Research Vol. 7 –

8. K. Nithya kala, K. Vidya kala and S. Poornima, 2012..Micro finance – an anti poverty vaccine for rural India.International journal of marketing, financial services & management research Vol.1 No. 1, , ISSN 2277 3622

9. Dr. B.B. Mansuri , 2010. microfinancing through self help groups- a case study of bank linkage programme. Sri krishna international research & educational consortium volume 1, issue 3 (December, 2010) issn 2229-4104

10. Sanjay kanthi Das. Perception of Group Members on Self Help Groups' Impact: An Empirical Study. International Journal of Business and Management (IJBM) Volume (1) : Issue (1) 13 by

11. Lakshmi and Vadivalagan. Impact of self help groups on empowerment of women: a study in Dharmapuri district. Tamilnadu by http://jms.nonolympictimes.org/articles/5.pdf

12. Charles o. ondoro, dorine omena,2012. Effect of microfinance services on the financial empowerment of youth in migori county, kenya Business and management review vol. 2(3) pp. 22 – 35 may, 2012 issn: 2047 - 0398

13. Chintamani prasad patnaik, 2012. Micro finance role in poverty alleviation and economic growth- a study in gajapati dstrict. International journal of social sciences and interdisciplinary research vol.1 no. 3, march 2012, issn 2277 3630

13. Dr. Anita soni ,2012. Analysis of financial performance of micro finance industry International journal of marketing, financial and services & management research vol.1 no. 4, april 2012, issn 2277 3622

14. O.O. Akanji- cbn. ,Micro-finance as a strategy for poverty reduction.Economic & financial review, vol. 39 n0. 4

15. Joe Remenyi .,Introduction: microfinance and poverty reduction., international and community development, deakin university

16. Appah, ebimobowei, john, m. sophia, and soreh wisdom,2012. An analysis of microfinance and poverty reduction in bayelsa state of Nigeria. .Kuwait chapter of
arabian journal of business and management review vol. 1, no.7; march 2012

17. Savita Shankar,2013. Financial inclusion in india: Do microfinance institutions address access barriers?ACRN journal of entrepreneurship perspectives vol. 2, issue 1, p. 60-74, ISSN 2224-9729

18. DR. B.B. Mansuri ,2010. Microfinancing through self help groups- a case study of bank linkage programme of NABARD- Apjrbm volume 1, issue 3 (december, 2010) issn 2229-4104

19. N. Manimekala, 2004. impact of various forms of micro financing on women-, submitted to department of women and child development ministry of human resource development government of india 2004

20. Nichel Halouni and Prof Younes boujelbene, 2011. Micro finance and social performance in aafrica- Indian Journal of Finance, vol 58.

21. M.V.S. Mahendra ,2011.The empowerment of women through microfinance-A Case Study of rangareddy district, AP, India. Indian Journal of Finance, vol 5,

CASE STUDY- 2
Self-help Groups Bank Linkage Programme in India: A study with reference to Andhra Pradesh

*Dr.S.S.S.DURGA GANESH
*Associate Professor in Commerce, Mrs. AVN College, Visakhapatnam

**V.M.VEENA
**Research Scholar, DCMS, Andhra University, Visakhapatnam

Abstract

The Self-Help Group Bank Linkage Programme (SHG-BLP) was an attempt to bring the 'unbanked' poor into the formal banking system and to inculcate among the poor the thrift and credit habits, a natural corollary is for the group members to adapt into seeking more and better livelihood opportunities with access to credit from formal financial institutions. The SHG-BLP has crossed many milestones - from linking a pilot of 500 SHGs of rural poor two decades ago to cross 8 million groups a year ago. Similarly from a total savings corpus of a few thousands of Indian rupees in the early years to a whopping Rs.27,000 crore today, from a few crore of bank credit to a credit outstanding of Rs.40,000 crore and disbursements touching Rs.20,000 crore during 2012-13. The SHG Bank Linkage is a great success story in Andhra Pradesh. In the current financial year, the government of Andhra Pradesh has facilitated Rs. 3966.82 crores of Bank Loans to 1.6lakhs SHGs up to end of October, 2013. The motive behind SHG-BLP is to combine the access to low-cost financial services with a process of self management and development. It is considered as most successful, promising and widely accepted model in India. The tremendous impact on the social status of the poor rural women becoming bread earners of their households through the instrument of SHGs has been highly commended by many researchers. The mushrooming of the Micro Finance Institutions (MFIs) smelling the 'business opportunities' with the poor, also led to an unhealthy trend of more and more credit being pumped without proper appraisal of the loanees and before assessing their capacity to repay. The grave crisis of confidence of MFIs and subsequent developments has had a highly negative impact on the micro credit initiative in the country had led to SHG-BLP. It is a pilot project started by NABARD is widely accepted model as one of the largest and successful one in the world. The present study is analytical and based upon secondary data which has been collected from different published reports, journals and existing available literature. The objective of this study is to evaluate the progress and impact of self help group bank linkage programme in Andhra Pradesh. The bank linkage programme for women self help groups is about Rs.20,000 crore and in five years time the government wants to increase this to Rs.1,00,000 crore.

Introduction

The Self-Help Group (SHG) movement originated in Bangladesh under the Leadership of Noble Laureate Mohamed Yunus. It is a noble mission-an innovative concept that has its roots in Bangladesh and also touched every part of the globe. In order to achieve the mission of reaching those families who did not access to credit by any formal financial institution and, therefore, were dependent on informal sources and moneylenders, the National Bank for Agriculture and Rural Development (NABARD) introduced the 'SHG - Bank Linkage Programme (SHG-BLP)' as a pilot project in1992. SHGs have emerged as popular method of working with people in recent years. Since SHG based micro-finance programmes cover a large number of women. SHG-BLP has an important bearing on women's social, economical and cultural empowerment. The SHG today have become a vehicle to purse diverse developmental agendas since its impact SHGs on the psychological, economical and social well being. It is all happened due to fast growing of the SHG-BLP model in the country. SHG-BLP was developed in India to provide finance to the vast rural poor. In this programme, the informal SHGs are credit linked with the formal financial institutions.

SHG-BLP has emerged as a dominant, relevant and effective prorgramme in India. It is flexible, independence creating, and imparts freedom of savings and borrowing according to the heterogeneous needs and requirements of the group members. SHG is a homogeneous group, comprising 15-20 members (mostly women), where members first pool in their savings and give out small loans to needy members. Once the SHG successfully undertakes savings and credit operations from its own resources, it can borrow from a bank SHG-BLP to enhance its pool of resources. SHGs are small, cohesive and participative groups of the poor, who pool their thrift regularly and use it to make small interest bearing loans to members and in the process, learn the nuances of financial discipline. Subsequently they graduate to access bank credit to augment their resources for lending to their members in need of financial assistance for meeting their credit needs.   Over the years the pooled resources of the SHGs become a sizeable corpus, which complimented by higher volume of bank loan enables them to take up livelihood activities which results in improving their standard of living.

Through SHG-Bank Linkage, the Reserve Bank of India(RBI) and National Bank for Agriculture and Rural Development (NABARD) has promoted relationship banking, i.e., 'improving the existing relationship between the poor and the bankers with the social intermediation of the NGOs.' The SHG-BLP in India is rapidly expanding its outreach under the pioneering initiative of NABARD, the monitoring and supervision of RBI, and the promotional policies of the government of India. At the grass root level, the programme is being implemented by the commercial banks, cooperatives, and regional rural banks, with government agencies. The state government's also implementing this programme with different names. The government of Andhra Pradesh is committed to social and economic empowerment of women. It has adopted micro credit as a tool to attain the same and had taken the SHG-Bank Linkage program as a mass movement since 1998-99 onwards in the State to achieve the goal.

Andhra Pradesh is vigorously implementing this programme under the banner of Indira KranthiPatham and covered 1.6 lakhs SHGs under SHG-BLP. Today SHGs play a major role in poverty alleviation in rural India. They have changed the life of many individuals /groups for the better. This is considered not only a tool for poverty alleviation, but also has proved to be appropriate social and human development. The SHG-BLP has provided a more favorable environment for enhancing India's potential for greater equitable growth with empowerment while considering the positive signs in their performance. The present study is analytical and based upon secondary data which has been collected from different published reports, journals and existing available literature. The objective of this study is to evaluate the progress and impact of self help group bank linkage programme in India and Andhra Pradesh.

Dr.C.Rangarajan, Chairman of The Economic Advisory Council to the Prime Minister said on the occasion of Microfinance India 2010 Summit in New Delhi that 'greater linkage between banks and Self Help Groups (SHGs) and expansion of the Business Correspondent (BC) model were likely to bring a surge in the microfinance sector.' The Bank-SHG linkage programme has an important role to play with the addition of the BC model.'

SHG-Bank Linkage Model
The 'Status of Microfinance in India' report observed that a successful programme such as the SHG-BLP, which could link millions of rural poor to the formal banking system, could have been the main instrument for financial literacy and financial inclusion in the country. There are a number of plausible ways by which matured SHGs could have been participants in the financial inclusion initiative, including being agents of providing direct banking services to the millions of households at their doorsteps, as a low-cost and efficient alternative.

As on March-end 2013, the total number of SHGs linked with banks stood at 73.18 lakh, with savings aggregating Rs. 8,217 Crore. Further 44.51 lakh SHGs had loans outstanding aggregating Rs. 39,375 Crore. This achievement might have been happened due to regular and voluntary savings and internal lending. The SHG-BLP model is the largest financial inclusion programme in the world. (The Business Line-Oct 18, 2013).

A SHG after completing a period of 6 months is rated by the Branch Manager of the bank to which it is savings linked, on certain parameters. If the SHG passes the rating exercise, the bank extends it a loan which is known as credit linkage. SHGs are rated by banks every time they take a loan from the bank. Therefore, it calls for continuous best practices by SHGs for getting repeat dosage of credit. The rate of interest charged by the bank for a loan to SHG is the Prime Lending Rate (PLR) of the bank which is in the range of about 12 per cent per annum. SHGs in some of the states in the country enjoy the benefit of interest subvention. SHGs in Andhra Pradesh pay only 3 per cent interest on bank loans and the balance 9 per cent is reimbursed by government of Andhra Pradesh. Similarly, SHGs in Karnataka also enjoy the benefit of interest subvention besides waiver of stamp duty on loan documents. This is one of the positive impacts of the programme in reducing the interest burden of the members and avoiding the exploitation of the poor by informal agencies, particularly money lenders, commission agents, etc.

It is worth mentioning that the recovery performance of banks is almost satisfactory. Almost all the banks have reported that more than or equal to 95 per cent recovery was done. The bankers are generally happy about the recovery performance under their SHG portfolio what is more gladdening is the fact that there are no coercive methods in recovery of loans.

Table -I: Overall progress under SHG-Bank Linkage for last 3 years
(Rs.Crores)

Particulars		2010-11		2011-12		2012-13	
		No. of SHGs (lakh)	Amount	No. of SHGs (lakh)	Amount	No. of SHGs (lakh)	Amount
SHG Savings with Banks as on 31 March 2013	Total SHGs	74.62 (7.3%)	7016.30 (13.2%)	79.60 (6.7%)	6551.41 (-6.7%)	73.18 (-8.1%)	8217.25 (25.4%)
	All Women SHGs	60.98 (14.8%)	5298.65 (17.8%)	62.99 (3.3%)	5104.33 (-3.7%)	59.38 (-5.7%)	6514.86 (27.6%)
Loans Disbursed to SHGs during the year	Total SHGs	11.96 (-24.6%)	14547.73 (0.01%)	11.48 (-4%)	16534.77 (13.7%)	12.20 (6.3%)	20585.36 (24.5%)
	All Women SHGs	10.17 (-21.4%)	12622.33 (1.6%)	9.23 (-9.2%)	14132.02 (12.0%)	10.37 (12.4%)	17854.31 (26.3%)
Loans Outstanding against SHGs as on 31 March2013	Total SHGs	47.87 (-1.3%)	31221.17 (11.4%)	43.54 (-9.0%)	36340.00 (16.4%)	44.51 (2.2%)	39375.30 (8.4%)
	All Women SHGs	39.84 (2.2%)	26123.75 (13.4%)	36.49 (-8.4%)	30465.28 (16.6%)	37.57 (2.9%)	32840.04 (7.8%)

(Figures in the parenthesis indicates growth/decline over the previous year)
Source: Status of Microfinance in India 2012-13

The bank linkage programme for women self help groups is about Rs.20000 crore and in five years time the government wants to increase this to Rs.1,00,000 crore.

The SHG Banlk Linkage Programme has the following objectives:
a) To develop mutual faith and confidence between the rural poor and bankers.
b) To combine sensitivity, flexibility and responses of the informal credit system with the strength of administration capabilities, technical strength and the financial resources of the formal financial institutions.
c) To expand credit flow/ financial services to the rural poor with less transaction costs.
d) To alleviate poverty and empower the women.

Findings

It is observed from the table-I shows that there is a decline in the number of SHGs savings linked with banks to the extent of 8.1 per cent during the year 2012-13 for the first time since the SHG-BLP was launched, though the savings harnessed by SHGs grew by 25.4 per cent. It is evident that this decline is in spite of more number of new SHGs savings linked to banks during the year pointing to existing SHGs gone out of the Banks linkage programme during the year. This decline can be attributed to banks now reporting only operative savings accounts of SHGs and in few instances of banks closing down accounts with 'nil' balances. Further, as banks were advised to switch to system generated (core banking solution) reporting only, this has also led to 'data cleansing' and more accurate reporting of operative (and not cumulative) SHG accounts.

It is also observed from the loans disbursed to SHGs during the year shows that the declining trend in the number of SHGs being extended fresh loans by banks for the last 3 years has been reversed this year with the number going up from 11.48 lakhs during 2011-12 to 12.20 lakhs during 2012-13 (an increase of over 6 per cent). The quantum of fresh loans issued during the year also went up by nearly 25 per cent to Rs. 20,585 Crore. The number of SHGs availing fresh loans by banks showed an increase of 6.3 per cent during the year and the quantum of fresh loans issued increased by 24.5 per cent over the previous year. It is also observed that the banks are lending more to credible SHGs, providing repeat finances to SHGs with a sound credit history.

From the above table it is also found that, the loans outstanding against SHGs shows that the number of SHGs having loans outstanding against grew by 2.2 per cent to 44.51 lakh as against 43.54 lakhs a year back while the amount of loan outstanding against them grew by 8.4 per cent and now stands at Rs. 39,375 Crore (Rs. 36,340 Crore last year). The growth in the loan outstanding of SHGs with banks (8.4 per cent) is almost 4 times the growth in the number of SHGs having outstanding loans with banks (2.2 per cent).

Social Impact and Empowerment

SHG Bank Linkage model pioneered by NABARD was not just meant for financial inclusion for rural poor women who usually belong to backward classes, scheduled castes and tribes. It had a holistic approach, i.e. besides financial inclusion, economic and social empowerment of poor women. Various studies conducted by NABARD, National Council of Applied Economic Research (NCEAR) and Institute for Social and Economic Change (ISEC) spoken in one voice about the paradigm change in the ways rural poor women think and act in the post-SHG phase. SHG members could undertake tasks like travelling alone to the next town or city, going alone to banks, offices of Tahsildar (revenue department) and hospitals, handling certain amount of money, addressing a forum and contesting for panchayat elections and others etc, with confidence in post-SHG phase. Studies also found that more than 70 per cent of women respondents reported improvement or even significant enhancement in their ability to face domestic problems. Overall findings indicate that the decision making capacity of women members with various SHG activities has improved drastically. SHG members were become part of the decision making process in all kinds of developmental activities of that village/mandal. Now SHGs are concentrating on educating their children's in English medium schools and acquiring lands and other type of assets and conducting marriages to their daughters splendidly. Members also reported in changing undesirable habits of their husbands. They are also participating in revamping the Public Distribution System (PDS), health and nutrition facilities. Finally SHGs are playing a major/dominant role in poverty alleviation in rural India. They have changed the life of many individuals/groups for better. The SHG-BLP has provided a more favorable environment for enhancing India's potential for greater equitable growth with empowerment while considering the positive signs in their performance.

It is the duty and responsibility of the central and state governments to socially empower the poor in terms of health, education and livelihood and there is no better conduit available other than SHGs to accomplish the task. Therefore, it is apparent that over the years, the SHG-BLP has invested sufficiently in building social capital in the country by way of organizing various training and capacity building programmes to SHG members at the time of formation itself besides financial assistance at low interest rates. This investment in the form of training and capacity building has enabled the rural poor woman to undertake responsibilities which she was not capable of taking up in pre-SHG situation.

Benefits to Banks

Till the early 1990s, the feeling among the bankers was that rural women do not have ability to save or borrow. SHG-Bank Linkage Model opened the eyes of many including the bankers towards rural poor women. It brought about an attitudinal change among the banking community and they no longer look SHG Bank Linkage Model as social sector banking. On the contrary, the nation has realized that loans to SHGs are one of the most profitable portfolios of any bank.

Banks while fulfilling their financial inclusion duties by extending the banking services to the rural poor have found SHG as a platform for reducing their transaction and risk cost. Imagine a scenario where all the members of 69,53,000 SHGs to be individually linked to banks. The cost of transacting with this huge segment would have been a big drain on banks' human and financial resources. By adopting the group approach, banks have reduced their transaction cost to a significant extent while dealing with the poor. Further, a portion of the groups' savings lying with the banks, estimated to be Rs. 6198.71 Crore as on 31 March 2010 is a significant source of low-cost deposits available with the banking community for profitable deployment.

The MFI model

It is given that MFIs are not the pioneers in microfinance. They have come into existence only after the SHG-Bank Linkage Model proved that poor is bankable. MFIs are not reaching to the unreached as they claim to be. Most of the MFIs are operating in places where the banking density is quite high in the country and credit to deposit ratio is satisfactory. MFIs are focusing more in irrigated areas of Andhra Pradesh, Tamil Nadu and Karnataka for their lending activities rather than reaching out to the poor in other regions of the country. The biggest bane in MFI model is transparency in interest rates.

MFIs do not spend time and resources in formation of groups and their capacity building. They usually poach members from established SHGs and form groups only to lend and recover loans. There is no capacity building to make them aware about the benefits of savings, smart borrowings, intelligent investments and financial discipline. In the SHG-Bank Linkage Model, capacity building gains precedence over credit. This has resulted in strengthening communities through investments in social capital.

SHG-BLP in Andhra Pradesh
In the financial year 2013, bank lending to SHGs was to the tune of over Rs.20,000 crore, out of which Rs.12,000 crore was distributed in Andhra Pradesh, Rs.2000 crore in Tamil Naidu, Rs.1600 crore in Karnataka and Rs.1000 crore in Kerala. It is obvious to say that 80 per cent of the amount was distributed in the southern part of the country and 60 per cent purely goes to Andhra Pradesh because of its commendable success of implementations of the programme in state.

The government of Andhra Pradesh is committed to social and economic empowerment of women. It has adopted micro credit as a tool to attain the same and had taken the SHG-Bank Linkage program as a mass movement since 1998-99 onwards in the State to achieve the goal. The activities of DWCRA and Velugu were integrated under a programme called Indira Kranti Patham in Andhra Pradesh. The basic objective of this integration is to implement various programmes for strengthening of self-help Groups with similar implementation strategy. The new scheme Indira Kranti Patham had been designed by clubbing Women Empowerment with Poverty Alleviation.

Indira Kranti Patham (IKP) is a statewide poverty reduction project to enable the rural poor to improve their livelihoods and quality of life through their own organizations. It aims to cover all the rural poor households in the state with a special focus on the 30 lakh poorest of the poor households. It is implemented by Society for Elimination of Rural Poverty (SERP), Dept of Rural Development, Govt of AP. SERP is an autonomous society registered under the societies act, and implements the project through District Rural Development Agencies (DRDAs) at the District level. The Chief Minister of Andhra Pradesh is the Chairperson of the Society. IKP builds on more than a decade long, statewide rural women's self-help movement. The focus is on deepening the process, providing an institutional structure and developing a framework for sustaining it for comprehensive poverty eradication. It is the single largest poverty reduction project in South Asia.

It works with 4,76,930 Self Help Groups federated into 28,080 Village Organizations (VO) and 700 Mandal Samakhyas (MS). The project mandate is to build strong institutions of the poor and enhance their livelihood opportunities so that the vulnerabilities of the poor are reduced. Community Investment Fund (CIF) is the major component of the project, which is provided to the SHGs/ VOs/ MSs to support wide range of activities for socio-economic empowerment of the Poor.

India might be the world's largest democracy, but it's also one of the most gender-skewed. Women remain under-represented at every level. The SHG-BPL has empowered the poor women by all means. Thus, a land where women have been discriminated for generations, thousands of poor illiterate women are spearheading a silent revolution. The remarkable success of women Self-Help Groups in Andhra Pradesh were well impressed by the world renowned personalities like former Presidents of USA, Bill Clinton and George Bush, the Micro Soft Wizard Bill Gates.

Financial Access

To encourage the poor including disadvantaged groups and communities to access the credit facility services seamlessly Community Investment Fund from project side, and linkages from bank side are provided to the poor women SHG members to improve their Livelihoods.CIF supports the poor in prioritizing livelihood needs by investments in sub-projects proposed and implemented by the Community Based Organizations(CBOs). SERP facilitated Rs.3244.98 crore of Bank Loans to 1,30,085 SHGs up to September 2012 in 2012-13. The cumulative CIF expenditure up to March,2012 is Rs.1088.07 crores and the total numbers of beneficiaries was 30,76,112 .The SHG Bank Linkage is a great success story in the state. The year wise progress from 2004-05 to March 2012-13 are shown in Table –II.

Table -II : SHG Bank Linkages

(Rs.Crores)

Year	Coverage of Groups	Amount of Loan	No. of Branches	Per Group Finance(Rs.)	Groups Per Branch
2004-05	2,61,254	1017.7	3,853	38,954	68
2005-06	2,88,711	2001.4	3,853	69,322	75
2006-07	3,66,489	3063.87	3,950	83,601	93
2007-08	4,31,515	5882.79	4,000	1,36,329	108
2008-09	4,83,601	6684.07	4,150	1,37,498	118
2009-10	4,13,625	6501.35	4,274	1,57,180	97
2010-11	3,89,444	7092.71	4,286	1,82,123	91
2011-12	3,52,485	8084.16	4,324	2,29,347	82
2012-13	4,54,561	11,128.00	4,915	2,44,808	92

Source: Indira kranthi Patham-Society for Elimination of Rural Poverty Progress
                        Report October,2013

It is also examined that Self help movement through savings has been taken up on a massive scale for poor rural women. The success of Self Help Groups in Andhra Pradesh has been a national model and presently has 10.59 lakh groups covering 1.6 crore of poor rural women. Interest free loans taken by them Rs.12,575 crore, Savings created by SHGs one rupee per day accumulated today Rs.15,000 crores (2013-14) this is equivalent to 10 per cent of AP state budget. Stree nidhi bank disbursed loans to SHGs in 2012-13 Rs.750 crores. This year 2013-14 expected to provide loans to SHGs Rs. 1600 crores

Findings

In the current financial year, SERP has facilitated Rs. 3,966.82 Crores of Bank Loans to 1,50,338 SHGs up to end of October, 2013. To reduce the financial burden on the self-help groups, the government of AP has announced an improved incentive scheme for the SHGs repaying installment promptly from the present PavalaVaddi to zero per cent interest (Vaddi Leni Runalu) with effective from 1.1.2012. All SHGs who have taken bank loans are eligible for Vaddi Leni Runalu, whose borrowings not exceeding Rs.5.00 lakhs. Under this scheme during 2013-14 an amount of Rs. 606.74 crores are to be disbursed to 7,57,325 SHGs up to October, 2013. 1098 Mandal Mahila Samakhyas (MMS) of SHGs in association with government of Andhra Pradesh have promoted 'STHREE NIDHI' Credit Cooperative Federation Ltd to address the issues of inadequate finance and to ensure timely availability of credit, preferably within 48 hours, for meeting emergent and other needs of the poorest of the poor. During this fiscal up to the end of October,2013 Rs.509.83 Crores were disbursed to 2,44,776 members of 60,525 SHGs in 22,465 VOs in 1059 mandals, thus the total amount disbursed upto end of October,2013 is Rs. 1241.49 Crores to 1, 78,191 SHGs.

The study shows that micro-finance programmes provided economic benefits to the people for whom the programmes were initiated. These benefits were mainly availability of savings and credit facility, access to credit for consumption and production, and use of credit for undertaking income generating activities.

Economic Benefits through SHG-BLP in AP

The finding that economic benefits were more pronounced in the project area of GramaVikas points to factors other than micro-finance at work. These are availability of larger funds for income generation mainly due to NABARD's Bank-SHG linkage programme and donor funds, and the existence of infrastructure (dairy marketing outlets). This leads to the hypothesis that the ability of the micro-finance programme to provide economic benefits depends on whether the factors are conducive for members to undertake income generating activities with the help of credit. Another important issue is sustainability of these programmes. Both the programmes depend somewhat heavily on donors for sustainability. The situation seems to be better in the project area of GramaVikas largely due to the presence of well functioning federation of SHGs, and larger amount of credit fund built with the help of donors and NABARD.

Further, over 35,000 women from villages across Andhra Pradesh are now using laptops to record financial activities of their SHGs because of their financial access with banks. Through the training programmes conducted "conducted by SERP from time to time, they are now able to operate the device and upload the data. SERP have selected the women who can identify English alphabets and are aware of terms such as income, expenditure, loan and repayment. The programme was sponsored by the World Bank. The laptops are owned by SERP, but are with the women. Nevertheless, it can be concluded that micro-finance programmes do provide the poor with access to credit, enable them to undertake income generation programmes and contribute to higher social enhancements in the villages.

Conclusion

SHG-Bank Linkage Programme is developed in India to provide finance to the vast rural poor. In this programme, the informal SHGs are credit linked with the formal financial institutions. It has emerged as a dominant, relevant and effective prorgramme in terms of borrowers and loans outstanding in India. It is flexible, independence creating, and imparts freedom of savings and borrowing according to the heterogeneous needs and requirements of the group members. The NABARD introduced the 'SHG-BLP' as a pilot project in 1992. Thereafter, RBI had advised commercial banks to participate actively in this programme. Subsequently, this programme was further extended to all Regional Rural Banks (RRBs) and Cooperative Banks. Today Self-help groups (SHGs) play a major role in poverty alleviation in rural India. SHGs have changed the life of many individuals/groups for the better. This is considered not only a tool for poverty alleviation, but also has proved to be relevant in social and human development. The SHG-Bank Linkage Programme has provided a more favorable environment for enhancing India's potential for greater equitable growth with empowerment while considering the positive signs in their performance. Because of its importance the government of India is planning to increase its outlay of bank linkage programme for women self help groups from Rs.20,000 crore to Rs.1,00,000 crore in next five years.

References

1. Das Sanjay Kanti.2012. Practices of Self Help Groups in Rural India: A Comparative Assessment on Quality and Impact, Economic Affairs 2012, Volume-57,Issue -2, ISSN:0424-2513.x ISSN:0976-4666 (Online).
2. India-Microfinance .2013. On line retrieved on November, 2013.
3. Indira KranthiPatham/ SERP AP.2013. Progress report of AP Government Oct 2013
4. Master Circulars on SHG-Bank linkage Programmes-Government of India July 01,2013
5. Misra and Puri. 2012. Indian Economy, Himalaya Publishing House, Mumbai.
6. NABARD .2012-13. Status of Microfinance in India - NABARD Annual Report 2012-13-The Business Line- October, 18,2013
7. NABARD. Financial Inclusion can be better achieved through self-help groups, www.**nabard**.org ,retrieved on Nov,2013
8. Rajasekhar, D. 2011. Micro-Finance, Poverty Alleviation and Empowerment of Women: A Study of Two NGOs from Andhra Pradesh and Karnataka,Retrieved on Nov2013
9. Uma Narang.2012. Impact of Self- Help Groups Bank Linkage Programme in India, International Journal of Trade and Commerce-IIARTC July-December 2012, Volume 1, No. 2, pp. 220-228 ISSN-2277-5811 (Print), ISSN 2278-9065 (Online)
10. VenkateshTagat. 2010. SHG-Bank Linkage Model-Why it is better?, An interview with Chief General Manager – NABARD Karnataka. http://indiamicrofinance.com/interview-dr-venkatesh-tagat-chief-general-manager-nabard-karnataka.html retrieved on Nov,2013
11. Venugopalan Puhazhendhi.2013. Micro Finance in India-State of the Sector Report 2012, SAGE Publications India Pvt Ltd, New Delhi

*****

CASE STUDY-3

A STUDY ON PSYCHOLOGICAL EMPOWERMENT OF SHG MEMBERS IN KRISHNA DISTRICT

*Dr.N.Subramanyam
**Mrs.N.Sailaja
***Mrs.G.Madhu Sri

Abstract

Microfinance has proved to be an effective tool for women empowerment. Microfinance includes micro credit, micro insurance and micro pension; etc.Micro credit is an extension of small loans to the poor to enable them to take up income generating activities. India now occupies a significant place and a niche in global microfinance through promotion of the self-help groups (SHGs) and the home grown SHG-Bank Linkage (SBL) model. The Indian model offers greater promise and potential to address poverty as it is focused on building social capital through providing access to financial services through linking with the mainstream. Though the access to credit has been seen as a motivational factor behind the formation of Self Help Groups (SHGs), SHGs have a potential that goes beyond mere economics of loan management. SHGs ensure people's participation in the development process as these are the grass root level democratic institutions of rural people. The vital function of the Self Help Group (SHG) programme is to provide access to credit in the context of poverty reduction and empowerment of women. With the aim to meet the millennium development goals and microfinance programme's role in supporting it, there has been an increasing expectation on their impact on women empowerment. However, the perception and expectations of the members of the SHGs vary from person to person. This paper focuses on the perceptions of the sample members, who are engaged in different income generating activities, in terms of psychological empowerment.

*Dr.N.Subramanyam, Professor, Department of Business Administration, SRK Institute of Technology, Enikepadu, Vijayawada._____ mail id:nsm.subramabnyam@gmail.com
**Mrs. N.Sailaja, Asst. Professor, Department of Business Administration, Vijaya Institute of Technology for Women,Enikepadu, Vijayawada. mail id:siri.sailu812@gmail.com

***Mrs. G. Madhu Sri, Research Scholar, Department of Business Administration, P.B.Siddhartha College of Arts & Science, Vijayawada, mail id: gaganasahasra@gmail.com.

1.0. Introduction:

Empowerment is essentially a bottom-up process rather than something that can be formulated as a top-down strategy understanding empowerment in this aspect means that development agencies cannot claim to 'Empower Women', women must empower themselves. The United Nations Development Programme (UNDP) has recently adopted a gender in development goal, which includes a commitment to advocating and promoting women in the political and economic decision-making at all levels. As a result, Indian women are being recognized as a separate target group after 1980, and the government begins to direct its effort towards mainstreaming of women into the national development process.

Three major approaches have been adopted one after the other by the government towards the development of women, namely, the welfare approach, the anti-poverty approach and the equity/equality approach. While the welfare approach lays stress on the importance of women's role as wife and mother and carriers of family welfare, the anti-poverty approach is built on two strategies: need for recognizing women's participation in development and exposing women's significant contribution to family income. There has been much effort taken to mobilize poor women and provide them with economic support through income generating projects and co-operative functioning. The equity/equality approach focusses on women's actual productive contribution and its aim is to ensure women's rightful and equal position in society through direct programs that would enhance women's activities in both the household as well as market spheres. Thus, the strategy for the empowerment of women has emerged in India.

An emphasis on empowerment of the individual level of analysis should not be taken to mean that sociopolitical or contexual factors are overlooked. Psychological Empowerment is not simply self-perceptions of competence but includes active engagement in one's community and an understanding of one's sociopolitical environment. Psychological Empowerment also includes learning about controlling troubles and learning how to face the problems. Thus, Psychological Empowerment should not be interpreted as individualism, the promotion of one ideology versus another, or merely an intra-psychic phenomenon. Rather, Psychological Empowerment includes beliefs that goals can be achieved, awareness about resources and factors. Psychological empowerment includes a sense of motivation to control or influence events. Decision making and problem solving skills and a critical awareness of one's sociopolitical environment was achieved as psychological empowering in the interactional component

1.1. Empowerment:

The term 'empower' literally refers to the power or authority given to a person to have independent control over his/her own life or the situation he/she lives in. It enables people to understand the reality of their environment and shape that environment if needed. Empowerment is a process that enlightens the people to go towards their destinations and improve their status. Particularly, empowerment liberates the people both mentally and physically. In every society there are powerful and powerless groups. Power is exercised in social, economic and political relations between individuals and groups. The excellence of power of an individual or group is, in turn, correlated to how many different kinds of resources they can access and control. It is a process of changing the existing power relations in favour of the poor and the marginalized women. It is a long-term process that requires changes in knowledge, attitude and behaviour of not only women, but also of men and the society at large. Therefore, the foremost aim of the empowerment of women is to provide those (women) with economic independence.

A working definition for this proposal is that empowerment refers to the process by which individuals, groups and communities become able to take control of their circumstances and achieve their own goals, thereby being able to work towards maximizing the quality of their lives (Adams 1990) The term "mutual aid group" will be used interchangeable with "self-help group"

1.2. Need for Women Empowerment:

Women represent 50 per cent of the world's population, produce half the world's food supply, account for 60 per cent of the working force, contribute up to 33.3 per cent of the official labour force, perform nearly 66.6 per cent of all working hours, receive 10 per cent of world economy but, surprisingly own less than one per cent of world's real estate. These data apparently justify that there is a need for Women Empowerment which shall be achieved only through providing opportunities and rights to basic civic amenities, education, equal wages; right to question, fight
against violence and injustice, make decision and express themselves. Hence, there is an urgent necessity to improve the status of women by well-conceived, planned development programmes which would have active community participation.

1.3. SHGs and Women Empowerment:

The Self Help Group concept has been in existence over the last two decades in India, but was predominantly applied in its rural areas. Initiatives by nongovernmental organisations (NGOs), policy decisions of the government, attention from donar agencies, and support by the National Agricultural Bank for Rural Development – all of these helped the Self Help Group Movement take off. Self Help Groups are seen to be a key vehicle for empowering women. Self Help Groups have brought about several changes in the society over the years. Some of them are listed below:
  ➤ SHG has improved the confidence and communication skills among its members.
  ➤ Awareness about various Government welfare schemes and participation of poor women in those schemes has increased.
  ➤ The economic status of SHG women has improved as they have taken up various economic activities.
  ➤ SHG women have come together breaking the caste and communal barriers.
  ➤ Higher level of participation of women in Gram Sabha and Panchayat Raj Institutions.
  ➤ Problems relating to lending have been solved to a greater extents
  ➤ It helps better nutrition and health.

1.4. Psychological Empowerment:

The conceptual development of psychological empowerment develops empowerment theory by explicitly defining a fundamental element necessary for understanding the other levels of analysis. Psychological empowerment may be distinguished from organisational or community empowerment, but it also influence and influenced by empowerment at other levles of analysis. The conceptualization of psychological empowerment that is presented is rooted firmly in a social action framework that includes community change, capacity building, and collectivity. Social change, however, may take many forms and may not necessarily result in a power struggle.

The term psychological empowerment is used to refer to empowerment at the individual level of analysis because it is intended to reflect a broader interpretation of the construct than simply intrapersonal characteristics (the term psychological refers to the study of both mind and behaviour). We define psychological empowerment as the ability to find the power within oneself to make choices and act upon them. This can be measured using outcome indicators such as self-efficacy or agency, feelings of autonomy, sense of self-worth, self-confidence or self-esteem.

Psychological Empowerment is defined by Levine and Perkins (1987) as the field that was born out of a commitment to addressing the problems of marginalized communities, an interest in preventing rather than treating mental health problems and a desire to work with disempowered communities to help them gain greater control over the resources and institutions that affected their lives

1.5. Objective of the Study:

> ➤ To find the perceptions of the sample respondents on the psychological impact of the SHG members.

1.6. Methodology:

The study uses both primary data and secondary data. Multi-stage random sampling method is used for the present study to collect primary data. Krishna district being selected for the present study. At the next level, two mandals (Kankipadu & Penamaluru) are selected for the present study. From each mandal, 50 SHG members, who are engaged in income generating activities, are selected randomly. Thus, the total sample size is 100. Primary data was collected from the 100 sample respondents using pre-tested questionnaire.

Sample Distribution

Table: 1.1: Vijayawada (Rural)

Sl. No.	Name of the mandal	Total No. of SHGs	No of SHG members	No. of SHG Members Taken for sample
1	Penamaluru	2039	20916	50
2	Kankipadu	1178	11931	50
	Total	7786	80216	100

1.7. SHG at Glance in Krishna District: Krishna District has a total of 49 mandals in the district. Out of 3, 48,493 rural households projected 348493 HHs (100%) are mobilized in the SHGs. A total 3,48,493(100%) of Poorest of the poor HHs are covered in to SHGs. Out of 1,18,117 SC HHs projected 1,18,117 HHs 100%) are mobilized in to SHGs. Out of 24,253 ST HHs projected 24,253(100%) are mobilized in to SHGs. There are 60,176 SHGs with a membership of 6, 61,936 women in the district as on August 2013.

1.8. PERCEPTION OF RESPONDENTS ON PSYCHOLOGICAL IMPACT:

The SHG provides scope for the improvement of mind and development of the body of an individual. The psychological impact constitutes improving confidence, awareness on self-reliance, societal status, improving literacy and communication skills and improving leadership skills. The perception of members on the psychological impact has been analyzed with the help of five statements, namely, SHG creates confidence to face problems, creates awareness about self-reliance, gives societal status, improves literacy and communication skills and improves leadership skills.

1.8.1. Confidence to face Problems: Table – 1.2 indicates distribution of the respondents by their opinion on whether membership in SHGs creates confidence to face problems. It is noted from the table that sample respondents constituting 68 per cent of the respondents have strongly agreed to this question, while 22 per cent of the respondents have agreed, whilst 7 per cent of the respondents are disagreed. On the other hand, 3 per cent of the respondents have strongly disagreed to this question.

Table 1.2: Distribution of the Sample Respondents by their Perception on Membership in SHG Creates Confidence to Face Problems

Category	Membership in SHG Create Confidence to Face Problems				Total
	Strongly agree	Agree	Disagree	Strongly Disagree	
Tailoring Women	5 (55.56)	4 (44.44)	0	0	9 (100.00)
Grocery shop business women	7 (87.50)	1 (12.50)	0	0	8 (100.00)
Fancy shop business women	11 (61.11)	5 (27.78)	2 (11.11)	0	18 (100.00)
Clothes business women	10 (58.83)	3 (17.65)	2 (11.76)	2 (11.76)	17 (100.00)
Vegetable vending business women	7 (87.50)	1 (12.50)	0	0	8 (100.00)
Fish vending business women	1 (50.00)	1 (50.00)	0	0	2 (100.00)
Dairy business women	2 (100.00)	0	0	0	2 (100.00)
Petty business women	18 (66.67)	6 (22.22)	2 (7.41)	1 (3.70)	27 (100.00)
Tiffin stalls business women	7 (77.78)	1 (11.11)	1 (11.11)	0	9 (100.00)
TOTAL	**68** (68.00)	**22** (22.00)	**7** (7.00)	**3** (3.00)	**100** (100.00)

In conclusion, SHGs create confidence to the sample members to face problems. Majority of the sample respondents reported confidence to face problems after joining SHGs. However, some of the respondents of some income generating activities only reported no confidence to face problems.

1.8.2. Awareness about Self-Reliance:

Table – 1.3 presents distribution of the respondents by their opinion on the statement that membership in SHGs creates awareness about self-reliance. Of the sample surveyed, 65 per cent of the respondents strongly agreed to this statement, 12 per cent of them agreed, 6 per cent of them expressed disagree and the rest 17 per cent strongly disagreed with this statement.

Table 1.3
Distribution of the Sample Respondents by their Perception on Membership in SHG Creates Awareness about Self-Reliance

Category	Membership in SHG Creates awareness about Self-Reliance				Total
	Strongly agree	Agree	Disagree	Strongly Disagree	
Tailoring Women	5 (55.56)	0	1 (11.11)	3 (33.33)	9 (100.00)
Grocery shop business women	7 (87.50)	1 (12.50)	0	0	8 (100.00)
Fancy shop business women	11 (61.11)	3 (16.67)	0	4 (22.22)	18 (100.00)
Clothes business women	11 (64.71)	2 (11.76)	1 (5.88)	3 (17.65)	17 (100.00)
Vegetable vending business women	7 (87.50)	0	0	1 (12.50)	8 (100.00)
Fish vending business women	0	0	0	2 (100.00)	2 (100.00)
Dairy business women	2 (100.00)	0	0	0	2 (100.00)
Petty business women	16 (59.27)	4 (14.81)	3 (11.11)	4 (14.81)	27 (100.00)
Tiffin stalls business women	6 (66.67)	2 (22.22)	1 (11.11)	0	9 (100.00)
TOTAL	**65** (65.00)	**12** (12.00)	**6** (6.00)	**17** (17.00)	**100** **(100.00)**

In conclusion, by and large most of the respondents felt that membership in SHGs create awareness about self-reliance. The situation is different across the strata. It is observed that majority of the respondents of all income generating activities with exception of fish vending business women reported that SHGs create awareness about self reliance, while entire fish vending business women felt that it doesn't do so.

1.8.3. Social Status:

Table – 1.4 shows distribution of the respondents by their opinion on the statement that membership in SHGs gives social status. The data shows that 63 per cent of the respondents opined that they strongly agreed with this statement, while 25 per cent of the respondents agreed with this statement and 3 per cent of the respondents stated no objection. As against this, merely 9 per cent of the respondents disagreed with this statement.

Table 1.4

Distribution of the Sample Respondents by their Perception on Membership in SHG gives Social Status

Category	Membership in SHG gives Social Status				Total
	Strongly agree	Agree	Disagree	Strongly Disagree	
Tailoring Women	6 (66.67)	1 (11.11)	1 (11.11)	1 (11.11)	9 (100.00)
Grocery shop business women	7 (87.50)	0	0	1 (12.50)	8 (100.00)
Fancy shop business women	9 (50.00)	7 (38.89)	0	2 (11.11)	18 (100.00)
Clothes business women	9 (52.95)	5 (29.41)	1 (5.88)	2 (11.76)	17 (100.00)
Vegetable vending business women	7 (87.50)	0	0	1 (12.50)	8 (100.00)
Fish vending business women	1 (50.00)	0	0	1 (50.00)	2 (100.00)
Dairy business women	2 (100.00)	0	0	0	2 (100.00)
Petty business women	16 (59.27)	9 (33.33)	1 (3.70)	1 (3.70)	27 (100.00)
Tiffin stalls business women	6 (66.67)	3 (33.33)	0	0	9 (100.00)
TOTAL	**63** (63.00)	**25** (25.00)	**3** (3.00)	**9** (9.00)	**100** **(100.00)**

It is concluded that by and large majority of the respondents felt that membership in SHGs gives social status. Interestingly, majority of the respondents of all income generating activities also stated the same. However, half of the fish vending business women and a few of the respondents of some of the income generating activities disagreed with this statement.

1.8.4. Literacy and Communication Skills:

Sample respondents are asked to express their opinion on the statement that membership in SHGs improves literacy and communication skills. Table – 1.5 shows distribution of the respondents by their opinion on the statement that membership in SHGs improves literacy and communication skills. Of the sample surveyed, 63 per cent of the respondents strongly agreed with this statement, 28 per cent of the respondents agreed, one per cent of the respondents stated no objection, 6 per cent of the respondents disagreed and the rest 3 per cent of the respondents strongly disagreed.

Table 1.5

Distribution of the Sample Respondents by their Perception on Membership in SHG Improves Literacy & Communication Skills

Category	Membership in SHG improves Literacy & Communication Skills				Total
	Strongly Agree	Agree	Disagree	Strongly Disagree	
Tailoring Women	5 (55.56)	4 (44.44)	0	0	9 (100.00)
Grocery shop business women	7 (87.50)	1 (12.50)	0	0	8 (100.00)
Fancy shop business women	11 (61.11)	6 (33.33)	1 (5.56)	0	18 (100.00)
Clothes business women	8 (47.06)	6 (35.30)	2 (11.76)	1 (5.88)	17 (100.00)
Vegetable vending business women	8 (100.00)	0	0	0	8 (100.00)
Fish vending business women	1 (50.00)	0	1 (50.00)	0	2 (100.00)
Dairy business women	2 (100.00)	0	0	0	2 (100.00)
Petty business women	15 (55.57)	9 (33.33)	1 (3.70)	2 (7.40)	27 (100.00)
Tiffin stalls business women	6 (66.67)	2 (22.22)	1 (11.11)	0	9 (100.00)
TOTAL	**63** (63.00)	**28** (28.00)	**6** (6.00)	**3** (3.00)	**100** **(100.00)**

It is concluded that on the whole majority of the respondents feel that membership in SHGs improves literacy and communication skills. The same is observed across the strata also. However, half of the fish vending business women reported that literacy and communication skills are not improved after joining SHGs.

1.8.5. Leadership Skills:

Table–1.6 depicts distribution of the respondents by their opinion on the statement that membership in SHGs improves leadership skills. It is evident from the table that 58 per cent of the respondents have strongly agreed with this statement, while 17 per cent of the respondents have agreed with this statement, whilst another 17 per cent of the respondents disagreed to this statement and a little percentage of the respondents strongly disagreed with this statement. Some of the respondents stated no objection to this statement (6 per cent).

Table 1.6

Distribution of the Sample Respondents by their Perception on Membership in SHG Improves Leadership Skills

Category	Membership in SHG improves Leadership Skills				Total
	Strongly Agree	Agree	Disagree	Strongly Disagree	
Tailoring Women	5 (55.56)	1 (11.11)	3 (33.33)	0	9 (100.00)
Grocery shop business women	7 (87.50)	0	1 (12.50)	0	8 (100.00)
Fancy shop business women	8 (44.44)	5 (27.78)	0	5 (27.78)	18 (100.00)
Clothes business women	10 (58.82)	3 (17.65)	4 (23.53)	0	17 (100.00)
Vegetable vending business women	7 (87.50)	0	0	1 (12.50)	8 (100.00)
Fish vending business women	0	1 (50.00)	1 (50.00)	0	2 (100.00)
Dairy business women	2 (100.00)	0	0	0	2 (100.00)
Petty business women	13 (48.16)	12 (44.44)	1 (3.70)	1 (3.70)	27 (100.00)
Tiffin stalls business women	6 (66.67)	2 (22.22)	1 (11.11)	0	9 (100.00)
TOTAL	**58** (58.00)	**24** (24.00)	**11** (11.00)	**7** (7.00)	**100** **(100.00)**

On the whole, majority of the sample respondents have the feeling that membership in SHGs improves leadership skill. Across the strata, all categories of respondents except fish vending business women strongly agreed with this statement, while one half of the fish vending business
women have agreed with this statement.

1.9. Findings of the Study:

➢ Business training can be benefit poor women entrepreneurs for empowerment when it is carefully designed to complement their existing skills and address their most pressing needs.

➢ Women's general education and literacy rate are important if they are to reach their full potential and become empowered. Illiteracy creates a situation of dependency on others that can limit an individual's prospects for empowerment. The literacy and education contribute to empowerment.

➢ In addition to education disadvantages, one of the most difficult challenges that many women are facing is when they start or expand business, the balancing of their business responsibilities with their household responsibilities. In many cases, women's business remains small and concentrated in less profitable due to the time constraints.

1.10. Suggestions:

From the above observations, the researcher feels that the policy makers can focus on the following issues and design appropriate policy to strengthen the impact of SHGs.The SHG members are to be properly educated about the fruits of this co-operative type of movement.The male members of the families should be made to play a supportive role. Training in the business activities of the members is the need of the hour. Self-confidence is one of the most crucial components of change for empowerment, yet it is also one of the most difficult tasks to measure or assess. Self-confidence is a complex concept relating to both women's perception of their capabilities and their actual level of skills and capabilities.

1.11. Conclusion:

SHGs role in the empowerment of women is significant in many aspects including socio-psycho and economic aspects. To sum-up, it can be said that majority of the respondents opined that membership in SHGs has positive psychological impact. The same is observed among different categories of respondents also. There was a remarkable improvement in psychological empowerment of SHG members.SHGs contributed towards personal empowerment in terms of collective efficiency, pro-active attitudes, self-esteem and self efficacy. The SHG woman has a greater access to knowledge and the resources, a greater autonomy in decision-making, a greater ability to plan life, a greater control over circumstances that influence life and the ability to overcome the restrictions and constraints imposed by customs, beliefs and practices. However, comparatively, sample fish vending business women are found to be somehow far away from the positive impact of the SHGs.

References:
1. "Women Entrepreneurship-Financial Inclusion and Micro Financing for Self Help Groups in Andhra Pradesh" by Anitha Devi, B V H Kameswara Sastry, S.Srininvasa Rao, BS Publications.
2. www.serpap.gov.in
3. Reports collected from DRDA office.
4. Anita Panda., (2004), "SHG – ABook for Many", The Co-operator, Volume 42, No. 6, pp. 264-66.
5. Suguna, B. (2002), "Strategies for Empowerment of Rural Women", Social Welfare,49(5), pp. 3-6

CASE STUDY-4

Entrepreneurship Development of Rural Women through Self Help Groups – A Case Study in Krishna District

Dr. Rajesh. C.Jampala
Professor & Head,
Department of Business Administration,
P.B Siddhartha College of Arts & Science,
Vijayawada,
Andhra Pradesh -520 008
Email: rajeshjampala@yahoo.com

Mrs G. Madhu Sri
Research Scholar,
Department of Commerce and Business Administration
P.B. Siddhartha College of Arts and Science,
Vijayawada – 520 010.
Email: gaganasahasra@gmail.com

Abstract

Empowerment of women has emerged as an important issue in recent times. Empowerment is an active, multidimensional process, which should enable women to realize their full identity and power in all spheres of life. Empowerment in the context of women's development is a way of defining, challenging and overcoming barriers in a women's life through which she increases her ability to shape her life and environment. Women must be empowered by enhancing their awareness, knowledge; skills and technology use efficiency, thereby, facilitating overall development of the society. The concept of Self Help Groups (SHGs) is proving to be a helpful instrument for the women empowerment. Entrepreneurship development and income generating activities are a feasible solution for empowering women. It generates income and also provides flexible working hours according to the needs of homemakers. The Self Help Groups (SHGs) have paved the way for economic independence of rural women. The members of SHGs in rural areas are involved in Micro –Entrepreneurships. Through that, they are becoming economically independent and are getting good recognition in the society. This paper deals with the success stories of the rural poor SHG members showing exemplary entrepreneurial qualities to come out of the vicious circle of poverty and indebtedness with the help of SHGs in Krishna District.

Keywords: Empowerment, Entrepreneurship development, Self Help Groups

1.1.Introduction:

India envisions a future in which Indian women are independent and self-reliant. In various national policies and developmental programmes, emphasis has been given on organizing women in Self Help Groups and thus, marks the beginning of a major process of empowering women. The concept of Self Help Groups (SHGs) is proving to be a helpful instrument for the women entrepreneurship in rural areas. SHG is an organization of rural poor, particularly of women that deliver micro credit to undertake the entrepreneurial activity.

The participation of women in income generating activities for the family has been increasing over time. Female work participations not only increase their family income but also bring economic independence among women in the households. SHGs play a pivotal role in women entrepreneurs. There are greater opportunities for rural women to establish and run a micro enterprise; many women SHGs are involved in farm and non-farm activities like handicrafts, tailoring, catering services which give immense scope for women to uplift the economic standard. NGOs give training to SHG members in all these activities. The government of Andhra Pradesh encourages the SHG activities and marketing of their products. Now a day, women have realized the importance of self employment.

There have been many success stories of the poor SHG members showing exemplary entrepreneurial qualities to come out of the vicious circle of poverty and indebtedness with the help of SHGs. The tremendous impact on the social status of the poor rural women becoming bread earners of their households through the instrument of SHGs has been highly commended by many researchers. The impressive performance under Self Help Groups- Bank Linkage Programme (SHG-BLP) prompted other developmental agencies like the Government Departments to depend heavily on such groups to take the development efforts forward. A large number of service deliveries of the Government Departments are now contracted to SHG members in preference to private contractors largely prompted by their devotion and efficiency. The success of SHG-BLP will be assessed not on the basis of savings or credit linkage or on social capital leveraged, but on the basis of the improvement in the quality of lives of its members.

1.2.Areas of Micro-Enterprise Development:

Depending on number of factors ranging from landholdings, subsidiary occupations, agro climatic conditions and socio-personal characteristics of the rural women and her family member the areas of micro-enterprises also differ from place to place. The micro enterprises are classified under three major heads:

1.2.1. **Micro Enterprise development related to agriculture and allied agricultural activities** like cultivating to organic vegetables, flowers, oil seeds and seed production are some of the areas besides taking up mushroom growing and bee –keeping. Some more areas can be like dehydration of fruits and vegetables, canning or bottling of pickles, chutneys, jams, squashes, dairy and other products that are ready to eat.

1.2.2. **Micro-Enterprise development related to livestock management activities** like diary farming, poultry farm, livestock feed production and production of vermi composting using the animal waste can be an important area in which women can utilize both her technical skills and raw materials from the farm and livestock to earn substantial income and small scale agro-processing units.

1.2.3. **Micro – Enterprise development related to household based operations** like knitting, stitching, weaving, embroidery, bakery and flour milling, petty shops, food preparation and preservation.

1.3. Advantages of Entrepreneurship among Rural Women:

Empowering women particularly rural women is a challenge. Micro enterprises in rural area can help to meet these challenges. Micro – enterprises not only enhance national productivity, generate employment but also help to develop economic independence, personal and social capabilities among rural women. Following are some of the personal and social capabilities, which were developed as result of taking up enterprise among rural women.

> Economic empowerment
> Improved standard of living
> Self confidence
> Enhance awareness
> Sense of achievement
> Increased social interaction
> Engaged in political activities
> Increased participation level in gram sabha meeting
> Improvement in leadership qualities
> Involvement in solving problems related to women and community
> Decision making capacity in family and community

Economic empowerment of women by micro entrepreneurship led to the empowerment of women in many things such as socio-economic opportunity, property rights, political representation, social equality, personal right, family development, market development, community development and at last the nation development.

1.3. Objective of the Study: The specific objective of the present study is given below:

1. To document the success stories of Self Help Group Members in Krishna District, Andhra Pradesh.

1.4. Methodology of the Study:

The study uses both primary data and secondary data. Multi-stage random sampling method is used for the present study to collect primary data. Krishna district being selected for the present study. At the next level, two mandals (Kankipadu & Penamaluru) are selected for the present study. From each mandal, 25 SHG members, who are engaged in income generating activities, are selected randomly. Thus, the total sample size is 50. Primary data was collected with the help of specific interview schedule by for personally interviewing the respondents.

Sample Distribution

Table: 1.1

Vijayawada (Rural)

Sl. No.	Name of the mandal	Total No. of SHGs	No of SHG members	No. of SHG Members Taken for sample
1	Penamaluru	2039	20916	25
2	Kankipadu	1178	11931	25
	Total	**7786**	**80216**	**50**

1.5. SHG at Glance in Krishna District:

Krishna District has a total of 49 mandals in the district. Out of 3, 48,493 rural households projected 348493 HHs (100%) are mobilized in the SHGs. A total 3,48,493(100%) of Poorest of the poor HHs are covered in to SHGs. Out of 1,18,117 SC HHs projected 1,18,117 HHs 100%) are mobilized in to SHGs. Out of 24,253 ST HHs projected 24,253(100%) are mobilized in to SHGs. There are 60,176 SHGs with a membership of 6, 61,936 women in the district as on August 2013.

Table 1.2: Details of SHGs, VOs and MSs:

Sl. No.	Particulars	No.
1	No.of women SHGs	60176
2	No.of women SHG members	661936
3	Average group size	11
4	No.of VOs existing	2057
5	No.of MSs existing	49
6	Disabled SHG	1203
7	No.of members covered	8936
8	Average groups size of Disabled SHGs	7.42
9	No.of MVSs	3

1.6. Need for the Study:

Case studies of SHG members were conducted to supplement the findings of the impact survey. Case studies have been successfully used as a research tool by social scientists to investigate a wide range of developmental issues. They may be defined as a detailed analysis or an intensive study of a person or group and are usually carried out by conducting an in-depth interview of a person or a group. In this study, a few case studies of individual members of SHGs were carried out to determine what factors led to their success or failure. Some of these case studies may also be seen as exemplary models for replication. Case studies were expected to highlight unique cases as well, to provide answers, support and provide insights on the data collected through the survey.In all, there are stories of individual members who have been extremely successful in their own business ventures. There are women who have shown leadership qualities and demonstrated good examples of women's empowerment.

Case Study No-1

a.	Name of the Member	: Yesamma
b.	Name of the Group	: Yesamma Group
c.	Mandal	: Penamaluru
d.	Contact	: 9885287336

Yesamma is privilaged to be a member of SHG. She is good at savings and got an opportunity to enter first linkage. She wisely chose to invest on catering and cooking. She uses to prepare all food items at home, supply them on orders and has become a successful entrepreneur in the business. She uses to get numerous orders from the customers and based on the need sometimes she use to go to the houses of the customers to cook. She has become successful business woman and wanted to improve the prospects of her business with good financial profits by availing more loan amount as a financial assistance from the government. She is now confident enough to repay the loan amount in instalment within a due time.

Case Study No-2

a. Name of the Member   : Lakshmi
b. Name of the Group   : Lakshmi Group
c. Mandal   : Penamaluru

Lakshmi proved to be a very successful woman in her vegetable business after joining as a SHG member. She started her business with a very meagre amount what she received under her first linkage. But now she is in a position to make good profits out of it. She could enjoy the gradual development and progress in her business because of her sincere hard work and commitment towards the work.

Case Study No-3

a. Name of the Member   : Ratna Kumari
b. Name of the Group   : Indira Group
c. Mandal   : Penamaluru
d. Contact   : 9701696864

Ratna Kumari joined in SHG to avail the benefit of gas stove. She also took the initative to motivate many women to join as a member in SHG to avail the facility of cooking gas with stove. She concentrated specially on economically backword people to join in SHG. If any member in the group is having a problem Ratnakumari takes the responsibility of reporting the problem to the higher authourities (officials) and she do her best to resolve the problems of groups as well as group members. She is very active and supportive member in SHG. Her unselfish service to the group members makes the group strong and she was appointed as an EO President to improve her support.

Case Study No-4

a. Name of the Member   : Udayakumari . V
b. Name of the Group   : Nicy Group
c. Mandal   : Penamaluru
d. Contact   : 9553868849

Udaya Kumari is a confident woman entrepreneur. She joined in SHG and started clothes business. She is benefited by learning new techniques and methods in improving the business. She is very happy and thankful to the government for its wonderful support and financial assistance specially to the women to improve their talents and hidden support skills. Perhaps according to her this financial support is born to women to improve their living standards without depending on anybody.

Case Study No-5

a. Name of the Member   : Subbalakshmi
b. Name of the Group   : Priyadarshini Group
c. Mandal   : Kankipadu

Subbalakshmi being the member of SHG is proudly saying that, she is able to earn good income without depending on her husband. She is able to clear the loan by paying regular instalments to the bank. Before joining in SHG, she is an individual but after joining she became as a good entrepreneur by purchasing a sewing machine. The membership in SHG made her as a perfect individual, self-sufficient and also economically strong.

Case Study No-6

a.	Name of the Member	: Gonthemma . M
b.	Name of the Group	: Surya Group
c.	Mandal	: Kankipadu

Gonthemma is a lady with lot of interest for providing good education to her children. She heard the SHG concept from her neighbour and joined as a member in Surya group. She utilised her first linkage amount in eggs business. She buys eggs from the wholesaler and sells them to the retailer. Out of this business she is getting Rs.300 profit per day. She is very much contented with this business and the profit out of it. She is really happy that she could able to provide quality education to her children after joining in SHG.

Case Study No-7

a.	Name of the Member	: Rani . D
b.	Name of the Group	: Jhansi Rani Group
c.	Mandal	: Kankipadu
d.	Contact	: 8125437837

Rani is expressing her happiness to be a part of SHG. Before joining SHG she does not have financial stability in her family. She use to lead stressful life along with her family members due to financial crisis. Later she came to know about SHG programme through some of her friends. Without any hesitation she joined in this group to improve income for the upliftment of her family. She availed the first linkage facility in the year 2005 and started a small retail shop at her house. Though she failed to get an expected result out of this business she is able to pay the instalments properly to the bank with in due date. In the year 2007 she became eligible to avail the second linkage form SHG and purchased a grinder and zigzag machine. This fetched her with good income and she could see little money out of this business. The savings amount is again invested by her on the business of manufacturing paper plates (Istarakulu). She bought a machine of manufacturing paper plates. She started improving slowly in her business with good income. Her husband also helps her in distribution of these plates to the shops. She has become a successful business woman and is able to purchase a plot of land and also constructed a house. By using all the above income sources in a proper manner she could prove herself as a perfect entrepreneur.

Case Study No-8

a.	Name of the Member	: Lalitha Kalpana
b.	Name of the Group	: Tirupatamma Swayam Sahayaka Sangham
c.	Mandal	: Old Rajeev Nagar
d.	Contact	: 9550008814

B.Lalitha Kalpana belongs to Tirupatamma Swayam Sahayaka Sangham. She has lost of interest to work, but her husband never encouraged her to work. Through her sister she came to know about SHG and joined in the group. She received loan from SHG and bought computer and started DEO work at home. She could convince her husband to work at home. She is able to fulfil her dream of working through SHG and its financial help. She is getting good income and is very happy about her achievements. She feels proud to say that she is a member of SHG and she could stand on her own feet. She got the opportunity to use her talent through SHG.

Case Study No-9

a.	Name of the Member	: D.Jyothi

    b. Name of the Group   **: Vijayalakshmi Mahila Dwakra Group**
    c. Mandal   **: Rama Nagar**

D.Jyothi, a member of Vijayalakshmi Mahila Dwakra Group want to work anywhere to get satisfaction. She joined in SHG and got loan from the government. After getting loan she motivated her team and invested the amount on 'Mid Day Meals' programme. She with the help of all group members use to cook for the children in the afternoons for lunch in government school. Government is spending Rs 4.30 paise for lunch on each child, excluding rice. All the group members are getting little profit out of this programme. They can live their lives comfortably and peacefully with the amount what they are getting out of this.

Case Study No-10
    a. Name of the Member   **: Lakshmi**
    b. Name of the Group   **: Ganesh Mahila Podupu Sangham**
    c. Mandal   **: Ramalingeswar Nagar**
    d. Contact   **: 9966615767**

Lakshmi is a confident woman. Her husband has an idea of purchasing marble machines long back to start a own business, but due to the lack of amount/money they could not buy the machines. Later Lakshmi came to know about SHG and she joined in the group and got loan. They invested this amount on purchase of 2 marble machines and started their own business. She got a special recognition in her family for her financial support. She feels very proud of it and greatful to government for establishing SHG's and helping economically backward families.

1.7. Findings of the Study:

- ❖ Self Help Groups (SHGs) have been successful in empowering rural women through entrepreneurial activities.
- ❖ Increase in income, expenditure and saving habits of rural women were observed. The SHGs had major impact on social and economic life of rural women.
- ❖ The study revealed an increase in social recognition of self, status of family in the society, size of social circle and involvement in intra family and entrepreneurial decision making.
- ❖ There was an increase in self confidence, self reliance and independence of rural women due to the involvement in the entrepreneurial and other activities of SHGs.
- ❖ SHGs could be linked to literacy programmes run by government and it could be made an integral part of SHG activities. Raised literacy level could be helpful for the SHG members to overcome cognitive constraints and to understand government policies, technical understanding and gaining required skills.
- ❖ Rural women could be motivated to avail finances for starting the entrepreneurial activities. Awareness need to be created about various credit facilities, financial incentives and subsidies through Self Help Groups.
- ❖ As women were found technologically less empowered, they are to be imposed to the technologies which are labour saving, drudgery reducing, income generating and productivity increasing.

❖ Entrepreneurship education and trainings could be introduced at all levels from basic education. It could be helpful in inducing positive self concept, self reliance, self confidence and independence in rural women.

1.8. Conclusion:

Women's entrepreneurship is both about women's position in society *and* about the role of entrepreneurship in the same society. Women entrepreneurs faced many obstacles specifically in market their product (including family responsibilities) that have to be overcome in order to give them access to the same opportunities as men. In addition, in some countries, women may experience obstacles with respect to holding property and entering contracts. Increased participation of women in the labour force is a prerequisite for improving the position of women in society and self-employed women. Particularly the entry of rural women in micro enterprises will be encouraged and aggravated.

Rural women can do wonders by their effectual and competent involvement in entrepreneurial activities. The rural women are having basic indigenous knowledge, skill, potential and resources to establish and manage enterprise. Now, what is the need is knowledge regarding accessibility to loans, various funding agencies, procedure regarding certification, awareness on government welfare programmes, motivation, technical skill and support from family, government and other organization. More over formation and strengthening of rural women Entrepreneurs network must be encouraged. Women entrepreneur networks are major sources of knowledge about women's entrepreneurship and they are increasingly recognized as a valuable tool for its development and promotion. This network helps to give lectures, printed material imparting first hand technical knowledge in production, processing, procurement, management and marketing among the other women. This will motivate other rural women to engage in micro entrepreneurship with the right assistance and they can strengthen their capacities besides adding to the family income and national productivity.

References:

1. "Women Entrepreneurship-Financial Inclusion and Micro Financing for Self Help Groups in Andhra Pradesh" by Anitha Devi, B V H Kameswara Sastry, S.Srininvasa Rao, BS Publications.
2. DRDA reports collected from Krishan District office
3. www.serpap.gov.in
4. http://www.rural.nic.in/
5. www.rd.ap.gov.in/
6. www.nird.org.in

CASE STUDY-5

Role of Microfinance Institutions in Entrepreneurship Development in Visakhapatnam District, Andhra Pradesh, India

Dr. N. R. Mohan Prakash
Assistant Professor,
Department of Marketing,
GITAM Institute of Management,
GITAM University, Visakhapatnma,

Abstract

Microfinance has been playing an important role in rural and semi-urban entrepreneurial development in Andhra Pradesh since its formation. Andhra Pradesh is a state of rich natural resource as well as healthy human resources potential to take up self employment. Microfinance and entrepreneurship help as a combine tool to contribute in development of an economy, particularly in Andhra Pradesh the combined contribution of these to are very much essential to cater the need of employability of people belongs to rural and semi-urban areas . Since formation of the state the people of Andhra Pradesh have been showing interest to earn money through self employment schemes by staring khadi and village industries in rural areas. The foremost objectives of this paper is to see the role of microfinance institutions in entrepreneurship development and also measure the level of satisfaction of microfinance institutions clients toward their respective banks considering primary source of data at state level. The sample of 300 microfinance bank clients residing in Andhra Pradesh has been interviewed. Data analysis and interpretation are the strength of this paper, descriptive analysis use in this paper and also non parametric test chi-square and Kruskal-Walli and Mann-Whitney test used. This study concludes that microfinance institutions play a significant role in entrepreneurship development in Andhra Pradesh and some of the clients who are taking loan from the public sector banks they use this amount to start a business than the other ones who use it for marriage, education house building purpose etc.
Keywords: Microfinance institution, Entrepreneurship, Mann-Whitney

INTRODUCTION

Microfinance to small enterprises in developing countries like India is very much required to cater the needs of poor people who want to start a small business with a limited amount of capital. In developing countries there are nearly 90 percent of the people which have lack of access to financial services from the institutions, either for credit or saving purpose. Especially for the poor who already have lack assets this situation become more critical for them. In microenterprises generally there is need for small capital but it is still difficult for the poor people to manage even that small quantity of capital. Resultantly, these lacks of capital hinder the growth of microenterprise (Robinson, 2002). Entrepreneurship is one of the commonly terms used in business, commerce and management, economics and other related disciplines. Entrepreneurship is an economic activity of an individual or a group of people to start a new business to serve or meet the needs of customers particularly and society at large by means of innovation, creativity, leadership, profit maximization. Entrepreneurship helps in the process to increase economic growth, employment generation, increase national income and also creating innovation (Ismailov and Zahid, 2008).

Two schools of thought mainly discuss about entrepreneurship as: Schumpeter's theory of entrepreneurship and Austrian theory of entrepreneurial discovery. The Schumpeter theory explains entrepreneurship as innovation with a combination of tool and forces and the different methods to produce new innovative products as for the Austrian theory of entrepreneurship, entrepreneur anticipating market and need of customers exactly and correctly and produce more cheaply than competitor and earn profit. (Swedburg, 2000).

Historical Perspective of Microfinance

Microfinance hits the history in Bangladesh when Dr. Muhammad Younus, Father of Microfinance, lend the first micro loan from his own pocket. The purpose is to save these poor people from the local moneylenders who charge high interest rates and also to establish income generating activity for them. In 1976, Muhammad Younus launch the research project to provide microcredit and banking services to the poor people in his nation. In addition to that, microcredit program is based on unique mechanism such as group lending, social collateral and distinctive payment methods. It isn't based on checking credit history, income sources and bank balances but works on character based lending and thus managed to give loans to those who lacking credit histories. They are also denied of access to conventional finance. In 1983, Mohammad Younus formally establishes a Grameen bank which is a milestone in the development of the microfinance industry. The objective of this bank is to give small loans at affordable rates to poor people, especially to women. The high number of clients and extremely high repayments rates is an impressive achievement for the bank. The microcredit program has not been restricted to Bangladesh as the similar activities are also under way in different parts of the world including Indonesia (1972), India (1990s) and, more importantly, in Latin America where microcredit operations were rapidly developed. In the end, Dr. Muhammad Younus is awarded a Nobel peace prize for his great achievement in 2006 (Bateman, 2010).

Significance, Sources and Characteristics of Microfinance

Microfinance is one of better tools to reduce poverty, increase economic growth and development in the economy. Asian Development Bank (ADB) defines microfinance as the provision of a broad range of financial services such as deposits, loans, payment services, money transfers, and insurance to poor and low income households and, their microenterprises (ADB, 2000).

Microfinance has three types of sources formal institutions such as rural banks and co-operatives, semi-formal institutions, such as nongovernment organizations (NGOs) and informal sources such as money lenders and shopkeepers. Microfinance provides two types of services financial services and non-financial services. Financial services include saving, microcredit, money transfer, micro insurance etc. Non-financial services include training, counseling, education, health etc. In both microfinance and micro entrepreneurship the common object is the creation of employment opportunities for the poor people and also indicts decrease poverty.

Microfinance institutions support two types of micro entrepreneurs: one is potential micro entrepreneur and the second is existing micro entrepreneur. The micro entrepreneurs mean the creation and the existing entrepreneurs mean the expansion of that entrepreneurship. Microfinance Institutions assist potential micro entrepreneurs by providing financing and training to enable them to start a business activity. This help to potential micro entrepreneurs is for pro-poor mostly. The objective of targeting the poor is to make them able to start their own business and enabling them to increase their revenues and to reduce their level of poverty. Microfinance institutions also provide services to existing micro entrepreneurs. Other financial services available to the existing micro entrepreneurs are money transfer using mobile banking to facilitate their transfers and other financial operations, micro insurance to insure their business operations and the unexpected that affect the smooth functioning of the business like the sickness or the death of the micro entrepreneur. The microfinance institutions also offer non-financial services to existing micro entrepreneurs enabling them to expand and develop their activities, their skills and to empower them. The nonfinancial services supply to existing micro entrepreneurs is managerial training, technical assistance, and analysis of the sector of activity (Ledger wood, 1998).

Various studies have been conducted before on role of microfinance in entrepreneurship development but there is not a single study available on role microfinance institutions in entrepreneurship development. So the present study contributes in this context and finds out the role of microfinance institutions in entrepreneurship development in Andhra Pradesh.

Next session, briefly, explains overview of microfinance and entrepreneurship in India. Section II explains literature review, Section III theoretical link of microfinance and entrepreneurship development, Section IV consists on methodology used in paper. Section V discusses the results drawn from the estimations. Section VI presents the conclusion and some policy implications which are based upon the study.

Overview of Microfinance and Entrepreneurship in India

India is perhaps the largest emerging market for microfinance. Over the past decade, the microfinance sector has been growing in India at a fairly steady pace. Though no microfinance institution (MFI) in India has yet reached anywhere near the scale of the well-known Bangladeshi MFIs, the sector in India is characterised by a wide diversity of methodologies and legal forms. However, very few Indian MFIs have achieved sustainability yet. Sustainability itself has to be seen in a broader sense than just financial sustainability. The sustainability of demand, of the MFI's mission, of its ownership and governance structure and the legal and regulatory framework under which it works, are all contributory to overall sustainability of an MFI. Further, the sustainability of an MFI by itself may not be enough unless a full-fledged micro-finance sector (MFS) is established on sustainable lines.

The important objective of microfinance is poverty reduction and social mobilization, the government of India doing efforts to establish and improve the foundations of microfinance in banking sector.

There is a huge unmet demand for micro-finance in India. Bridging the demand supply gap requires an environment that attracts large numbers of microfinance providers. There is a need to adopt a three track approach, using mutually complementary strategies:

- Incentivising existing mainstream financial service providers (apex financial institutions, such as NABARD, SIDBI and HUDCO, commercial banks, insurance companies, co-operatives, and NBFCs) to enter the microfinance sector as a serious business proposition.
- Encouraging new microfinance institutions (MFIs) with a supportive policy and regulatory framework and financial resources to enlarge and expand their services.
- Building a strong demand system in the form of community-based development financial institutions (CDFIs), with the help of NGOs and others.

There are many aspects of the existing legal and regulatory framework, which discourage mainstream FIs from increasing outreach and achieving sustainability in microfinance. Further growth in microfinance can only be possible by redressing these limitations in the legal and regulatory framework. These constraints apply both to mainstream FIs and to alternative MFIs.

Small loans have been historically seen by banks as a social obligation rather than a potential business opportunity. The leadership and managers of mainstream FIs see the small loan market as difficult to serve, risky and having a low or negative net spread. Contributing to this position has been the fact that poverty alleviation related small loans (IRDP, DRI, SC/ST)2 have been utilised historically as a tool for disbursing political patronage, undermining the norm that loans must be repaid. This has made bankers cynical about lending to the poor. However, over the last three years, some strides have been made to re-engage mainstream FIs into micro-credit.

The concept of Local Area Banks (LABs), with a lower start up equity of Rs 50 million, has not yet been operationalised by the RBI. The Regional Rural Banks Act does not permit any private shareholding in any RRBs, and the Cooperatives Acts of all states do not permit district level coop banks to be set up except by the state government. The result of these two laws together is that rural credit has been a monopoly of state owned institutions.

The only exception is private finance "companies" – so called, but not actually companies under the Companies Act. These entities are not allowed to take deposits, and thus their source of funds is the owners' personal funds and borrowings from relatives. They can, however, extend credit and thousands of them are thriving doing so. Their interest rates are usually three to five percent per month. However, due to their unincorporated status, they cannot borrow from banks/FIs and grow substantially.

To incorporate, at the moment there are only two options – either be a co-operative or be an NBFC (non-banking finance company). If an MFI opts to be an NBFC, it finds it very difficult to mobilise the minimum start-up equity of Rs 20 million. Even where it does have any equity, borrowing from Indian financial institutions are highly restricted due to the negative image of NBFCs in general. Further, even deposit mobilisation is not possible at least for the first three to four years, till a satisfactory rating is obtained. That leaves the option of borrowing from foreign institutions, which is difficult in the first place. MFIs taking foreign currency loans are subject to exchange rate risks, which they would not be able to handle. Very few foreign institutions are willing to give rupee denominated loans. Thus, in summary, currently there is no facilitative framework to promote private sector, for-profit MFIs in India. It is desirable to build a strong demand system in the form of community-based development financial institutions (CDFIs), with the help of NGOs and others. Such a system is required to

- convert latent demand into effective demand,
- wean away microfinance customers from moneylenders,
- remove the expectation of low interest rate and capital subsidies that have spoiled borrowers over the years
- restore the repayment norm, and
- build local stake in grassroots financial structures

A member owned and member managed CDFI is possible when small groupings such as five person joint liability groups or 20 member SHGs federate into a CDFI without losing their character and autonomy. These CDFIs may be unregistered or registered. If registered, they may choose to be societies, trusts, mutually aided co-operative societies (MACS) or even nonbanking finance companies (NBFCs). Such CDFIs require capacity building inputs to manage higher volumes and transactions. In certain states, there is a possibility to set up MFIs under progressive cooperative legislation, such as the AP Mutually Aided Co-operative Societies Act 1995, in Andhra Pradesh. Similar Acts have come up in Bihar, Jammu and Kashmir and are on the anvil in Orissa, Tamilnadu and Madhya Pradesh. Having explained the three tracks for building the microfinance sector in India, we focus on track 2 (MFIs), as other presenters from India will be dealing with tracks 1 (mainstream FIs) and (CDFIs).

Indian Microfinance can be chronologically classified into four phases. The four stages are:
- Phase I: 1900s – 1969 : Cooperative Movement
- Phase II: 1969 - 1991 : State Driven through National Banks and emergence of NGOs
- Phase III: 1992 – 2000 : SHGs Bank Linkage program and Growth of NGO-MFIs
- Phase IV: 2000 – today : Commercialization of Microfinance

While each phase represents distinct features of its own, there are some overlaps and crosscutting themes among them. An overriding feature of Indian Microfinance throughout its evolution is its focus on poverty alleviation in rural areas. This focus has broadly determined the approach and operations of microfinance in India. In addition to this Indian microfinance is characterized by existence of both State and Civil Society Organization in delivery of microfinance services while private players joining the wagon during phase IV. In context of Indian Microfinance, it is important to note that each phase was influenced not only by learning from earlier phase but also from development discourse, government policies and international trends in microscope eco-space among other things. The remaining section describes each phase in detail.

Indian Microfinance today is a dynamic space with multitude of players offering various products and services to low income clients with different approaches. Banking system along with other legal forms such as NBFCs, Section 25 companies, cooperatives and NGO-MFIs all are approaching rural markets. Many new forms of relationships are emerging among these entities to leverage on each other's strength. However, despite such new developments the penetration of microfinance remains low and spread highly skewed in Southern India. Indeed there are ample gaps to be filled and this would lead to further changes in Microfinance space in future.

LITERATURE REVIEW

Different studies have been conducted on different aspects of microfinance such as importance of microfinance, beginning of microfinance, performance of microfinance institutions, effectiveness of microfinance etc. However this study is concerned with role of microfinance on entrepreneurship development. The review below is presented the **Role of Microfinance in Entrepreneurial Development in various states of India**

International Labour Organisation (ILO) (1998) in its different projects concluded that microfinance had successfully increased micro-enterprises and self-employment of the clients. An ILO survey of 46 Microfinance Institutions (MFIs) in 24 different countries showed that 74 per cent of MFIs had "the self-employed" as clients, leaving it open whether these had some wage labourers or not, 17 per cent had primarily self-employed in their clientele and just 4 (9 per cent) had only a minority of self-employed amongst their clients.

Puhazhendhi and Satyasai (2000) in their study commissioned by NABARD covered 560 sample households from 223 SHGs spread over 11 states across India. For assessing the impact of the programme, a comparison of pre- and post-SHG situation was made. With a view to quantify the empowerment of SHG members, economic and social empowerment index was computed for each household by using the scoring technique. The findings of this study showed 33 per cent rise in average annual income from pre- to post-SHG situation. Forty per cent of this incremental income was generated by non-farm sector activities. The estimated employment days per household worked out to 375 person days during post-SHG situation that had registered an increase of 17 per cent from pre-SHG situation. Sample households took up 200 additional economic activities by utilising 85 per cent of the borrowed funds for productive purposes. The share of families living below the poverty line was reduced by 20 per cent in post-SHG situation. The social empowerment of sample SHG members in terms of self-confidence, involvement in decision-making, better communication, etc. improved in a significant way.

Manimekalai and Rajeswari (2001) studied the socio-economic background of self-help group women in rural micro-enterprises in Tamil Nadu and examined the factors which had motivated the women to become SHG members and eventually as entrepreneurs. The researchers analysed the nature of economic activities and the performance in terms of growth indicators such as investment turnover, employment, sources of finance, product marketing and other related aspects and identified the problems faced by SHG women in running the enterprises. For the purpose of the study, a sample of 150 SHG members was selected who were studied according to the nature of their activities from 5 blocks of Tiruchirapalli district of Tamil Nadu. These groups were formed and promoted by an NGO. The nature of micro-enterprises run by the groups included trade, agriculture, animal husbandry, processing of food, tailoring, gem cutting, catering, petty shop, bamboo based units and agro-based units etc. The primary data pertained to the year 1999-2000. The SHG women were employed both in agricultural and non-agricultural activities. The study found that women SHGs earned the highest profit from agriculture, followed by trade related activities and catering services. A majority of sample units did not market their products outside the districts but sold these directly to the customers. The income of the SHG women almost doubled after taking up micro-enterprises. Majority of the respondents faced serious problems like non-availability of raw materials, lack of infrastructure facilities including marketing, lack of support from family members in running the enterprises etc. The provision of microfinance by the NGO to the women SHGs had helped the groups to achieve a measure of economic and social empowerment. It had developed a sense of leadership, organisational skill, management of various activities of a business, identifying raw materials, market and suitable diversification and modernisation.

Todd (2001) studied the impact of SHARE Microfinance Ltd. on its clients in Andhra Pradesh, India. The study compared 125 SHARE clients to 104 new clients who had yet to receive any exposure to the programme. All the SHARE clients had participated in the programme for at least three years. Todd created a poverty index composed of four elements: sources of income, productive assets, housing quality, and household dependency burden (the number of household members divided by the number of income earners). This index score helped Todd to document the extent to which clients had moved out of poverty. The results of the study showed that 76.8 per cent of the total clients had experienced a reduction in poverty including 38.4 per cent that shifted from very poor to moderate poor category and 17.6 per cent that had left poverty entirely. As compared to the incoming clients, mature clients were more likely to send their children to school and spend money for health purposes.

Chen and Donald (2001) in their study compared the impact on the clients who borrowed for self-employment and the clients who only saved with Self-Employed Women Association (SEWA) Bank without borrowing to the non-clients of Ahmedabad and Gujarat states of India where SEWA was based. The study was conducted in two rounds, i.e. in the years 1997 and 1999. It was observed that repeated borrowing was especially important, compared to one time borrowing. Repeated borrowers had greater income spent on food, household improvements and consumer durables and more likely to had girls enrolled in primary schools. Income of participant was over 25 per cent greater than that of saver and 56 per cent higher than the non-participant income. Savers too enjoyed household income 24 per cent greater than that of non- participants. These findings indicated that microfinance was quite effective.

Singh (2001) conducted a study on the socio-economic impact of microfinance programme in Uttar Pradesh. In order to study the impact, rural areas of Kanpur district were selected on account of highest number of credit linked SHGs as compared to other districts in the state. For the purpose of the study, out of 11 SHGs linked with RRB, one group in Beridayria village was selected. It was found that in pre-SHG situation most of the members were dependent on income from labour but in the post-SHG situation their main source of income was dairy. The survey showed that simple and quick credit delivery with lower interest rates in SHGs replaced the money-lenders. During pre-SHG some of the loans were taken for consumption purpose but in the post-SHG situation the loans were mainly taken for income generating purposes. The study showed that the average value of assets increased by 46 per cent and the annual income per household increased by 28 per cent in post-SHG periods. The most interesting feature of SHGs was compulsory savings even by cutting the necessary expenditures. Recovery rate was quite high which ranged from 95 to 100 per cent. The study also revealed that the commercial banks were not prompt in linking SHGs for loans.

Mishra et al. (2001) studied the impact of rural SHGs on generation of income and employment among the beneficiaries, identified the major constraints and problems faced by the groups, and suggested measures for overcoming these problems in Faizabad district of eastern Uttar Pradesh. For the purpose of the study, five SHGs in Amaniganj block of the district were selected randomly. It was observed that SHG members were mainly from OBC community whose main occupations were agriculture, small businesses, labour etc. Ninety-three per cent of the SHG members were male and only 7 per cent were female. Majority of the members lived below the poverty line. The average monthly savings ranged from Rs. 15 to Rs. 50. Repayment performance was good. The results of the survey showed that SHGs have helped to increase the income of the participants by 10 to 15 per cent. The major problems that the members faced were lack of training, credit and marketing facilities, entrepreneurship and high interest rate. It was suggested to involve Commercial Banks, RRBs and Primary agricultural co-operative societies to provide liberal credit at cheaper interest rate to the poor through SHGs.

Dahiya et al. (2001) in their research paper made a socio-economic analysis of the working of SHGs in Solan district of Himachal Pradesh. The data was collected from 54 SHG participants drawn from six SHGs from two development blocks of the district. The study revealed that members were mainly involved in small business and service/profession like bangle selling, tailorin g, marginal farming etc. The interest rate charged on internal lending ranged from 24 to 60 per cent and the bank interest rate was 12.5 per cent. The recovery performance both for internal and bank loans was 100 per cent. The study found that there was a considerable increase in annual income in post-SHG period. This increase was very high for the newly formed groups as compared to the older groups. The overall increase in annual income was 94.3 per cent in post-linkage period. The social impact was deep in empowering women folk, educational development of children and emancipation from social evils like drunkenness by male household members.

Gaonkar (2001) studied the impact of SHGs on women in Goa. For this purpose, the data was collected from 5 women SHGs situ ated in Bardez and Bicholim talukas in Goa. The study revealed that SHGs made a lasting impact on the lives of the poor and their quality of life was improved in terms of increase in income, savings, consumption expenditure, self-confidence, productive use offree time, getting opportunity to improve hidden talents and getting more importance in the family. It was found that individual loans were mostly utilised for productive purposes and the repayment of these loans was 100 per cent. The study concluded that the SHG movement could significantly contribute towards the reduction of poverty and unemployment in the rural sector of the economy.

Mishra and Hossain (2001) in their study assessed the impact on mahila-mandal (a rural SHG in Orissa) in terms of empowerment of rural women and employment generation through programme participation. The group was working under the development agency for the poor and tribal awakening, a leading NGO of

Kalahandi district. The impact was assessed, comparing the pre-1996 and post-SHG situation (2001) of the programme participants. The study found that till the year 2001, 26.67 per cent of the families started non-farm activities, 40 per cent adopted small family norms, 45 per cent consumed food with vegetables, 58 per cent had food security to manage the lean season and all the member families have become literate. The study revealed that the average net income per member per year increased from Rs. 6465 to Rs. 15325 through scientific cotton cultivation, livestock maintenance and small business like retail shop, dry fish trading etc. The group was maintaining successfully the fair price shop fulfilling the requirements of five nearby villages. Additional employment generated worked out to be 185 person days per member. In this way, the success of these mahila-mandals suggested that these could become a role model for other SHGs.

Nedumaran et al. (2001) conducted an empirical study on the impacts of SHGs in Tamil Nadu. Two districts of Tamil Nadu, namely, Erode and Tiruchirapalli were selected. One hundred and fifty members from 30 SHGs promoted by two NGOs – MYRADA and LEAD were surveyed. Primary data was collected through personal interview method during March-April 2001. The study showed that the average amount of group loans availed was positively associated with the group age. The annual net family income of the members in post-SHG situation was increased by 23 per cent over the pre-SHG situation. The study also indicated a considerable improvement in the social conditions of SHG participants after joining the group activities. The researchers also recommended the promotion of SHGs in rural areas, training to members and involvement of local NGOs in building SHGs for the overall improvement of the households.

Raghavendra (2001) evaluated the contribution made by microfinance programme initiated by Sahyadri Grameen Bank in Thyagarthi village in Shimoga district of Karnataka. The income generating economic activities and women's empowerment in rural areas was studied. For the purpose of study, three SHGs were personally interviewed and data was collected for the years 1994-1995 to 1999-2000. Out of these three SHGs first group was run by a forward community, second was run by SC/ST and the third was run by a backward community. The analyses revealed a significant change among the group members in diversifying income generating economic activities. The researcher found that the microfinance programme was financially sustainable. The members reported that they did not borrow from money-lenders anymore. It was found that the members of SHGs formed by forward community had created their own capital base. They were involved in diversifying farm-based activities into market-based activities. For the other two groups, resource constraint was found to be a detrimental factor to expand economic activities. The case study concluded that there was a great potential for implementing various programmes for the rural poor through SHGs.

Puhazhendhi and Badatya (2002) in a study commissioned by NABARD surveyed 115 SHG members from 60 SHGs in eastern India. They concluded that institutional credit had deepened and widened among the rural poor, while there had been substantial reduction of loans from money-le
nders and other informal sources. The findings of this study showed that 52 per cent of sample households registered 23 per cent rise in annual income and 30 per cent increase in asset ownership in post-SHG situation. About 72 per cent of the bank loan was used for income generating purpose and the remaining 28 per cent was for cons umption and other social functions and contingency purposes. The estimated employment days per household worked out to 405 person days during post-SHG

situation that had registered an increase of 34 per cent between pre- and post-SHG situations. Activity-wise, per cent increase was higher for non-farm activities (121 per cent) followed by off-farm activities (21 per cent) and farm activities (19 per cent). The social empowerment of sample SHG members in terms of self-confidence, involvement in decision-making, better communication, etc. improved in a significant way. It was also found that members in the older groups of five years and above were more socio-economically benefited as compared to the members in newly formed groups.

Kabeer and Noponen (2005) in their paper set out the findings of a socio-economic impact study of PRADAN's microfinance programme carried out in Jharkhand, one of the poorest states in India. The study was carried out in Godda, Dumka and Banka districts of Jharkhand. In order to study the impact of microfinance programme 400 SHG members were compared with 104 non-members in these three districts. The major objective of the study was to find out the impact of microfinance on the capacity of the participants to meet basic needs, livelihood base, asset position, saving and debt position and women's choice and agency. The findings of the study showed that as far as basic needs were concerned, the members had reported a more favourable overall food situation in terms of adequacy and diversity of diet as compared to non-members. They had better access to clean drinking water, improved housing with more rooms and doors. Members were sending greater number of children to school along with greater gender equity. Members were engaged in own cultivation and livestock rearing and less dependent on unskilled wage labour activities. Members had higher levels of savings and lower incidence of indebtedness to high interest of moneylenders as compared to non-members. As regards women's skills, knowledge and agency, members had acquired more practical skills and demonstrated greater awareness of government programme for the welfare of poor. However, there was less difference regarding participation in household decision-making. In both the groups, women made sole decisions in one-fifth of the households and a joint decision was made in about half of the households. Overall, the study showed that members were in a better position than non-members and the process of women empowerment had been initiated through the microfinance programme.

Misra (2006) in his paper discussed the factors and theoretical position associated with evolution of microfinance and then assessed the socio-economic impact of SHG bank linkage programme of microfinance in India. A field research was undertaken by the researcher to study the impact of microfinance programme covering 93 client households from 5 SHGs from 3 different locations of western and central part of India. The group members who were in the programme for at least two years were surveyed. It was found that all the group members were saving regularly at fixed intervals and dependence on money-lenders was eliminated for 2/3 of the clients. The social development index of group members measured on Likert scale showed a definite positive trend after joining SHGs. Loan repayment rate was also very high. But, while measuring economic development it was found that just 6 per cent of the members had taken up any economic activity in post-group formation period. Bank credit and savings were used overwhelming for consumption and other emergency needs. While the programme had a definite impact on building social capital, it had marginal impact on income level. It was found that group members were not willing to borrow to take up economic activity on account of credit risk and absence of skills to undertake some non-farm activities. Lack of technical skills a nd invasion of rural markets by big consumer goods companies reduced the scope for rural micro-enterprises. In the absence of any significant economic development, it was found that high loan repayment rate was made out of reduced consumption, increased working time as farm labour, borrowing from relatives, other groups in vicinity or in some cases from money-lenders also. So, reliance on high loans volume, outreach and repayment rate as a proxy for positive economic development ignored the issue of impact assessment at client level.

Yamuna (2007) studied the changes in the role and status of SHG participants in Solamadevi village of Coimbatore district. For the purpose of study primary data was collected from 54 SHG members through an interview schedule. The results of the study showed that all the participants who received bank loans under this scheme started their own businesses. There was an increase in the income level, savings, value of assets and household durables after joining the SHGs. It was also found that SHGs had developed women's relationships with government department and banking institutions. They had been equipped with leadership skills through various human resource training programmes and interaction with other SHGs. Women had got lot of courage and self confidence to speak for their rights after becoming SHG members.

Sarangi (2007) evaluated the impact of microfinance programme on rural poor households in some backward regions of Madhya Pradesh in India. For the purpose of study, Betul, a tribal region; and Sehore, a re latively prosperous region; were selected. The researcher examined three most popular group based microfinance programmes, i.e. government supported SGSY programme, NABARD's SHG bank linkage programme, and World Bank promoted Swashakti programme. One hundred eighty participants from two districts, and three programmes were selected through a multistage random sampling method. Non-participant households were selected with a ratio of 1:2 to participants in each village. In order to make comparisons, t-test, analysis of variance, and regression techniques were used. Impact assessment results showed a significant positive effect of programme participation on increase in the in come of the households. It was found that the income of households reporting self-employment in off-farm activities was much higher for the participant households than their counterparts. Intervention of PRADAN in promoting poultry, mushroom cultivation and sericulture among the participant households had helped diversifying their economic portfolio. Indicators of consumption items including clothing and footwear seemed to obtain high average values for the participant households than non-participants. It was also found that location factors contribute to the creation of opportunities for diversifying the economic portfolio and employment choices. The probit regression was applied to estimate the probability of participation as a function of level of per capita income, off-farm activities, work participation rate, education of principal earner of the household, adult literacy ratio, productive assets, agricultural land, distance index and years of operation of different microfinance programmes in the villages. The results indicated the exclusion of very poor households from participation in group-based credit programme. The probability of participation was low at the lower end of income distribution and it increased with the increase in per capita income of the household and declined with very high level of per capita income. The results also showed that the increase in share of off-farm earnings increased with increase in landholding. The returns seemed to be much higher for the very big landowners than the small farmers. The findings suggested that on the one hand, many of the very poor households were excluded from the programme, and on the other, the gains from participation of the programme were mostly observed for the better-off section of households, particularly those with high per capita income or the large landholders. He concluded that credit to serve as a sole instrument of poverty alleviation did not seem to be plausible, without other corroborative mechanisms that help in increasing the potential of credit use by the poor or the small farmer.

Borbora and Mahanta (2008) in their case study of Rashtriya Grameen Vikas Nidhi's (RGVN) credit and saving programme (CSP) in Assam examined the role of credit in generation of employment opportunities for the poor. They also assessed the role of SHGs in promoting the saving habits among the poor and the contribution of the programme in social and economic empowerment of the poor in general and of women in particular. The analysis of survey data revealed that 80 per cent of the members in the selected SHGs were from poor families. The members of the groups were engaged in gainful economic activities. It was found that the programme had succeeded in inculcating the habit of saving among the members. As many as 57.8 per cent of the members saved Rs. 200 to Rs. 500 and 42.2 per cent saved Rs. 501 to Rs. 1000 each. It also helped them to free themselves from the clutches of non-formal sources of credit. Forty-three per cent of the sample beneficiaries expanded their income generating activities. The SHGs had helped to set up a number of micro-enterprises for income generation. The focus of CSP was exclusively on rural poor and it adopted a credit delivery system designed specially for them with the support of specially trained staff and a supportive policy with no political intervention at any stage in the implementation of the programme. So, the CSP in Assam was found to be successful.

THEORETICAL LINK OF MICROFINANCE AND ENTREPRENEURSHIP DEVELOPMENT

For any business development, credit is an important thing. Absence of credit is a wall for investment and also for the economic growth. Access to credit can increase the adoption of new and more advance technologies which allow the poor households to expand their enterprises and improve their income level and reduce poverty. Availability of credit increases the level of household's productive and physical assets and also improves the consumption of the poor.

Olajide (1980) recognized two sources of credits for entrepreneurs named as internal and external. He found that when the internal funds increase from net flow due to entrepreneurial activities, the external funds also increase from loans extended by micro finance providers. Rural enterprise needs capital which is held by microfinance providers, as financing to microenterprise is universal not only in rural areas but even in urban areas. Credit for small and medium enterprises provides an important tool for the development of industrialization and improving the efficiency of the enterprise and increase productivity.

The clients of microfinance banks are mostly self-employed low income entrepreneurs in urban and rural areas and include traders, subsistence farmers, street vendors, service providers etc.

Methodology

Sampling

This study use primary data, which is collected from sampled population by preparing comprehensive questionnaire. **Visakhapatnam district** is an administrative division of Andhra Pradesh, India. The administrative headquarters of the Visakhapatnam District is Visakhapatnam.

According to the 2011 census Visakhapatnam district has a population of 4,288,113 (males 2,140,872 and females 2,147,241); this gives it a ranking of 44th in India (out of a total of 640) and 5th in its state. The district has a population density of 384 inhabitants per square kilometre (990 /sq mi). Its population growth rate over the decade 2001-2011 was 11.89 percent Visakhapatnam has a sex ratio of 1003 females for every 1000 males, and a literacy rate of 67.7 percent. The growth rate of population is 15.36 percent from 1991 to 2001. Rural population of the district is more than that of urban population. Rural population is 22,50,655, whereas the urban population is 2037458. The Scheduled Caste Population is 7.6 percentage of the total population, where as Scheduled Tribe Population is 14.55 percent (Wikipedia)

For this study the researcher has randomly selected three microfinance banks working in the district of Visakhapatnam. The banks selected are Canara Bank, Andhra Bank and State Bank of India. All the three are public sector banks extensively serving the rural customers to cater their needs of Microfinance. Sample size was used in this study is 150.

Table 1 : : Particulars of Sample Size

S.No.	Name of Bank	Size of the Respondents
1	Canara Bank	50
2	Andhra Bank	50
3	State Bank of India	50

This study uses purposive sampling as the data for the clients is not available and microfinance banks also do not provide their clients personal information. The data is collected by face to face interview of the respondents. The questionnaire consists of four major sections as: first section contains information of the respondents regarding their personal profiles, second section deals with business profile, third section inquires about the information regarding the facilities provided by the microfinance institutions (bank branches) to the clients and last section collected information regarding the amount of loan, type of entrepreneur training given by organization to the clients. SPSS software is used to analyze the data. Chi-Squire test is used only to investigate the association between banks and respondent's demographic characteristics (sex, area, age, income, education, profession and major source of family income). Non-parametric tests as: Kruskal-Wallis and Mann-Whitney tests are used for econometric analysis.

Results and Discussion

Results and discussion divided by in three sections first section base on descriptive analysis second section discuss role of institutions in entrepreneurship development and the third section deal with satisfaction of bank clients.

Descriptive analysis

The Figure 1 is showing that 26 percent of the clients are male and 74 percent are female. The greater proportion is male in the clients of the microfinance institution.

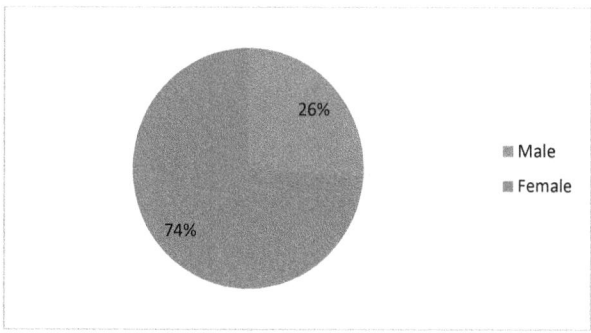

Figure .1: Gender of the Respondents

The Figure 2 is showing that 28 percent are those who live in urban areas and 72 percent are those who live in rural areas. This shows that most of the clients are from the urban areas.

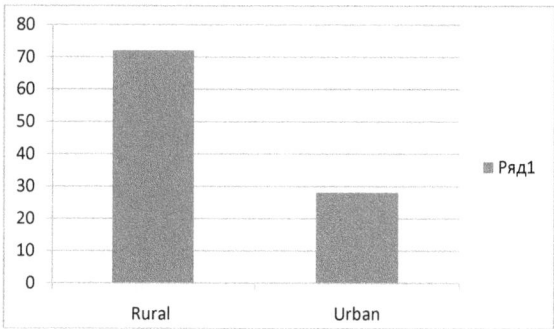

Figure .2: Location of the Respondents

People have different purpose to take loan from microfinance institutions such as for education, for social work, for marriage, for house building, for start a new business or finance their existing business. The Figure 1.3 is showing that most of the clients take loan for the purpose other than to start a business as 40 percent clients take loan to start a business while 60 percent are those that access to microfinance to take loan to meet the other needs of life.

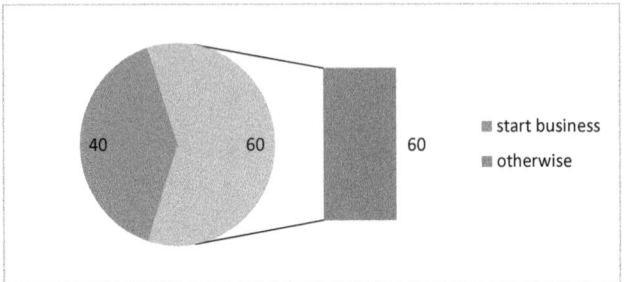

Fig 1.3: The Propose of the Loan taken by the Respondents

Figure 1.4 is showing that before the microfinance institution loan acquisition, only 37 percent respondents hold a business and 63 percent are those who don't hold the business. So microfinance loan play a vital role in business

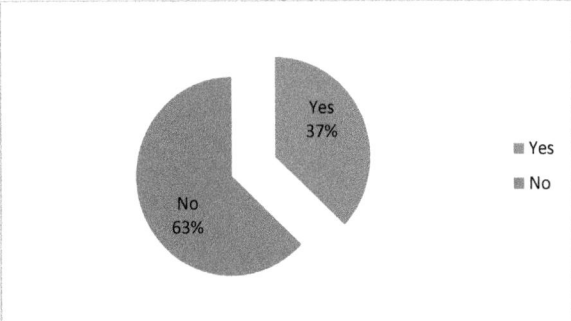

Fig. 1.4: Family Business before Taking a Loan from Microfinance Institution

Table 2 is showing the Demographic profile of the respondents in percentage. The variables as source of finance other than microfinance ($p = 0.042$) and purpose of loan ($p = 0.037$) are significant at 5 percent level and significantly differ between male and female clients. The statistics shows that out of total 37 percent clients, who says that they have access to finance other that microfinance institution, 16.1 percent are males and 20.9 percent are females while those who say they don't have finance other than microfinance institution are 63 percent in which 14.3 percent are males and 49.7 percent are females . As the purpose of loan, those who say that they have taken loan to start a business are 27.3 percent in which 16 percent are females clients and 11.3 percent are males and those who report that they have taken loan to support and strengthen the existing business are 67.3 percent in which 54.7 percent are females and 12.7 percent are males.The variables as profession of the respondents ($p= 0.085$), major source of income ($p = 0.077$) and education ($p = 0.083$) are significant at 10 percent level. Those who say they are government employee, .7 percent is female and 1.3 percent is males, 10 percent females and 3.3 percent males have private job holder and 58 percent female and 19.3 percent males report that they are self-business holder. Among those who inform that their major source of income of household is employment, 22 are female and 13 are males and the clients who say their major source of income is business, 53.3% are female and 15.3 percent are males. Most of the respondents' response is business as their major source of income. As education is also statistically significant and female are more educated as compare to the males.

Table 2: Demographic Profile of the Respondents in percentage

Variable	Gender		
Profession *** Government . job private job self-business agriculture Labor Unemployed	Male (percentage) 1.3 3.3 19.3 .0 .7 1.3	Female (percentage) .7 10 58 2 3.3 .0	Total (percentage) 2 13.3 77.3 2 4 1.3
Family business	Male	Female	Totals in Percentage
Yes	16.1	20.9	37
No	14.3	49.7	63
X² = 0.795 Sig=0.373			df=1
Major Source of Income***	Male (percentage)	Female (percentage)	Totals in Percentage
Agriculture	0	4	4
Employment	8.7	14.7	23.3
Business	15.3	53.3	68.7
Remittances	1.3	2	3.3
Others	7	0	7
X² = 8.443	df =4		Sig = 0.077
Education***	Male	Female	Total
Illiterate	14	3.3	17.3
Primary	6	8	14
Middle	4.7	18.7	23.3
Matriculation	4.7	22.7	27.3
Secondary	4.7	5.3	10.0
Graduation and above	2.7	5.3	8
X²=11.866	df=5		Sig=0.083
Purpose of Loan**	Male	Female	Total
To start a business	11.3	16	27.3
To strengthen existing business	12.7	54.7	67.3
For house construction	0	7	7
For marriage	0	7	7
Social work	7	0	7
Other purpose	1.3	3	4.3
X²=11.866	df=5		Sig= 0.037

*shows significance at 1%

**shows significance at 5%

***shows significance at 10 %

Table 3 is showing the Demographic profile of respondents by location in percentage. The variables as source of finance other than microfinance (p = 0.597) significant at 1 percent level and purpose of loan (p = 0.032) are significant at 5 percent level and significantly differ between rural and urban respondents. The statistics shows that total 26.7 percent respondents, who says that they have access to finance other than microfinance institution, 8.1 percent are urban and 18.1 percent are rural while those who say they don't have finance other than microfinance institution are 73.8 percent in which 19.5 percent are urban and 54.4 percent are rural . As the purpose of loan, those who say that they have taken loan to start a business are 27.3 percent in which 11.3 percent are urban respondents and 16 percent are rural and those who report that they have taken loan to support and strengthen the existing business are 67.3 percent in which 14 percent are urban and 53.3 percent are rural.

The variables as purpose of loan (p= 0.032) significant at 5 percent level. Those who say they are government employee 1.3 percent are urban and .7 percent is rural, 4 percent urban and 9.3 percent rural have private job holder and 20.7 percent urban and 56.7 percent rural report that they are self-business holder. Among those who inform that their major source of income of household is employment, 6.7 are urban and 16.7 are rural and the respondents who say their major source of income is business, 17.3 percent are urban and 51.3 percent are rural. Most of the respondents' response is business as their major source of income.

Table 3: Demographic of Respondents by Location in percentage

Variable	Location		
Profession	Rural (percentage)	Urban (percentage)	Total (percentage)
Government job	.7	1.3	2
private job	9.3	4	13.3
self- business	56.7	20.7	77.3
agriculture	.7	1.3	2
Labor	3.3	.7	4
Unemployed	1.3	.0	1.3
X^2 =5.743	df= 5		Sig = 0.332
Family Business	Rural(percentage)	Urban(percentage)	Total(percentage)
Yes	28.3	8.7	
No	44.6	18.4	37
			63
X^2 =0.404	df = 1		Sig = 0.525
Other Source of Finance	Rural(percentage)	Urban (percentage)	Total (percentage)
Yes	18.1	8.1	26.2
No	54.4	19.5	73.8
X^2 =0.280	df= 1		Sig = 0.597
Major Source of Income	Rural (percentage)	Urban (percentage)	Total (percentage)
agriculture	1.3	2.7	4
employment	16.7	6.7	23.3
business	51.3	17.3	68.7
remittances	2.7	.7	3.3
others	.0	.7	.7
X^2 = 7.573	df = 4		Sig = 0.108
Education	Rural (percentage)	Urban (percentage)	Total (percentage)
Illiterate	12.7	4.7	17.3

Primary	8	6	14
Middle	18.7	4.7	23.3
Matriculation	19.3	8	27.3
Secondary	6.7	3.3	10
Graduation and above	6.7	1.3	8
X² = 4.434	df = 5		Sig = 0.489
Purpose of Loan**	Rural (percentage)	Urban (percentage)	Total (percentage)
To start a business	16	11.3	27.3
	53.3	14	67.3
To strengthen existing business	.0	.7	.7
	.7	.0	.7
For house building	.7	.0	.7
For Marriage	1.3	2	3.3
Social work			
Other			
X² = 12.128	df = 5		Sig = 0.032

*shows significance at 1%
** shows significance at 5%
***shows significance at 10%

ROLE OF INSTITUTIONS IN ENTREPRENEURSHIP DEVELOPMENT

As stated earlier for the purpose of this study the researcher has selected three public sector banks, which are playing key role in entrepreneurship development through micro finance, those are Canara Bank, State Bank of India and Andhra Bank. Figure 5 shows Canara Bank clients use loan for the other purpose and State Bank clients use loan to start a business. Andhra Bank plays wider role to encourage its clients to start a new business than Canara Bank and State Bank of India

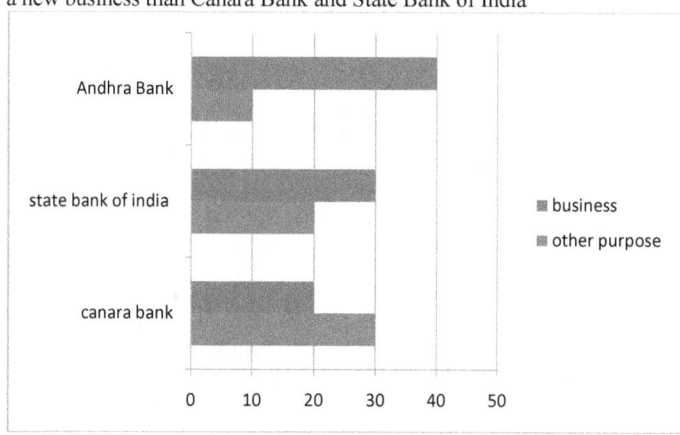

Fig. 5: Showing Loan Purpose –Entrepreneurship and MFI

Table 4: Microfinance institutions and entrepreneurship development

Variable	Name of MFI		
Entrepreneurship** Otherwise	Canara Bank %	State Bank of India %	Andhra Bank%
To start a business	22.0	22.7	15.3
	10.7	11.3	18.0
Chi square value = 6.130		df -= 2	Sig = 0.047

** shows significance at 5%

Table 4 is showing that the clients those who start a business differ significantly with respect to microfinance institutions. The p-value (0.047) is showing that it is significant at five percent level. Those who are taking loan from the Andhra bank, they use this amount to start a business than the other ones who use it for marriage, education etc. The 18 percent clients of the Andhra bank response that they have started a business with the amount of the taken loan than any other bank as 11.3 percent of State Bank of India and 10.7 percent of the Canara Bank.

      Kruskal-Wallis and Mann-Whitney Tests are nonparametric tests. Kruskal-Wallis test allow the comparison between more than two independent groups. It is used when three or more sets of scores are to be compared. The test statistics value for Kruskal-Wallis exceeds the critical level of 0.05 percent level, then the null hypothesis is rejected which means that the sample come from the different populations. The Mann-Whitney test is used only when to make the comparison between two set of groups only. This test set the null hypothesis as:

H0 = the population medians are same.

Table 5 Role of MFI in Entrepreneurship Development

Variable	Mean Rank	Sum Rank
Institution**	69.57	6261.50
Otherwise	83.79	5062.50
To start a business		
Mann-Whitney U test	2166.500	
Wilcoxon W test	6261.500	
Z value	-2.171	
Sig.	.030	

**significance at 5% level

Table 5 shows the role of microfinance institutions in entrepreneurship development which informs that the mean rank vale (83.79) for those who start a business is statistically differ in ranking to those who say otherwise (69.57). This is significant at 5 percent level of confidence as its p-value is (0.030).

Table 6 shows the ranking of the variables and test statistics of these variables as Mann-Whitney, Wilcoxon value, Z and p-values. The variables education of the clients (0.000) and other sources of income of the clients' families (0.007) highly significant at 1 percent level while the institutions (0.030), age of the respondents (0.019), profession of the respondents (0.032) are significant at 5 percent level. The mean rank value of the education with respect to start a business (95.92) is showing that the more the educated, the more the chances that he invest the amount of loan to start a business than the illiterate. The clients those who respond that they have other sources of finance else than micro credit, they have don't use it for starting a business than those of who say they don't invest in it business. The mean rank value (81.76) for those who report they don't use it to start a business in higher than those who invest it in other than business. The mean rank value (79.64) for the profession of the respondent is showing that it is low for those who to start a business than to otherwise. The mean rank value for the age is showing that (82.18) ranked high than that of who start a business among the other age level of the clients.

Table 6 Mann-Whitney Test

Name of Variables	Mean Rank	Test Statistics	
Institutions**		Mann-Whitney U	2165.500
Otherwise	69.57	Wilcoxon W	6261.500
To start a business	84.39	Z	-2.171
		Sig.	0.30
Gender of respondent		Mann-Whitney U	2655.000
		Wilcoxon W	4485.000
Otherwise	76.00	Z	-.277
To start a business	74.75	Sig.	.820
Area of respondent		Mann-Whitney U	2609.000
Otherwise	76.50	Wilcoxon W	4440.000
To start a business	74.00	Z	-.444
		Sig.	.657
Age of respondent**	82.18	Mann-Whitney U	2099.000
Otherwise	65.48	Wilcoxon W	3929.000
To start a business		Z	-2.338
		Sig.	.019
Income of respondent***		Mann-Whitney U	2252.500
		Wilcoxon W	4082.500
Otherwise	80.47	Z	-1.757
To start a business	68.69	Sig.	.079
Education of respondent*		Mann-Whitney U	1474.500
		Wilcoxon W	5569.500
Otherwise	61.88	Z	-4.805
To start a business	95.92	-Sig.	.000
Profession of respondent**		Mann-Whitney U	2291.500
		Wilcoxon W	4121.500
Otherwise	79.64	Z	-2.142
To start a business	68.69	Sig.	.032
Major source of respondent family income*		Mann-Whitney U	2126.500
		Wilcoxon W	3955.500
		Z	-2.706
Otherwise	81.76		
To start a business	65.92	Sig.	.007
Have you or any family member business before?		Mann-Whitney U	2548.000
		Wilcoxon W	4318.000
		Z	-.412
Otherwise	75.37	Sig.	.680
To start a business	73.19		
To what extent do you have links with business community?		Mann-Whitney U	2567.500
		Wilcoxon W	4397.500
		Z	-.961
	76.15	Sig.	.336
Otherwise	73.29		

To start a business			

*shows significance at 1% level
**shows significance at 5% level
***shows significance at 10% level

SATISFACTION OF BANK CLIENTS

Table 7 is showing the Kruskal-Wallis Test and ranking of the institutions, p-value and chi square values are also given. The variables as amount of loan (0.007) and attitude of staff (0.000) significant at 1 percent level of confidence and scheme of bank (0.036), quality of institution (0.019), purpose to take loan (0.048) are significant at 5 percent level of confidence. Interest rate and satisfied with help of microfinance institutions are statistically insignificant. Clients of Canara bank are highly satisfied with the amount of loan than the other bank clients the mean rank value for the Canara bank is (81.59) is higher than that of the other banks as State Bank of India (75.69) and Andhra Bank (71.51). The clients of the Andhra Bank report that they are highly satisfied with the attitude of the bank staff than the other banks as its mean rank value (92.54) is showing that it is highly ranked among the others. Clients of State Bank of India are highly satisfied with scheme of loan as the mean rank value for State Bank of India (83.34) is higher than the other banks as their mean rank is (65.17) for the Canara Bank and (79.49) for Andhra Bank. The clients of the Andhra Bank response that they are more satisfied with the quality of the institution that the other institution clients as its mean rank value (86.83) is also showing that it is highly ranked among the other banks. Those who take loan for the purpose to start a business are statistically significantly differing in their ranks as State Bank of India (52) is high in rank than the other banks.

Table 7 Kruskal-Wallis Test

Variables	Mean Rank	Test Statistics	
Satisfied with amount*		X^2	9.844
		df	2
Canara Bank	81.59	Sig.	.007
State Bank of India	75.69		
Andhra Bank	71.51		
Satisfied with scheme**		X^2	6.663
		df	2
Canara Bank	65.17	Sig.	.036
State Bank of India	83.34		
Andhra Bank	79.49		
Satisfied with attitude*		X^2	18.183
		df	2
Canara Bank	61.77	Sig	.000
State Bank of India	71.72		
Andhra Bank	92.54		
Satisfied with quality*		X^2	7.914
		df	2
Canara Bank	66.46	Sig	.019
State Bank of India	73.56		
Andhra Bank	86.83		
Satisfied with rate of Interest		X^2	2.084
		df	2

Canara Bank	72.10	Sig	.353
State Bank of India	81.79		
Andhra Bank	72.41		
Satisfied with MFI help		X^2	2.482
		df	2
Canara Bank	74.95	Sig.	.289
State Bank of India	70.01		
Andhra Bank	80.14		
Purpose of business**		X^2	6.089
		df	2
Canara Bank	49	Sig	.048
State Bank of India	52		
Andhra Bank	50		

*shows significance at 1% level
**shows significance at 5% level

Conclusion

Present study conduct on the role of microfinance in entrepreneurship development and also measure the level of satisfaction of microfinance institution clients towards their respective banks. In Kruskal Walli test, the variables are satisfied with amount of loan, scheme, attitude, quality and purpose of loan is significant. In Mann-Whitney test variables institutions, age, income, education, profession and major source of income are significant. Results of the study suggest that microfinance institutions playing a significant role in micro-enterprise development in Visakhapatnam district of Andhra Pradesh. Comparatively, clients of Andhra Bank are more likely to confirm that they initiated micro-business by taking the loan. As for clients satisfaction is concerned study suggests mix results. For Results concludes that clients of Canara bank more satisfied as compare to the other bank clients.

In policy implementations microfinance institutions should start training for the clients in future and educate them about the importance of business for the economy. Due to high constraints on credit availability hinder the way of entrepreneurship development so the government should facilitate for credit availability with low interest rates so that the individuals get credit on easy conditions to start a business and to finance their existing business.

REFERENCES

1. Borbora, S.; and Mahanta, R. (2008), "Microfinance Through Self Help Groups and its Impact: A Case of Rashtriya Grameen Vikas Nidhi-Credit and Saving Programme in Assam", in G. Sreeramulu (ed.), *Empowerment of Women Through Self Help Groups*, Kalpaz, New Delhi, pp. 42-43.
2. Chen, Martha A.; and Donald, Snodgrass (2001), "Managing Resources, Activities, and Risk in Urban India: The Impact of SEWA Bank", *United States Agency for International Development (USAID) and Assessing the Impact of Microenterprise Services (AIMS) Project*, Management Systems International, Washington, DC.
3. Dahiya, Prem Singh; Pandey, N.K.; and Karol, Anshuman (2001), "Socio-economic Evaluation of Self-help Groups in Solan District of Himachal Pradesh: Impact, Issues and Policy Implications", *Indian Journal of Agricultural Economics,* Vol. 56, No. 3, pp. 486-87.
4. Gaonkar, Rekha R. (2001), "Working and Impact of Self-Help Groups in Goa", *Indian Journal of Agricultural Economics,* Vol. 56, No. 3, p. 471.

5. ILO (1998), "Enterprise Creation by the Unemployed: The Role of Microfinance" Paper Presented in International Conference on Self-employment, Burlington, 24-26 September.

6. Kabeer, N.; and Noponen, Helzi (2005), "Social and Economic Impacts of PRADAN's Self Help Group Microfinance and Livelihoods Promotion Program: Analysis from Jharkhand, India", *Imp-Act: Improving the Impact of Microfinance on Poverty: Action Research Program Working Paper*, No. 11, University of Sussex, Brighton.

7. Manimekalai, M.; and Rajeswari, G. (2001), "Nature and Performance of Informal Self Help Groups- A Case from Tamilnadu", *Indian Journal of Agricultural Economics,* Vol. 56, No. 3, pp. 453-54.

8. Mishra, J. P.; Verma, R. R.; and Singh, V. K. (2001), "Socio-economic Analysis of Rural Selfhelp Groups Schemes in Block Amaniganj, District Faizabad (Uttar Pradesh)", *Indian Journal of Agricultural Economics,* Vol. 56, No. 3, pp. 473-74.

9. Mishra, S.N.; and Hossain, M.M. (2001), "A Study on the Working and Impact of Dharmadevi Mahila Mandal − A Rural Self-help Group in Kalahandi District of Orissa", *Indian Journal of Agricultural Economics,* Vol. 56, No. 3, pp. 480-81.

10. Mishra, S.N.; and Hossain, M.M. (2001), "A Study on the Working and Impact of Dharmadevi Mahila Mandal − A Rural Self-help Group in Kalahandi District of Orissa", *Indian Journal of Agricultural Economics,* Vol. 56, No. 3, pp. 480-81.

11. Misra, Alok (2006), "Microfinance in India and Millennium Development Goals: Maximising Impact on Poverty", Discussion Paper for Workshop on World Bank, Singapore, 18 September.

12. Nedumaran, S.; Palanisami, K.; and Swaminathan, L.P. (2001), "Performance and Impact of Self-help Groups in Tamil Nadu", *Indian Journal of Agricultural Economics,* Vol. 56, No. 3, pp. 471-72.

13. Puhazhendhi, V.; and Badatya, K.C. (2002), *SHG-Bank Linkage Programme for Rural Poor in India - An Impact Assessment,* Microcredit Innovations Department, National Bank for Agriculture and Rural Development, Mumbai.

14. Puhazhendhi, V.; and Satyasai, K.J.S. (2000), *Micro Finance for Rural People: An impact evaluation,* Microcredit Innovations Department, National Bank for Agriculture and Rural Development, Mumbai.

15. Raghavendra, T.S. (2001), "Performance Evaluation of Self Help Groups: A Case Study of Three Groups in Shimoga District", *Indian Journal of Agricultural Economics,* Vol. 56, No. 3, pp. 466-67.

16. Sarangi, Niranjan (2007), "Microfinance and the Rural Poor: Impact Assessment Based on Fieldwork in Madhya Pradesh, India", Paper Presented in Conference on Sustainable Development & Livelihoods, Delhi School of Economics, Delhi, 6-8 February.

17. Singh, D. K. (2001), "Impact of Self Help Groups on the Economy of Marginalized Farmers of Kanpur Dehat District of Uttar Pradesh−A Case Study", *Indian Journal of Agricultural Economics,* Vol. 56, No. 3, pp. 463-64.

18. Todd, Helen (2001), "Paths out of Poverty: The Impact of SHARE Microfinance Limited in Andhra Pradesh, India", Unpublished Report, Imp-Act, Brighton, UK.

19. Yamuna, G. (2007), "Women Empowerment Through Self-help Groups in Solamadevi Village" in V. S. Ganesamurthy (ed.), *India: Economic Empowerment of Women,* New Century, New Delhi.

Web References

1. Chakrabarti Rajesh (2005), The Indian Microfinance Experience-Accomplishments & Challenges. Available at http://papers.ssrn.com/sol3/papers.cfm?abstract_id=649854#PaperDownload

2. Deb, Alok Kumar (2006), World Cooperative Movement. Available at http://www.tripurainfo.com/citizen_services/helping_bytes/helping10.shtml

3. Intellecap (2007), Inverting the Pyramid: The Changing Face of Indian Microfinance. Available at http://www.microfinancegateway.org/files/49609_file_Intellecap_Inverting_the_Pyramid_Oct_2007.pdf

4. Jayasheela, Dinesha P.T. and V. Bas il Hans, (2008), Financial Inclusion and Microfinance in India: An Overview. Available at http://papers.ssrn.com/sol3/papers.cfm?abstract_id=1089680

5. Littlefield Elizabeth and Rosenberg Rich ard (2004), Microfinance and the Poor: Breaking Down Walls between Microfinance and Formal Finance. Available at http://collab2.cgap.org/gm/document-1.9.2712/BreakingDownWalls.pdf.

6. Misra Alok (2006) Microfinance in India and Millennium Development Goals: Maximizing Impact on Poverty. Available at : http://www2.warwick.ac.uk/fac/soc/csgr/activitiesnews/workshops/2006ws/world_bank/papers/misra.pdf

7. Throat Y S (2005) Centenary of Indian Cooperative Movement- Round Table on Cooperative Banking. Available at http://www.nabard.org/fileupload/DataBank/Speeches/md_speech_Shri%20Y.S.P.%20Thorat 1_070106.pdf

8. World Bank (2005), Microfinance in South Asia: Towards Financial Inclusionfor the Poor, 2005. Available at http://web.worldbank.org/WBSITE/EXTERNAL/COUNTRIES/SOUTHASIAEXT/0,,contentMDK:21404284~pagePK:146736~piPK:146830~theSitePK:223547,00.html

9. http://www.microfinancegateway.org/gm/document-1.1.9211/Microfinance%20in%20India.pdf

CASE STUDY-6

Implementation of CSR in Micro Finance to upscale skills deficiencies for micro credit borrowers in order to mitigate the rate of defaulters:

A Study of an Integrated Model

Dr. Anitha Kumari, Sankar Mukherjee

Abstract: Eradication of abject poverty through the financial literacy was aimed to be accomplished under the armoury of Micro-Finance. Financial Literacy for the economically

Marginalised people in India have been the core of concern under the perspective of micro- economy. Micro-Finance has been coined a paramount important tool to combat the social evil particularly the mother of social evils called poverty. But owing to the anamolities of different structural loop holes there has been a concern of cloud appears over the process and financial health and hygiene of micro-finance in India. Micro credit in terms of repayment from the borrowers has over shadows the natural flow of Micro-Finance operation across the entire Micro-Finance companies. This hermeneutics study strive to open the logjam of this non-payment mechanism to foster the capital infusion that leads to capacity of lending and further strengthen the micro credit fabrics for holistic social empowerment. In modern times, when globalization, economic liberalization brings the world trade into a single converging point, multi disciplinary role became more dynamic and multi-dimensional to cater the need for each others. Human Resource is one the discipline which has its strategic significance to every sphere. Micro Finance needs this strategic support mechanism from the HR to understand the actual root of the problems of intensity of non-payment across the borrowers. Hence, this secondary based study, like to explore the strategic role that HR can play to mitigate the risk of lending of micro credit and it can replenish the mutual confidence between lenders and borrowers for accomplishing the holistic social inclusiveness.

Dr. Anitha Kumari, Assistant Professor, Bengaluru School of Management, GITAM University

Sankar Mukherjee, Assistant Professor, Bengaluru School of Management, GITAM University, alapanmistu@gmail.com

Introduction:

"One small loan enables me to transform the live hood of my entire family. I have borrowed enough money to purchase a small cow. In three years i quadrupled my investment by selling cow milk and calves from original cow and constructed a new house for my family"................ Anwar Begam **(Bangladesh).**

The above statement signifies the success of Micro-Finance in Bangladesh which has been scripted in India to change the economy of rural landscape. Micro-Finance under the ambit of NBFCs (Non Banking Financial Corporations) is an instrument to arrest the financial inclusion that leads to holistic social inclusion for inclusive growth. The Rangarajan committee on Financial Inclusion defined Financial Inclusion as the "process of ensuring

access to financial service and timely adequate credit where needed by vulnerable groups such as weaker sections and low income groups at a affordable cost". Above definition clearly state that it is time and affordability factors which separate the characteristic of micro credit from other types of macro credits. First noble laureate from Bangladesh Mohammad Yunus and Grameen Bank received the citation stated that "Lasting peace cannot be achieved unless large population groups finds ways in which to break out poverty. Micro credit is one such means." Peace need to convert into pace to remain a substance of sustainability in the live hood of economically deprived section of the community. The main idea behind Micro Finance is that marginalised poor people in the rural, urban, semi-urban geography who cannot provides collaterals for seeking loan can facilitate with the provision of small loan to cater their productive and self sustaining activities.. Economic Emancipation of women has been a reality in today's competitive world became a substance of achievement by the catalyst role that Micro Finance has played. United Nation Capital Development Fund (UNCDF) has provided the fund to Bangladesh to project the micro finance on productive purpose such as rice cultivation, cattle fattening, and small scale entrupreunuial initiative. The definition of Micro Finance stands the means by which poor people convert the small sum of money into large lump sum (Rutherford, 1999).

Emergence of Micro-Finance: Global Footprint

Susus" of Ghana, "chit funds" in India, "tandas" in Mexico, "arisan" in Indonesia, "cheetu" in Sri Lanka, "tontines" in West Africa, and "pasanaku" in Bolivia, as well as numerous savings clubs and burial societies found all over the world represents the savings and credit groups entities have been operating since the centuries. As "necessity is the mother of Invention ", so Micro –Finance also emerge as a instrumental tool to alleviate poverty under the influence of widening economic , gender , color, race disparities around the world. Commercial Banking was considered as a striking force to narrowing the disparity gaps; fail to accomplish the desire goal. No of Unbanked people remain outside the boundaries of economic eco-system. Under this perspective formal credit and savings institution come forward to ponder the value delivery system through credit delivery mechanism through co-operative for the said section of unbanked marginalised people. Such initiative of credit delivery without collaterals was initiated by Irish Loan Fund System, in the early 1700 by noted Irish Nationalist Jonathan Swift. This idea made a wave and created 300 found to facilitate 20% of household in Ireland. People Bank, Credit Union, Savings and Credit Co-operative raised their existence in the decade of 1800 across Europe.

Former World Bank President James Wolfensohn once said "Microfinance fits squarely into the Bank's overall strategy. As you know, the Bank's mission is to reduce poverty and improve living standards by promoting sustainable growth and Investment in people through loans, technical assistance, and policy guidance. Microfinance contributes directly to this objective" .The emphasis on microfinance is reflected in microfinance being a key feature in Poverty Reduction Strategy Papers (PRSPs)

Micro-Finance: (1800-1900)

Money Laundering

Friedrich Wilhelm Raiffeisen and his supporters strived to rescue the rural populitation from money lenders by liberating them from the culture of economic dependency. This movement has engulfed entire Europe and cemented a movement called Co-operative movement which has spread across gradually in North America and Europe which later percolated down to developed and developing countries.

Micro-Finance: A Way Back In India

Micro Finance in India can trace its root in way back 1970, when a self employed women's association (SEWA) formed a co-operative movement called "*Shri Mahila SEWA Sahakari Bank*" to facilitate the banking service among unorganised in Ahmadabad city. Later in the decade of eighties it has spreader its wings in a luxurious form to make Micro Finance social weapons to empower the marginalised section in rural habitats. Today Micro Finance has become a multi-million dollar industry backed by different financial institutions such as Small Industries Development Bank for India (SIDB),National Bank for Agriculture and Rural Development (NBARD)as well private financial entities like ICICI Bank,

Emergence of Micro Finance under the back drop of Banking Sector in India

Emergence of banking sectors has taken the need of financing of rural people particularly the credit of marginalised section of rural inhabitants. Banking nationalization was aim to meet the credit necessities among vast landscape of rural India. There were various objective for Bank nationalization strategy expanding the outreach of financial service to the neglected sections (Singh,2005).But the objective remain a distant dream as the expectation to outreach programme for the financing for neglected sectors could not scale up to the desire platform. The object was highly laudable but sustainability of the objective could not reach owing to the Credit flow to the marginalised particularly rural women section remain a concern. Credit flow is the instrument which can have a substantive impact of rural poverty. Banking sector fails to develop right mechanism to overcome this gap.

Agriculture & Micro-Finance

Industrial Revolution could not deter the prosperity of agricultural sector. So thrust of Micro-Finance focused on developing agricultural modernization. Latin America has experience such modalities in their rural area. This decade has seen more government intervention in giving credit to reduce the feudalistic relation between lenders and farmers in rural area. In most cases, these new banks for the poor were not owned by the poor themselves, as they had been in Europe, but by government agencies or private banks. Over the years, these institutions became inefficient and at times, abusive.

Between the 1950s and 1970s, governments and donors focused on providing agricultural credit to small and marginal farmers, in hopes of raising productivity and incomes. These efforts to expand access to agricultural credit emphasized supply-led government interventions in the form of targeted credit through state-owned development finance institutions, or farmers' cooperatives in some cases, that received concessional loans and on-lent to customers at below-market interest rates. These subsidized schemes were rarely successful. Rural development banks suffered massive erosion of their capital base due to subsidized lending rates and poor repayment discipline and the funds did not always reach the poor, often ending up concentrated in the hands of better-off farmers.

Meanwhile, starting in the 1970s, experimental programs in Bangladesh, Brazil, and a few other countries extended tiny loans to groups of poor women to invest in micro-businesses. This type of microenterprise credit was based on solidarity group lending in which every member of a group guaranteed the repayment of all members. These "microenterprise lending" programs had an almost exclusive focus on credit for income generating activities (in some cases accompanied by forced savings schemes) targeting very poor (often women) borrowers.

Grameen Bank and New Dimension of Micro Finance

In Bangladesh, Professor Muhammad Yunus addressed the banking problem faced by the poor through a programme of action-research. With his graduate students in Chittagong University in 1976, he designed an experimental credit programme to serve them. It spread rapidly to hundreds of villages. Through a special relationship with rural banks, he disbursed and recovered thousands of loans, but the bankers refused to take over the project at the end of the pilot phase. They feared it was too expensive and risky in spite of his success. Eventually, through the support of donors, the Grameen Bank was founded in 1983 and now serves more than 4 million borrowers. The initial success of Grameen Bank also stimulated the establishment of several other giant microfinance institutions like BRAC, ASA, Proshika, etc.

Through the 1980s, the policy of targeted, subsidized rural credit came under a slow but increasing attack as evidence mounted of the disappointing performance of directed credit programs, especially poor loan recovery, high administrative costs, agricultural development bank insolvency, and accrual of a disproportionate share of the benefits of subsidized credit to larger farmers. The basic tenets underlying the traditional directed credit approach were debunked and supplanted by a new school of thought called the "financial systems approach", which viewed credit not as a productive input necessary for agricultural development but as just one type of financial service that should be freely priced to guarantee its permanent supply and eliminate rationing. The financial systems school held that the emphasis on interest rate ceilings and credit subsidies retarded the development of financial intermediaries, discouraged intermediation between savers and investors, and benefited larger scale producers more than small scale, low-income producers.

Meanwhile, microcredit programs throughout the world improved upon the original methodologies and defied conventional wisdom about financing the poor. First, they showed that poor people, especially women, had excellent repayment rates among the better programs, rates that were better than the formal financial sectors of most developing countries. Second, the poor were willing and able to pay interest rates that allowed microfinance institutions (MFIs) to cover their costs.

1990s

These two features - high repayment and cost-recovery interest rates - permitted some MFIs to achieve long-term sustainability and reach large numbers of clients. The 1990s saw growing enthusiasm for promoting microfinance as a strategy for poverty alleviation. The microfinance sector blossomed in many countries, leading to multiple financial services firms serving the needs of micro entrepreneurs and poor households. These gains, however, tended to concentrate in urban and densely populated rural areas.

It was not until the mid-1990s that the term "microcredit" began to be replaced by a new term that included not only credit, but also savings and other financial services. "Microfinance" emerged as the term of choice to refer to a range of financial services to the poor, that included not only credit, but also savings and other services such as insurance and money transfers.

Micro Credit: In the Cross Road of Technology Driven Century

Post economic reform and rapid urbanization has tweaked the way for micro-credits and its long term responsibilities. The beginning of new millennium has witnessed a slew of eventful incidents in accordance with the stream of progress with the pace of technology driven socio-economical development. The evolution of micro-finance has had different approaches which have gained its momentum in this decade. There are array of actual problems under the umbrella of multi dimensional factors has marked the Micro-Finance industries prospect into a tardy affairs. This study has underpinned the following impediment that highlights the proceeding and subsequent progress of this industry is being furnished to understand the actual source of the bottlenecks for further expansion of Micro Finance ails Non Banking Financial Corporation (NBFCs) to adopt an alternative inter-disciplinary approach to stir the growth rate towards sustainability.

Micro Finance: A Mission to be accomplished in the Millennium:

Miscellaneous milestone are to be attained within the framework of invisible influence of ever growing demand of society under the realm of the broader respect of nation. India, a nation being depend on agrarian economy dominated by post independence has shifted its major share of agriculture contribution on Gross Domestic Product(GDP)(17.5%) to more on service sector on account of the demand of technology driven approaches from the past decade's manual mechanism owing to steeper span of narrowing trade barriers across globe under the impact of globalization. But, real data says a reverse picture when phenomena meet with reality. We as a nation still struggling to arrest financial Inclusion that leads to Inclusive Growth. Disparities across gender, sex, race, caste, creed etc has been widening in proportionate as economic prosperity has been captivated within the possession of elite section, neo-middle class, and creamy layers of the society. The prime object for economic liberalization still remains as a distant dream on account of marginalised section's non participation in economic ecosystem. Financial Inclusion is the most buzz word in India as per the laid down directive issued by Reserve Bank of India

Micro-Credit a Panacea:

Financial Inclusion for Unbanked to eradicate Abject Poverty

Although agriculture contribution in GPD is in continuing decline, but the impact of agriculture remain standstill in the fabric of Indian Economy. Ever five year plan focus more on agriculture credit which is still in demand particularly for marginalised peasant to irk their live hood. HYV (High Yielding Varity) and Genetic Modified Crop (GM) has augmented the quantity and quality of production, but operational expenses for accessibility to technology being still restricted due to finance ails credit. Therefore, Planning Commission in every five years plan laid down the importance of rapid and progressive instiualisation of timely and sufficient credit support for the easy accessibility of agricultural technology for the deprive marginalised farmers. Financial Inclusion is need of the hour for this section that dwells in the mass landscape of rural habitats. Finance by the name of rural credit is catered to the growing by the Micro-Finance institutes

Micro-Finance and Women Empowerment: Made For Each Other

An antidote for gender Equality, gender Illiteracy, Child Mortality, mitigates the risk of disease

Empowerment is a holistic concept comprising multi-dimensional approaches in the different aspect of life. Stromquist (1993) identified four interdependent Dimensions of empowerment – cognitive, psychological, economic, and political. Cognitive empowerment refers to knowledge about, and understanding of, the conditions and causes of subordination. Psychological empowerment relates to the development of self-esteem and self-confidence enabling powerless individuals' or group to recognise their own power and to motivate those into action. Economic empowerment is the ability to earn and control economic resources. Political empowerment involves the ability to analyse one's world and to organize and mobilise for social change. Acharya and Ghirme (2005) identified three dimensions of women's empowerment- economic, social and political. According to them each component of these dimensions reinforces each other. The economic aspects include increasing women's access to, and command over tangible and intangible resources, such as wealth,
Property, employment, knowledge and information. Social aspects include changing Discriminatory ideology and culture, which determine the environment for women's Existence. Finally, political process must increase women's presence and influence in the power structure.

However, Garba (1999:131) adopted two genetic concepts of dimensions of Empowerment with respect to women: the static and dynamic. The former emphasizes Women's empowerment in terms of their capacities to participate in decisions making That directly or indirectly affect their lives, and to influence those decisions. This refers to the notion of women having an effective voice. Women are also assumed to be disempowered when they cannot influence decisions that alter their lives. The Static concept of empowerment leads to exogenous empowerment strategies. Exogenous
Strategies are those built on the premise that disempowered groups can be empowered by external individuals or groups in the way so that an effective voice could be given to women. The exogenous empowerment strategy implies a top-down approach. .
Lastly it can be said that the process of women's empowerment highly depends on the existence of alternatives. Women may be aware of the conditions of their oppression, but if they see no viable alternatives, if there are no choices available, they can only turn their anger inwards, into frustration and bitterness, or into (religious) acceptance of suffering. Such exogenous approach towards the development of the women, there are various sift in the policy approach of GOI(Government Of India) in the last forty years from concepts of "welfare" (1970s), to "Development"(1980s), and now the " Empowerment" in 1990s. (Behuria, 2004). The first noble laureate of Bangladesh Mohammad Yunus has taken the same exogenous approach to hand over the economic power to women through disbursing the micro credit in considering the multiple factors in aiming rural women emancipation. Self Help Group (SHG) movement was one of the steps forward in this direction by becoming one of the first micro lending to women in groups that has been eclipsed by the rise of MFIs in the last decade. India, with 1,270,272,105 (1.27 billion) people is the second most populous country in the world, rural population 68% represent from rural habitats.Economicaly active rural women population contributing 31% out of total

women population 35,98,17171. Basically SHG are being part of the micro finance institutions aimed at helping the poor to easily obtain financial service like savings, credit, and insurance. The SHS-Bank linkage Programme (SBLP) is a milestone strategy to improve rural people access to formal credit system in a cost effective and sustainable manner by making use of SHGs. Over ninety percentage of the SHGs link with banks were found to be exclusive women SHGs. There has been much debate in the gender and development literature on how to achieve women's empowerment, with this debate often pointing on whether Microfinance programmes do in fact empower women (Jayaweera, 1997). Does access to credit automatically lead to empowerment? – This question is increasingly being Asked by academics who are working on the impact analysis of microfinance on women (Cheston and Kuhn, 2002). Kantor (2003) identified a similar question: opportunity to income earning can improve women's status within the household or do social norms and practices intervene to make access to resources alone insufficient to challenge intra-household gender relations in some contexts? These questions are critical for understanding Changes in gender relations and the contribution of microfinance to women's Empowerment. Several studies (Chaudhary, 2005; Garba, 1999; Gulati, 1996 etc.) have indicated that access to credit and income cannot lead to the Empowerment of women instead those are associated with processes of changes in the power structure. Therefore, it is important to make a conceptual distinction between projects that seek to reduce poverty and enhance productivity and those that seek to empower women, as the strategies adopted could be different. Cheston and Kuhn (2002) pointed out that the ability of a woman to be empowered through access to financial services depends on many factors – some of them linked to her individual situation and abilities, and others dependent upon her environment and the status of women as a group. So Status of women as a group ensure micro credit through SHGs develop the credit delivery mechanism into distinctive dimension to empower rural women in order to eradicates the menace of the society such as gender inequality, child mortality, illiteracy.

So, Professor Muhammad Yunus, the founder of "Grameen Bank" and its Managing Director, reasoned that if financial resources can be made available to the poor people on terms and conditions that are appropriate and reasonable, "these millions of small people with their millions of small pursuits can add up to create the biggest development wonder." The above statement signifies the role of rural women is the instrumental catalyst to create a long and sustainable wealth in order to expedite the wheel of rural inclusive social development.

Economic Sustainability and Micro Finance: A Road Ahead

Sustainability is a word indices the nature of respective practices of any kind. Micro finance as a instrument of rural development rely on several factors link with socio-economical aspects. Technological progresses, Commercilization, rapid urbanization are the most influential indicators to stir the growth of rural micro economy. Sustainability of Micro credit in appropriate mechanism depends of the said factors. Moreover, to gain the momentum of business it is finance that is imperative or others factors are equally important is area where academician and practioners invest their school of thoughts in several aspect. Economic sustainability has its myriad ways to attain its long standing objective. By only providing finance is barely a means to make the wheel of economic activities run. But the direction of destination can only be guided through the right mechanism of its timely execution makes the road of success into sustainability of success.

"Give a man a fish he eats for a day, teach a man to fish he eats for a life time"..... This Chinese proverb has its succinct validity to understand the value of the word" Economic Sustainability". The ethos of Micro Finance and its vital need in developing nations specially those grappling with the changes of poverty alleviation and unemployment. Micro finance is often considered to be just about giving micro credit to the financially challenged population, but essence of Micro finance to attain financial inclusion that is the fundamental conduit for extending financial service to unbanked sections of population. The sector has evolved vastly ever since the noble laureate Muhammad Yunus laid the foundation of modern MFIs with establishment of Grameen Bank, Bangladesh which has transformed the dynamic of rural economy. He was conferred the noble in the discipline of peace not in the economics on account of his contribution to bring the peace within the rural economy by providing them a weapon of peace called economic stability. Hence, Micro finance can be an instrumental force in developing financial inclusion that leads to '**inclusive growth**' resulted in economic sustainability across all the demographics.

Analysis:

Crises at the bottom of the Pyramid

Back ground of the Crises...

I. The microfinance industry in India is in the mid of the most severe crisis in its 25 year history. The genesis of the crisis lies with the actions taken by the government of the southern state of Andhra Pradesh in October 2010, when it passed legislation by shutting down all private sector microfinance institutions ("MFIs") operating in the state. In the first half of FY2011, MFIs in Andhra Pradesh disbursed Rs 5,000 crore ($1.13 billion) to borrowers; in the second half of FY2011, these same MFIs could only disburse Rs 8.5 crore ($1.9 million)i. The Andhra Pradesh Government's stated aim was to protect the poor although the penultimate actions have resulted in a substantial (600-fold) decrease in financing to the very poorest of India's citizens. The AP government's actions have eventually shut off finance to these most vulnerable of India's citizens.

II. The direct effect of the enactment of the Andhra Pradesh (AP) Act has been to deny millions of India's poorest citizen's access to basic financial services. The impact of the AP Act has the potential to affect 450 million people creating a severe shortage of much needed finance to the rural poor, India's most vulnerable inhabitants

III. The AP government's claims that private sector MFIs are exploiting India's poor by charging uneven interest rates and practicing coercive recovery techniques cannot be substantiated Based on numbers from SERP, it appears that the suicide rates amongst MFI borrowers are dramatically lower than the statistical average in the entire state of Andhra Pradesh.

IV. Private sector MFIs have demonstrated to be the most scalable and sustainable way of helping the Indian government meet its stated policy of encouraging "financial inclusion" for the 450 million people in India who are currently "unbanked", i.e., with no access to basic finance.

V. The Malegam Committee's recommendations and their broad acceptance by the RBI give rise to a number of concerns, and the constraints proposed around loan limits, interest rates, provisioning norms and capital requirements must be revisited to avoid unintended and deleterious consequences that could permanently impact private sector MFIs.

Statement of the Problem

A research published International Journal of Management Research Development (IJMRD) on "A study on recent trend and problem in using Micro Finance service in India" has revealed different cause and factor effect on Micro finance problems that is the indicators of sluggish pace of Micro finance institutes in India. Problems have featured in the following table to further analysis.

Table 1: Problem identify in availing Micro Finance

SL NO	FACTORS	WEIGHTED MEAN
1	Charge more Interest on Loan	4.12
2	Use of undue influence in delay of loan settlement	4.34
3	Unnecessary delay cause in availing service	3.89
4	Document support expected for credit	4.01
5	Low interest for Micro savings	3.78
6	Micro Insurance is not suitable to cover survivals	4.21
7	Charges are very high	3.57
8	Official support is not satisfactory	4.21
9	No involvement of provision on micro finance service	3.57
10	No chance for getting business and technical support	3.82
11	Lack of finance support for starting business	3.92
12	No subsidy offered at worse time	3.99
13	Failed to support live hood	3.43
14	Consumed more productive hours	3.73

(Source: Research Published on IJMRD, March 2013)

The above table drawn from the primary data is the testimony of myriad nature of problems being confronted in the centre stage of Micro Finance sector in India. Andhra Pradesh legislation act, 2010 is the result of the core operation impediments that has been a perinerial loop holes in MF sector. From the weighted mean it is substantiated that loan repayment, documentation hazards, interest charge, post loan follow up are the areas of profound concern. Data also suggests that MFI approach is under the confinement of restrictive practices. This study examines the core area of repayment problem generates from the gap of lending and payments. No chance of getting technical and business support is one of the major area that generate multiple layers of problems which is the main aim of this study to find an win –win solution. In a nutshell it can be stated that merely lending micro credit produce non productive resource that leads to regular failure of repayment. Failure in repayment creates Non Performing Assets (NPA) for MFIs as well other financial institutes such as banks, NABARD etc.This study seeks a resolution of this core problem to enhance the skill competencies of rural micro credit borrowers to support their business function in right direction in order to facilitates the timely repayment to build trust between borrowers and lenders (MFs) in resulting the sustainability of the Micro-Finance.

Credit Recovery Vs Long Term Sustainability

Technology that has been changing its functioning in a rapid space under the influence of growing needs and post adaptation across all the countries owing to the impact factor of globalization, is paving the way to foster the pace of financial inclusion. Above problem identifies the areas which need to be nurtured in a right manner to unveil the value delivery system of MF objective in a holistic accomplishment. A whole new way of lending that hinge on a peer-to-peer (P2P) or e-micro finance model has been a widely accepted tool of MF as a websites publishes a list of loan seekers from NGOs or a MFIs. A innovative platform where the prospective lenders chooses the borrowers of his or her choice, makes payment through an online platform and gets monthly or quartly payment on the loan, with 6-8 per cent returns. The facilitating online platform retains 1-5-2 percent as their own fees. Hence, the end cost for a borrower comes anywhere between 15-16 per cent. Some of the international fame of business fraternities like former CEO of Citibank, Vikram Pandit, Infosys former CFO V Balakrishnnan, Skype co-founder Toivo Annus, Jayprakesh Parekh one of the founder of Sony entertainment has joined in the bandwagon of P2P or e-microfinance as a attracting high profile individuals, both as investor and lenders.

So long journey of this new breed of micro finance has been a centre of attraction. Social lending platform turns into a mammoth opportunity for MF is going to replace an offshoot of conventional Grameen lending model is need to be seen as a self-regulated and self controlled repayment risk reduction. Cost of borrowing and the cost of repayment with off bite transparency can bring the most desirous result out of the multiple repayment bottlenecks. Social media platform also can contribute to the gain of financial literacy that is a stream roller in reducing the micro credit defaulters and hence boost the financial health of MFIs.This P2P or e-MF model and social media intervention can be a key stepping stone to induce financial literacy through business consultancy among unbanked rural borrowers of micro credit in order to further strengthen the relationship between MFs and borrowers. Moreover, the uncertainty of repayment of loan will reduce significantly on account of in timely and viable business consultation that gives the right direction and dimension of business to the borrowers based on various factorial analysis that help them to pay loan timely leads to the sustainability of their business.

Methodology

Data sources:
The data collected for the study includes secondary data. The various sources used to collect secondary data include research papers, journals, articles and annual reports of banks. Data from the Microfinance information exchange (MIX) and various other websites.
Methods:
The methodology of study includes collection of secondary data from various research articles, journals, Magazines and the web sites related to Micro finance

Scope of the Study

The scope of the research is limited to the role of microfinance institutions leading to social inclusion in India through CSR way. The skill enhancement Programme (SEP) was used to increase the performance of the recovery of loans sanctioned through MFIs in India. This study does not take into account the MFIs in various other geographical regions in the world.

Objective of the Study

1. To study the process of financial inclusion in India.
2. To study the role of NGOS under CSR initiative in loan recovery.
3. To create a model for ensuring effective recovery for Micro Finance.
4. To examine the mechanism of bring Financial Literacy among rural borrowers
5. To understand the role and significance of CSR in order to bring the rate of defaulters under control in Micro finance Sector

CSR: Impact and its role to resolve the recovery mechanism

Analysis:

Corporate Social Responsibility is a social practices exercised by corporate in understanding the business responsibility towards society. Adam Smith, the father of economics as we know, is famous for advocating *"laissez faire"* or leaving thing alone, when it comes to regulate business activities. He argued that there is an "invisible hand" that guide the actions of the individual for, while they strenuously pursue self –interest in the product they make and sell, in the process, they are satisfying other's needs and thereby society's welfare. Social responsibility inks with corporate social responsibility as profit evolves from the cluster of the society. Academician as well practioners are in debates in identifying CSR as an integral part of business. But after the enactment of company act, 2013 by GOI (Government of India) to contribute 2% of their profits has widen up the spectrum of CSR value driven proposition. From the cheque book Phrinalthrophy to the core area of business, CSR has evolved across its wings of importance in practising core business activities. It is not mealy a resipocrative responsibility(R-R) to the society, but an imperative business practices. Social activism becomes an integral part in running business owing to the ever changing dynamics of business environment under the fabric of globalization, liberalization.

Micro Finance and CSR: Hand in Hands

MF is itself a part of social responsibility draws many debates. Recent incident in AP has raised the question about MF responsibility towards social inclusion. Farmer's suicide in AP and post government legislation amplified the role and significance of CSR in MF. MFIs should initiate another social responsibility under the ambit of CSR, to educate the borrowers and through financial literacy. Moreover, it is imperative for MFIs to understand the demographical factors that influence the rural borrowers to pay their loans in timely and systematic manner. Hence, MFIs social responsibility plays a major and substantive significance in developing the human resource competencies in repaying the loan. CSR as a part of MFI's business activity has a distinctive and transparent accountability towards their borrowers and the society.

A thrush of skill enhancement mechanism: Area of CSR in MFIs

This study has undergone a slew of factors in identifying the root cause of non repayment of micro credit that overshadows the prospect of MFIs growth and social inclusion. While understanding the core factor behind the growing number of defaulters, it has been found that there is a wide gap of business practice and core skill competencies according to the need of the respective business demand. Hence, bridging this gap is a challenge that every MFIs are facing to facilitate loan recovery mechanism.CSR by MFIs can be a game changer to enhance the scope of skill development that can works as a instrumental tool to drive the right business to the right borrowers and rekindle a right sprit to make actual entrepreneur.MFIs need to energise this CSR activism by outsourcing it through Non Governmental Organizations (NGOs) in the area of skill enhancement through imparting of right training and right advocacy of business practice among rural micro credit beneficial, ascertain the local demographical factors depends on respective rural habitats.

A few facts to nurture

This study identifies plethora of findings in respect to availability factors and subsequent growing numbers of defaulters in Micro finance sectors. All the problems that MFIs in India are facing are combination of internal as well exogenous factors. Earlier research has shown undue settlement in loan and timely official supports are two core problematic factors in availing MF.On the contrary other secondary data as well AP episode also indicates that there is another piece of puzzle that needs fitting for micro finance to make a real dent in poverty. It is understood that the borrower are least capable of income expansion not only for capital adequacy but also in competencies in knowledge and skills. Hence, proper capital utilization in a right way can further induce capital enrichment.MFIs need to understand the deficiencies in imparting skill enhancement programme among rural borrowers to explore the scope of optimization of their loan in producing and creating social wealth. This onerous responsibility can be paved through wings of corporate responsibility that need to be outsourced and promoted through the hand and hands approaches with NGOS.

Micro Finance and its Sustainability through value creation: A CSR way

This study depicts the value that can be created through micro credit delivery for the social development under collaborative and collective exchange of responsibilities within MFIs and borrowers. There are numerical hurdles that have been supplicating a road block in the growth path of expansion of MFIs.Value delivery mechanism produce sustainability to unlock the further value proposition. Secondary data from multiple sources substantiate a wide range of value delivery flaws in applying the right mechanism for accomplishing suntentive and sustainable value proposition.NABARD promoted SHG-Bank linkage programme, joint liability groups (JLG) on the line of SHGs are working in a uniform direction to gain collective repayment obligation. But repayment and loan recovery is subject to various risks owing to its nature because repayment period is barely a few weeks or months. So, from this limited tenure of repayment indicates high possibility of payment default. Under this perspective this study suggests an innovation integrated model linking CSR and MF to deliver a value chain delivery system between MFIs and the respective rural borrowers. Micro finance Institutes need to invest in CSR by connecting NGOs in imparting financial literacy training and skill development to enhance the core competencies of borrowers. Over and above under the CSR initiative they should solicit the experts opinion of respective NGOs based on the respective rural area to give business advice depends on the demand of the respective local geographies to catapult the business need. This integrated CSR programme that has been figured out in the below diagram can be antidotes to ascertain the actual problems and subsequent remedies to bring sustainability of micro finance programme.

Summary of the Model: Integration between CSR and Micro Finance

The below diagram of the model depicts the value that can produce by an integrated way linking CSR and Micro finance in aiming to reduce the number of micro credit defaulters as well sustainability of Micro Finance business eco-system. Capacity of income expansion is a major area which jeopardise the payment structure in Micro finance. Infusing capital does not ensure capital expansion until investment of the respective capital goes into right business path. This is the need of the hour of MFIs to ascertain the root cause and develop an action oriented mechanism. This study has suggested through this below model a CSR approach by the MFIs that can resolve this core repayment problem of borrowers. Understanding the existing skills of the borrowers imparting right skill enhancement training along with guiding them to invest in right business according to their (borrowers) skills can ensure the return on investment (ROI). Model shows an integrated association between MFIs NGOs under the ambit of social responsibility to tender skill enhancement programme to the micro credit beneficial for constituting a win-win proposition. Micro finance institute need to outsource this skill enhancement programme (SEP) to local NGOs who has an expertise in skill development in the respective geographies. NGOs will identify the skills from the borrowers through data analysis, followed by identification of business opportunities, gap analysis, competencies training to ensure need based credit disbursement to the loan aspirants. Apart from the training and development NGOs will ensure the business consultancy followed by monitoring and timely evaluation of the borrower's business progress. The third phase of the integrated process will produce timely and systematic repayment of micro loan. Moreover, it will boost up the trust between MFIs and respective Joint Liability Groups (JLG).On the contrary if any groups unable to pay loan on time as a defaulter, NGOs will have a close contact with the group and restructure the group business activities with further enhancement of their skill through another round of training. Meanwhile, the timely repayment borrowers (JLG) will join with NGO to become a role model for the defaulters. They will actively participate in the training programme and share their expertise to the bidding entrepreneurs. This cyclic process is a composite illustration of integrated approach to accomplish the objective of Micro finance Institutes to reduce the level of defaulters and subsequent wealth creation. Implementation of this model not only reduce the number of micro credit defaulters, but also reduce the risk of Non Performing Assets (NPA) to the banks as they lend the loan to MFIs.

An Integrated Model: Micro Finance and CSR

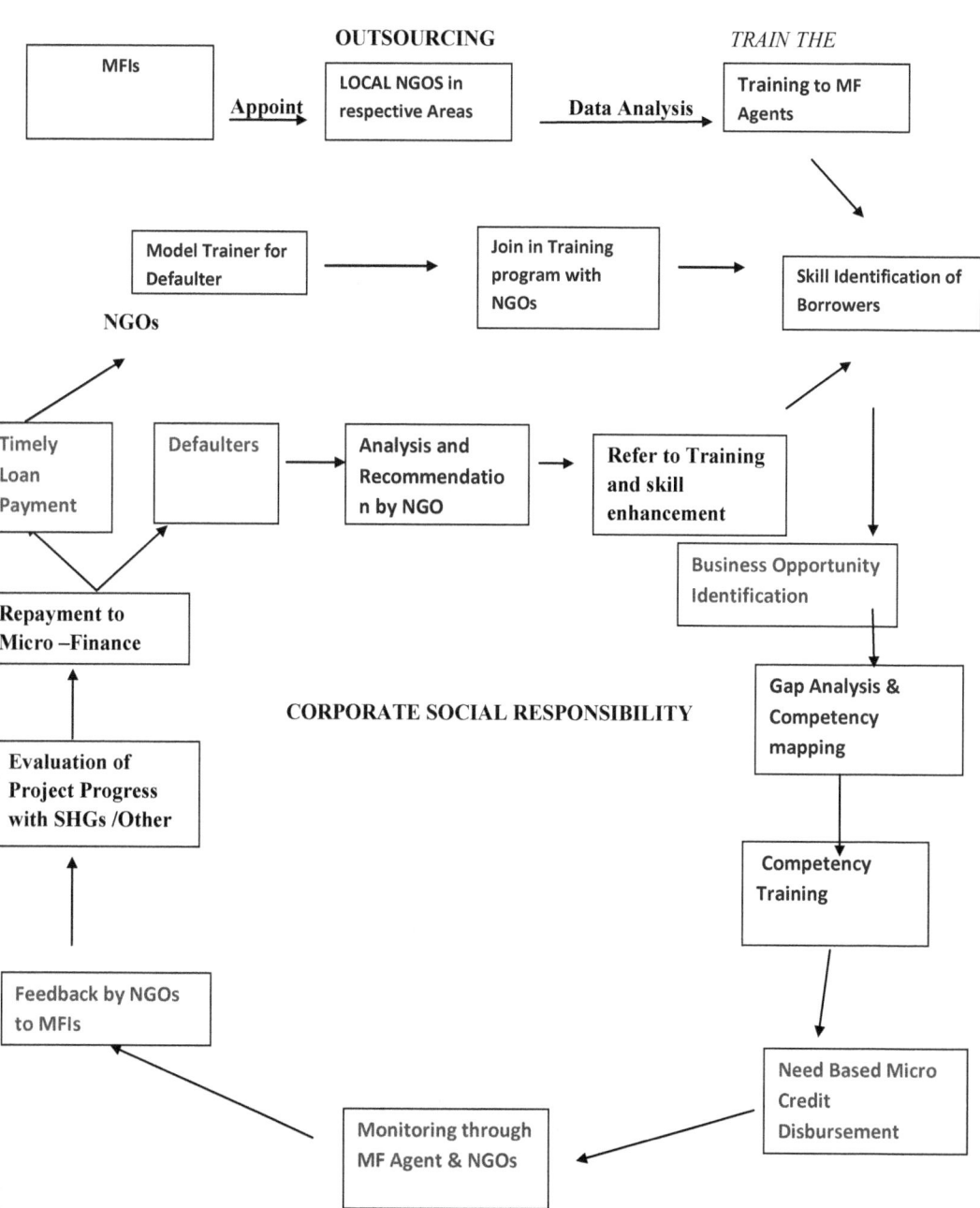

Conclusion

This secondary based hermeneutics study has focused different aspect of Micro credit in India. Micro finance is social instruments that need to be nurtured in an appropriate mechanism to make it a sustainable weapons to combat various social menace particularly poverty. But the growth of MF has been a major concern owing to its nature of disbursement of micro credit. It has a unique proposition in disbursing loan to the marginalised section in comparison to Banks. A slew of defaulters as a group has marred the growth prospect of MF in recent past. Vulnerability of MF lies in loan disbursement and loan repayment. So, this study aim to unveil the areas of thrust to minimized this process of financial exchange. The gap between capital infusion and capital recovery has been highlighted through this study and come up with a model that can be a weapon to bring down this gap. An integrated model under the influence of CSR from MFIs is an antidote to gain the viability and sustainability of Micro Finance. Skill enhancement program (SEP) under CSR initiative will be a boon to capital infusion and post capital recovery that can produce trust building as well social inclusion.

REFERENCES:

1. Anbuoli.P. (2013), " A Study on recent trends and Problems to using Micro Finance Services in India", IJMRD,VOL-3,

2. APMAS, Optimizing SHGs, October 2005NO-1, P-77-84

3. Behuria, Anita (2004): 'Women Empowerment Through Self-help Groups', Human Touch, 1(5), Aug.

4. Basu, Priya and Srivastava (2005): 'Scaling-Up Microfinance for Rural Poor', Policy Research Working Paper 3646, The World Bank, South Asia Region, Finance and Private Sector Development Unit, June.

5. IFAD, IFAD microfinance Project – India Chapter, September 2003

6. Kumaran, K P (2002): 'Role of Self Help Groups in Promoting Micro Enterprises Through Micro Credit: An Empirical Study', Journal of Rural Development, Vol 21 (2), NIRD, Hyderabad,

7. Kropp, Dr. Erhard W. & Suran, Dr. B.S., Linking Banks and (Financial) Self Help Groups in India – An Assessment, November 2002

8. NABARD, SHG Bank Linkage Model-wise Cumulative Position upto 31 March 2005

9. NABARD (2000): 'Ten Years of SHG-Bank Linkage: 1992-2002", NABARD and Microfinance.

10. Reserve Bank of India, Report of the Internal Group to Examine Issues Relating to Rural Credit and Microfinance, July 2005

11. Singh, Kavaljit, Banking Sector Liberalization in India: Some Distributing Trends, ASED, August 29, 2005

12. The Micro Finance Review, Journal of the centre for Micro Finance Research, Bankers Institute of Rural Development Lucknow,2009

WEB

1.Consolidation of data on Indian MFIs at www.mixmarket.org

2.http://indiamicrofinance.com/wp-content/uploads/2010/10/Andhra-MFI-Ordinance.pdf

3. AP Microfinance Ordinance - "Whereas these SHGs are being exploited by private Micro Finance Institutions (MFIs)through usurious interest rates and coercive means of recovery resulting in their impoverishment & in some cases leading to suicides, it is expedient to make provisions for protecting the interests of the SHGs, by regulating the money lending transactions by the money lending MFIs and to achieve greater transparency in such transactions in the State of Andhra Pradesh"

4.The Ordinance became law in December 2010 with the enactment of the APA

5. http://indiamicrofinance.com/wp-content/uploads/2011/01/Malegam-Report-Issues-Microfinance-Ind

6. http://www.microfinancefocus.com/content/exclusive-54-microfinance-related-suicides-ap-says-serp-reportia.pdf

.